Mediation Advocacy: Representing Clients in Mediation

Mediation Advocacy: Representing Clients in Mediation

Stephen Walker MA (Oxon), FCIArb
Solicitor and Accredited Mediator

Bloomsbury Professional

Bloomsbury Professional Limited, Maxwelton House, 41–43 Boltro Road, Haywards Heath,West Sussex RH16 1BJ

© Stephen Walker 2015

Cover image © Two Associates

Bloomsbury Professional is an imprint of Bloomsbury Publishing plc

A CIP Catalogue record for this book is available from the British Library.

Every effort has been taken to ensure the accuracy of the contents of this book. However, neither the authors nor the publishers can accept any responsibility for any loss occasioned to any person acting or refraining from acting in reliance on any statement contained in the book.

ISBN: 978 1 78043 792 7

Typeset by Phoenix Photosetting, Chatham, Kent
Printed and bound in the United Kingdom by CPI Group (UK) Ltd, Croydon, CR0 4YY

Preface

A white flag

In 2013 I wrote a book with David Smith, *Advising and Representing Clients at Mediation*. We deliberately avoided using the words 'mediation advocacy'. At page 3 we described the confusion that exists within the mediation community about what to call people who attend mediations with their clients. There were many suggestions, such as advocates, advisers, assistants or even skilled helpers. We decided to refer to them as 'mediation representatives.'

We had two objections to the words advocate or advocacy:

- They imply that the principal role of the representative is to argue a case and to win the argument both by the persuasive presentation of supporting evidence and points and by the demolition of the opposing arguments.

- For many people, the word 'advocate' implies some sort of legal standing or qualification. After all barristers are often referred to as advocates. In Edinburgh, for example, there is the Advocates' Library.

I have given up the fight.

The phrase 'mediation advocacy ' is too embedded. It is an important part of being a mediator or an advocate (or representative) to know when to abandon a position and move on to something else more constructive.

So this book is called *Mediation Advocacy*. It is intended to help advocates and their clients get the best out of the mediation process in the UK, especially those who may be under time pressure. The book is based on the experience of mediators in England and Wales and from other jurisdictions and focuses on what happens in practice in mediations rather than in theory. It explains how people actually make decisions, especially when under stress and in confrontational circumstances.

Mediation Advocacy develops in more detail some of the themes in the previous book and takes account of the many helpful comments received from readers and reviewers. It is more accessible to the non-lawyer advocate or reader and includes checklists, flowcharts, tips, precedents and templates.

The core of the book is civil and commercial mediation. It also refers to family, workplace and community mediation. The reason why they are given less prominence is that at the moment, as these mediations are conducted in the UK, there is less scope for advocates; the parties are usually not represented at these types of mediations.

I have included a chapter on self-advocacy (**Chapter 19**) to help unrepresented clients. Self-advocacy is not used in the sense that it is often is the United States of representing yourself against health authorities or insurance companies. It just means that you are attending a mediation on your own without a representative.

There are also sections discussing what advocates can do to prepare their clients for mediation even if they are not going to represent them at the mediation itself.

Green flag

Overview of the mediation scene

20 July 2014 was a very significant date in the history of British mediation. For years mediators in the UK have been complaining about the poor take-up for mediations. What can be done to increase the take up has been discussed at great length at many conferences and gatherings of mediators. One comment is always made. We need to see a mediation in a TV soap opera.

The good news is that it has happened.

Where?	In Coronation Street.
When?	On 20 July 2014.
How?	Leanne and Nick Tilsley went to a mediation with a mediator called Charlie Kemp, played by the actor Oliver Porter.

Was there rejoicing amongst the mediation community? No there was not. There was only expressions of dismay at the way in which the mediation was portrayed. Of course Leanne and Nick did not settle. It was a family mediation and being in a soap opera these two high conflict individuals engaged in high conflict behaviour. However, the word 'mediation' and the concept of a mediator has now at least been aired on primetime television in the UK.

At the other end of the cultural scale mediation is now a topic in the most difficult academic examination known to the Western world. This is the entrance examination for Prize Fellows of All Souls College Oxford, an institution dedicated to the intellectual and academic elite. It has no undergraduates, but great wealth, tradition and prestige. In the past it has not been renowned for being in tune with modern trends. But in Paper LAW 1 of the Fellowship Examination in September 2013, question 22 read: 'Is the recent trend towards mediation at the expense of litigation to be welcomed?'

So mediation as a concept has now penetrated both ends of the cultural and intellectual spectrum of the UK.

Mediation is now also well established as a topic for discussion in the media, both traditional print and digital as well as in social media – not only amongst lawyers but also in the emerging new trades of dispute resolution professionals or conflict management professionals.

The scope of mediation is expanding. It is no longer limited to civil and commercial disputes in which legal proceedings have been issued. Community mediation is now well established and available to local authorities and social services departments, used by them to deal with antisocial behaviour. In schools there is now peer mediation. Workplace mediation is increasingly common. The NHS announced in August 2014 that it was offering mediation to resolve disputes involving NHS trusts.

The number of mediations and mediators has increased. The best estimate is that there are now 5,000–6,000. Some 900 new mediators a year are being trained. The number of lawyers who have received some sort of mediation training is increasing. Mediation is now taught on the Bar course. It is a component in many university law courses. The judiciary are giving it more, if not always consistent, support.

Red flag

Looking back over the last 20 years there are three themes discernible in the current scene which cause concern.

Maturity

The market for mediation is now mature. There are well-established mediation providers and trainers. There is a steady stream of new mediators coming into the market. Users of mediation, in particular solicitors and barristers have greater experience of the process. It is now a recognised and established part of the English legal system.

The current economic and financial climate has spurred the judiciary on to support mediation. Lord Justice Briggs, in *PGF II SA v OMFS Company 1 Limited* [2013] EWCA Civ 1288, recently said:

> '[Thirdly], the constraints which now affect the provision of state resources for the conduct of civil litigation (and which appear likely to do so for the foreseeable future) call for an ever-increasing focus upon means of ensuring that court time, both for trial and for case management, is proportionately directly towards those disputes which really need it, with an ever-increasing responsibility thrown upon the parties to civil litigation to engage in ADR, wherever that offers a reasonable prospect of producing a just settlement at proportionate cost.

He concluded in para 56 by saying:

> 'The court's task in encouraging the more proportionate conduct civil litigation is so important in current economic circumstances that is appropriate to emphasise that message by a sanction which, even little more vigorous I would have preferred, nevertheless operates pour *enourager les autres*.'

As part of this maturity there is greater diversity. There is a wide range of mediation service providers and styles available. Some providers have gone out of business but new ones have come into the market. There are elite groups, law firms and barristers chambers which have set up their own panels. Some providers just provide administrative services, whilst others offer advice and career development for their members. There is wide range of prices.

Mediators increasingly come from non-legal backgrounds. The traditional facilitative model of mediation has been adapted and supplemented. There is a danger that the buyer of mediation services might be confused or overwhelmed by the choice of philosophies, styles and prices.

Sophistication

With greater maturity of the market, the users of mediation have become more sophisticated. They are now familiar with the process. At times it appears that a tension is growing between the users and the mediators who increasingly report that at mediation it is the lawyers who try to game the mediator. It becomes a tactical tussle as they demonstrate to their clients that they know what the mediator is up to.

Mediators are being encouraged to try new models of mediation. Increasingly they are told that no mediator can be wholly evaluative or facilitative. They have to be eclectic, taking in a range of tools for their toolkit, including transformative and narrative mediation. In addition they are being told that ODR (online dispute resolution) will transform the way they work and carry on business. Is it a threat or an opportunity? Will it lead to mediation becoming commoditised? These questions keep commentators and academics busy.

Academics are providing more research on what they perceive it is that mediators do and call for further research. Conferences and special interest groups proliferate.

The colonisation of mediation by lawyers is now a recurrent theme amongst academic commentators. Titles such as *Mediation Law: Journey through Institutionalism to Juridification* appear. Practitioners such as Peter Adler report from the United States that the original ideals of mediation have been lost. It has ceased to be an alternative method of dispute resolution but is now part of the mainstream legal system. Its purpose is to save judicial times and resources.

The increasing number of legal decisions on matters such as the enforceability of agreements to mediate or settlements made at mediation mean that lawyers become more involved. Non-lawyers are increasingly wary of going to mediation without a lawyer.

Mediation is going the way of arbitration cry the commentators – and that is not a good thing.

Asymmetry

Although the supply of mediators with an increased range of skills and experiences is growing, the demand is lagging behind. In 2014, there were 795,227 civil cases issued between January and June. The Sixth Annual Survey published in 2014 by the Centre for Effective Dispute Resolution (CEDR) shows that the number of civil and commercial mediations carried out rose by 9 per cent since 2012. There were 9,500 civil and commercial mediations This number excludes family and community mediations but includes scheme mediations. Even so it is a very small number. There are 10,726 firms of solicitors in England and Wales. It works out at less than one mediation per firm per year. The best estimate is that there are now 5,000–6,000 mediators. Some 900 new mediators a year are being trained

In the 1930s, F E Smith (who, as Lord Birkenhead, was a Lord Chancellor) described the English Bar as a profession of 2,000 with work for 1,000 being carried out by 500. The English mediation community, it could be said, is a cottage industry of 6,000 with work for 500 being carried out by 100.

According to the CEDR survey, 85 per cent of mediations were carried out by 130 mediators. Less than 25 per ent of mediators carried out more than 20 mediations in a year.

Large commercial firms of solicitors say that they would prefer mediators to charge more and prepare better and do fewer mediations. Other firms of solicitors want to pay less and there is downward pressure on fees.

A second manifestation of asymmetry is shown in the City of London Survey carried out in October 2014. This shows the disparity between what the end-users of mediation want, ie the clients, and what the advisers and trainers think that they want. This is discussed in more detail in **Chapter 5.**

The three themes of maturity, sophistication and asymmetry come together in the growth of an increasingly specialised and accredited activity known as mediation advocacy (see **Chapter 6**).

It is hoped that this book will be of use to those who want to keep up to date with what his actually happening at mediations. I have drawn on the works of Professors D J Kahnneman, R Caldini and R Dobelli and recommend their books to all readers.

Finally ...

Finally, I respectfully adopt the approach of Tom Bingham in *The Rule Of Law* and have used 'he' rather than 'he or she' and in his words 'hope that this will be understood in an unchauvinistic, gender-neutral way'

The law is stated as at 1 January 2015

Stephen Walker
January 2015

Dedication

To Alison, Robert, Duncan and Lizzie who make it all worthwhile and taught me the value of mediation.

Contents

Table of Statutes

Table of Statutory Instruments

Table of Cases

Glossary

ACAS	Advisory, Conciliation and Arbitration Service.
ADR	Alternative dispute resolution – usually defined as alternative to litigation in the courts. It has other definitions such as appropriate dispute resolution or amicable dispute resolution.
ADR Group	A mediation provider and trainer set up in 1989.
Adjudication	Adjudicative dispute resolution procedure for construction industry providing provisional but quick decisions. See the Housing Grants, Construction and Regeneration Act 1996, Pt 11, as amended by the Local Democracy, Economic Development and Construction Act 2009, ss 138–145.
Adjudicative	Any dispute resolution process where the parties appoint a third party to make a decision on their dispute.
Agreement to mediate/ mediation agreement	A written agreement to engage in a mediation. Not the same as a Settlement Agreement, which is signed at the end of a successful mediation and records the terms of the settlement reached.
Arbitration	Adjudicative dispute resolution process under which the parties agree in writing to submit their dispute for decision by an impartial tribunal appointed under an agreed procedure.
Arb/Med	A hybrid process. An arbitration is conducted. Before the arbitrator publishes the award the parties attend a mediation with the arbitrator acting as the mediator. See also MED/ARB.
ATE	After the event insurance – usually only covers costs.
BATNA	Best Alternative To A Negotiated Settlement.
BTE	Before the event insurance – usually only covers costs.
Caucus	A private and confidential meeting at a mediation between the mediator and a party and its advisers. Also known as a private session.
CAMS	Court of Appeal Mediation Scheme.
CEDR	Centre for Effective Dispute Resolution – a mediation provider and trainer. Set up in 1990.
CFA	Conditional Fee Agreement. This is not a contingency fee arrangement, but the lawyers are only paid if they win, in which case they are paid their base fee and a mark up.
CIA	Chartered Institute of Arbitrators.
Clerksroom	A mediation provider.
CMC	Civil Mediation Council.
CPR	Civil Procedure Rules 1998 (SI 1998/3132) which set out the procedural rules for litigation in the High Court and county court.

Glossary

Court settlement	A form of mediation provided by judges in the Construction and Technology Court.
CRT Score	Cognitive reflection test: a test designed to assess the ability to suppress intuitive and spontaneous wrong answers in favour of reflective and deliberative ones.
CSP	Court settlement process
DBA	Damages based agreement. This is a contingency fee arrangement introduced in April 2013 as part of the Jackson reforms.
eADR	Electronic ADR.
ED	Expert determination.
EE	Expert evaluation
ENE	Early Neutral Evaluation.
EU Directive	Directive 2008/52/EC – applies to cross-border disputes where the mediation commenced after 6 April 2011. Implemented in the UK by SI 2011/1133 and the CPR Amendment Rules 2011.
FMC	Family Mediation Council.
ICC	International Chamber of Commerce.
iDR	Internet dispute resolution.
IMI	International Mediation Institute.
Intake Meeting	Initial meeting held by a family mediator with the parties.
JAMS	JAMS Inc, formerly Judicial Arbitration and Mediation Services, founded in the United States in 1979 by retired judges as a provider of dispute resolution services.
Jordan Order	A court order requiring the parties to file witness statements saying why they consider the use of ADR to be unreasonable in their case.
JSM	Joint Settlement Meeting. A meeting of the parties and usually their representatives to negotiate a settlement. Also referred to as a Three Room Meeting. Common in personal injury cases.
Litigation funding	Money provided by a third party to pay for litigation.
Mediation	A non-adjudicative dispute resolution process.
Med/Arb	A hybrid dispute resolution procedure. The parties conduct a mediation. If it does not result in settlement they appoint the mediator to act as arbitrator. He conducts an arbitration in the usual way.
MENDALOA	Mediation after last offer arbitration.
MIAM	Mediation information assessment meeting. Used in family proceedings.
MLATNA	Most Likely Alternative To A Negotiated Settlement.

MoJ	Ministry of Justice.
MSEO	Mediation Settlement Enforcement Order under which an agreement made through mediation in a cross-border dispute within the European Union can be recorded in a court order.
Non-adjudicative	A form of alternative dispute resolution in which agreement is reached by the parties.
ODR	Online dispute resolution.
Part 36 Offer	An offer to settle made by any party to litigation under Pt 36 of the Civil Procedure Rules.
PATNA	Probable Alternative To A Negotiated Settlement.
PI	Professional indemnity insurance. Taken out by professionals to provide cover for claims for negligence or breach of contract in the performance of their professional duties.
PIN	Positions, Interests and Needs.
PMA	Pre-mediation analysis.
RATNA	Realistic Alternative To A Negotiated Settlement.
RICS	Royal Institution of Chartered Surveyors.
RTM	Round-table meeting (see also Joint Settlement Meeting and Three Room Meeting). The parties and their representatives meet on a without prejudice basis to discuss settlement.
SCMA	Standing Conference of Mediation Advocates – a trade association for those specialising in representing clients at mediation, and a training body.
SCMS	Small claims mediation scheme. A free scheme in county courts for lower value cases usually conducted by telephone with an hour time limit.
TCC	Technology and Construction Court, a specialist division of the High Court.
Tomlin Order	A consent order in litigation, which records a settlement in a schedule and stays proceedings except for the purpose of implementing the terms in the schedule. It is not a judgment. But judgment can be entered without starting new proceedings if there is breach of the settlement.
TPN	A third party neutral, such as a mediator.
Ungley Order	A court order requiring parties to consider ADR, (note: not just mediation) and, if a party considers ADR to be unsuitable, to be prepared to justify that view at the conclusion of the trial.
WATNA	Worst Alternative To A Negotiated Agreement.

Useful Websites

EU	europa.eu/civiljustice/adr/adr_eu_code_conduct_en
CMC	www.civilmediation.org
Commercial Court	www.justice.gov.uk/courts/admiralty-and-commercial-courts guide
T&C Court	www.justice.gov.uk/courts/tech-court/tech-con-court-guide.
IMI	www.imimediation.org
ICC	www.iccwbo.org
ADR Group	www.adrgroup.co.uk
CEDR	www.cedr.com
CIARB	www.ciarb.org
FMC	www.familymediationcouncil.org.uk
Mercantile Court	www.justice.gov.uk/courts/mercantile-court/mercantile-court-guide
MoJ	www.justice.gov.uk/

Part A
Introduction to Mediation Advocacy and the Mediation Process

Chapter 1

Introduction to ADR

Introduction

> This chapter deals with:
>
> ● A test
>
> ● Core principles
>
> ● The current mediation scene
>
> ● Current development of mediation advocacy
>
> ● Who needs to know about it
>
> ● Scope of the book

1.01   In this chapter, the concept that in order to make good decisions you need to know how decisions are made is introduced along with the eight core organising principles of the book. Three other sets of principles, which recur in the book, are introduced and explained. This is intended to reduce repetition and duplication later and to provide a framework for the reader when working through the rest of the book.

A test

> Look at the three questions below. Answer them as quickly as you can. Do not think long and hard about them. Write down all three answers before reading further.
>
> ### Question one
>
> A bat and the ball cost £1.10p. If the bat costs a £1 more how much is the ball?
>
> ### Question two
>
> In a clothes factory five machines take exactly five minutes to make five blouses. How many minutes does it take 100 machines to make 100 blouses?

> **Question 3**
>
> A pond has weeds growing on it. The weeds grow quickly. Each day they double the area they take up. If it takes 48 days for the pond to be completely covered by weeds how many days will it take to be half covered?
>
> Intuitive answers are 10 pence, 100 minutes and 24 days.
>
> These are from the cognitive reflection test (CRT) developed by Prof Shane Frederick. The actual answers are £.05, 5 minutes, and 47 days.
>
> An interesting further finding was that those with higher CRT scores tended to choose the riskier option and gamble. This is especially true for men. Those with lower scores tended to prefer a bird in the hand.
>
> People with higher CRT scores can control their impulses and are less prone to fall foul of hyperbolic discounting.
>
> What is hyperbolic discounting?
>
> The answer is at **para 18.11**.
>
> This book introduces the concept that to make good decisions you need to know how decisions are made. A good working knowledge of this is essential for a skilled mediation advocate. This is discussed in more detail in **Chapters 16** and **18.**

Working definitions

Mediation

1.02   There is no single universal definition of mediation, but a conventional workable definition is:

> 'Mediation is a voluntary, confidential process in which the parties to a dispute can, with the help of a neutral intermediary meet to work out their own settlement.'

Negotiation

There are hundreds of definitions of negotiation, but a working one is:

> ' Negotiation is a process in which two or more parties talk to each other in order to persuade each other to do something which each wants and the other may be reluctant to do.'

Eight core principles

This book is organised around eight core principles:

(1) Mediation is for making peace not war

(2) Peace is made by negotiating deals.

(3) Not every negotiation is a mediation but every mediation is a negotiation.

(4) The process of negotiation is a process of the mutual recognition of reality: your own and the other person's.

(5) Deals are made by discussing proposals not by arguing.

(6) Preparation for mediation is preparation for peace talks.

(7) Negotiation leads to action. It is different from a discussion or debate. A successful negotiation leads to a decision, which leads to action.

(8) People make decisions and settlements for their reasons not for yours.

Three core concepts

1 What lawyers do

1.03　Lawyers perform three different tasks:

(1) Analysis

(2) Advice

(3) Advocacy

2 Three classic stages of mediation

(1) Exploring

(2) Exchanging

(3) Formulating

3 Actual stages of mediation

(1) Advocacy

(2) Problem-solving

(3) Negotiation

The mediation advocate's three Rs

(1) Rebalance

(2) Reorientate

(3) Recognise

In the next section these principles are explained in more detail with commentary on each of them.

Eight core principles

Principle 1: Mediation is for making peace not war

1.04   If the parties want to fight they go to court. Mediation is not a pseudo day in court. If the parties want to make peace they come to mediation. The only purpose of going to mediation is to make peace. That requires a different skill set and a different mindset. This is discussed in **Chapters 5** and **6**.

Principle 2: Peace is made by negotiating deals

1.05   This is a self-evident truth, but one overlooked at mediation where advocates try to pulverise the other side into submission with a barrage of legal points and authorities and a fusillade of threats.

Once both sides have exhausted their ammunition and they look for the common ground not the battleground there is progress towards making peace.

The implications of this fourth mediation process are discussed at **Chapters 6**, **9** and **16**.

Principle 3: Not every negotiation is a mediation, but every mediation is a negotiation

1.06   It is central tenet of this book that the only difference between a negotiation and a mediation is that a third party is involved. This view is not universally accepted. Many object to mediation being considered as merely assisted negotiation. They think that it is a much richer and ambitious process. This is discussed in more detail in **Chapter 4**.

It is also a tenet of this book, based upon practical experience, that at mediation there are several negotiations taking place. These are:

- the negotiation between the parties through the mediator;
- the negotiation between the parties direct, without the mediator;
- the private negotiation which each party has with the mediator; and
- the public or joint negotiation which the parties have with the mediator and each other.

Principle 4: The process of negotiation is a process of the mutual recognition of reality – your own and the other person's

1.07   Both sides to a negotiation have to be very clear in their own minds what their goals are and what they can afford to pay for them. In other words, what is the outcome worth to them? To be able to trade effectively, they have to know not only what they have, but what the other side wants and what it is worth to them.

Parties to a negotiation need to find out what reality is – both their own and the other person's by trading, listening, and asking. These three activities do not always come naturally to negotiators, particularly lawyers or professional commercial negotiators. They are skills that can be recognised, learned and practised.

There is a debate about whether good negotiators are born or made. Some people seem to have a natural aptitude. Others appear to be able to negotiate instinctively. In fact, key skills for negotiators can be taught and therefore, with sufficient interest, and application can be learned. By repeated practice and reflection they become habitual and instinctive.

Many professional skills described as being instinctive are in fact the product of accelerated repeated experience.

These key skills of listening, asking and trading are discussed in detail in **Chapters 6** and **16**.

Principle 5: Deals are made by discussing proposals, not by arguing

1.08   When people argue they are trying to establish who is right. When they negotiate they are trying to establish what is the right thing to do.

Effective negotiators ask: how can we make this proposal work for each other?

Of course people disagree. They try and persuade the other side to agree with them. People do sometimes change their mind during negotiations but what causes them to do this is not being proved they are wrong by forensic argument.

In other words negotiators need to expand the common ground to find what the proposal is that sufficiently meets the goals of all the parties so that they can agree to do it, and then do it.

Trading blows and points does not move the parties towards a deal. Trading information and concessions does.

A question to be asked is whether, in essence, a negotiation to buy a company or sell a property is different in kind from a negotiation to settle a dispute. If the view is taken, which it is in this book, that there is essentially no difference, then it has to be asked why negotiation would be seen as an adversarial process. This question is discussed in more detail in **Chapter 16**.

The key skills identified under Principle 2 that are discussed in more detail in **Chapter 6** are also relevant.

Principle 6: Preparation for mediation is preparation for peace talks

1.09 This follows from Principle 1. The implications for mediations are discussed in **Chapter 7**. In a nutshell: spend less time polishing up the best legal points and camouflaging the weak ones and more time on working out how to structure settlements.

Principle 7: Negotiation leads to action – it is different from a discussion or debate – a successful negotiation leads to a decision, which leads to action

1.10 At mediations the parties make their own decision, unlike in court, where the judge makes it for them. Therefore parties must be ready, willing and able to make decisions. The implications of this for mediations are discussed in **Chapter 10**.

Principle 8: People make decisions and settlements for their reasons not yours

1.11 People decide to settle a dispute or buy a property because it suits them. They do not do it because it suits you. At mediations do not spend time trying to prove you are right. Spend time framing a proposal that is right for them and you.

Three core concepts

What lawyers do

1.12 Lawyers perform three different tasks:

- Analysis
- Advice
- Advocacy

Clients take a problem to their lawyers who find out as much information as they can about it. They study the documents. They try to work out what has happened. They analyse the legal and factual issues. On the basis of this analysis they give advice to their clients on what their position is and what the options are. The bolder ones may actually advise their clients what to do.

Lawyers write to the other side with what their client's demands are and the reasons why they are entitled to make them. They respond to the other side's counter-arguments and proposals. They repeat the reasons why their client is right. In other words they argue their client's position concentrating on maximising the positives and minimising the negatives. This is advocacy.

Lawyers may take the case and their advocacy to the ultimate level and argue their client's case before a court or tribunal in an attempt to secure a finding or judgment in their client's favour, which establishes that they were right.

It is essential that both the lawyers and their clients understand which of the three functions at any one time the lawyer is performing. The three stages are not necessarily sequential, although they often are.

At mediations it is frequently apparent that sometimes an advocate seems to believe that they are advising their clients and analysing their problems when they are in fact engaged in advocacy. This applies even if the only person that the advocates are trying to persuade are themselves and that they are still entitled to hold the same view that they have been expressing for the last 18 months.

The way in which the three tasks and different functions of the lawyer role are engaged during the mediation process is discussed in detail in **Chapter 6**.

Three classic stages of mediation

1.13   There are three classic stages which mediators are trained to take parties at mediation through the during the mediation process. These are:

- Exploring

- Exchanging

- Formulating

Exploration

In this stage the mediator wants to find out what each party regards as important in the dispute and what it thinks the other party regards as important. He is looking for answers to three questions:

- What is important?

- Why is it important ?

- How do you want to achieve it?

He does this through a combination of open questions and active listening (see **Chapter 9**).

Exchange

The mediator is now:

- finding out what each side needs to know about the other's position;

- trying to fill in gaps in each side's information and understanding. If people have different information they are more likely to have different opinions. The more shared information they have the less scope there is for differing opinions. In this way the mediator is already trying to expand the common ground; and

- able to correct misunderstandings. In any dispute there is always an element of misunderstanding arising out of poor communication. By the time most parties come to mediation they are not communicating directly with each other. They are usually doing it through third parties and in particular through lawyers. The mediator can unblock the channels of communication.

At all times the mediator respects the confidentiality of the process and only discloses to each party what he has been authorised to disclose.

Formulation

In this stage the mediator is:

- working with each party to formulate proposals for settlement; and
- communicating the responses to proposals and helping with reformulation.

As Principle 2 says, settlements are achieved by the parties discussing proposals not by arguing points of evidence or law. The sooner the parties put proposals on the table that can be discussed the more chance they are giving themselves of achieving a settlement on the day. It is for this reason that this book emphasises the importance of parties formulating potential settlement proposals as part of their preparation before they attend the mediation (see **Chapter 7**).

Three actual stages of mediation

1.14   Three phases have been observed as occurring in most civil and commercial mediations. These are:

- Advocacy
- Problem-solving
- Negotiation

They are not strictly sequential. Some mediators in their Opening Statement at the Joint Opening Session tell the parties that they have observed this pattern.

In the advocacy phase the parties themselves, through their representatives, tell the mediator all the points that they will tell the judge if the case does not settle.

In the problem-solving phase the parties, with the help of the mediator, explore to find out if they have the necessary building blocks to construct a settlement. Is a settlement, although desirable, actually doable?

In the negotiation phase the parties have decided that a settlement is both desirable and doable and they are concentrating on agreeing the terms and figures.

The mediator will make the obvious point that the sooner the parties can move from the advocacy phase into the problem-solving phase the more chance they are giving themselves of settling on the day.

In the messy world of real mediation these three stages run alongside the three classic stages and intermingle. The job of the mediator is to manage the process.

The different ways in which mediators do this and the different ways in which advocates can help or hinder the process are described in more detail in **Chapters 6** and **9.**

The mediation advocate's three Rs

1.15 The three lessons which this book invite advocates to absorb are the need to:

(1) **Rebalance** Too many advocates when preparing for mediation concentrate on presenting their case not on formulating and structuring settlements. In a well-conducted mediation most of the time and energy will be spent considering proposals for settlement, not about arguing points of law and evidence. Preparation for mediation has to be rebalanced. This is explained in more detail in **Chapter 7**.

(2) **Reorientate** Representatives (and clients) at mediation and in particular lawyers have to realise that the focus of the process is on devising settlement proposals. They are at mediation to make peace not war. They have to reorientate themselves away from adversarial, forensic debate and argument. This is explained in more detail in **Chapter 6**. To avoid duplication, additional tips on advocacy are included in **Chapter 19** on self-advocacy (see the flowcharts at **paras 19.06** and **19.09**).

(3) **Recognise** Representatives whether lawyers or not and also clients now have available to them much greater knowledge and insight about how they behave when processing information and negotiating. The results of research carried out by neuroscientists and behavioural economists show that much of our decision-making suffers from inherent flaws.

It is important that clients and their advisers have access to information about these cognitive biases and heuristics so that advocates can recognise and neutralise them. If representatives do not recognise them and leave them untreated, their decision-making process will malfunction, which can prejudice the outcome of negotiations for their clients. This is discussed in **Chapter 18**.

The mediation scene

1.16 The preface to this book highlights some green and red flags. In addition certain features can be identified. Although the job of mediators is to promote agreement, they disagree a lot. In the interests of lowering temperatures and using non-confrontational language these conflicts are reframed as dualisms. Some of them have been apparent for some time. Others are emerging. Their existence does influence the provision of mediation services and the conduct of mediation in the UK. Advocates need to be aware of them.

Dualisms

1.17 There are ten dualisms that can currently be clearly observed on the mediation scene.

- **Lawyers v non-lawyers** There is an increasing polarisation between mediators who are lawyers and those who are non-lawyers. Rival organisations representing their respective interests have been established. Some, such as the ADR Group, make a conscious effort to be inclusive to mediators of all backgrounds (see **Chapter 3**).

- **Therapists v problem solvers** The mediation river is fed by these two tributaries. There is increasing polarisation between those who think that mediation is to solve problems and those who think it is to heal people and produce resolutions not just solutions (see **Chapter 4**).

- **Evaluators v facilitators** This is the traditional division between the models of mediation. Facilitative is the classic original style where the mediator helps the parties find a solution and does not volunteer his own solution or opinions. Its supporters say that evaluative mediation is an oxymoron. Evaluative mediation, where the mediator does give his opinion on the legal and commercial merits of the case and the settlement, is increasingly popular. Its supporters say that facilitative mediation is an oxymoron (see **Chapter 4**).

- **Case v dispute** There is a continuing confusion between a case which is the legal formulation of a disputant's position and the dispute itself. Not all the elements of a dispute can be encompassed within the legal formulation. It is the dispute that has to be settled at mediation, not just the case. This is still problem solving not resolving underlying conflicts. This confusion does influence the way people prepare for and conduct mediations (see **Chapter 11**).

- **Critics v creators** It is much easier to criticise something than to create something. At mediations the parties aided by their advocates are very ready to criticise each other. The lawyers love debating the legal merits of the cases – this is what they are trained to do and they are good at it. Hence, mediators ask advocates to supply them with silver bullets they can fire at the other side. It is harder to create a settlement that will meet the needs of the decision makers on all sides (see **Chapters 6** and **7**).

- **Trainers v practitioners** Many mediators complain that there is more money to be made out of training then mediating and that trainers are mediators who cannot earn enough by mediating. The growth in the number of mediations is not enough to satisfy the growth in the number of newly trained mediators (see **Chapter 3**).

- **Calling v business** Not all mediators mediate to make money. Some want to do good and spread the word. They have developed new models of mediation and criticise the hijacking of mediation by lawyers and judges (see **Chapter 4**).

- **Regulators v free marketeer** This split is not unique to the mediation community but it is very distinct. There is very little regulation or even effective accreditation at present (see **Chapter 3**).

- **Art v science** Traditionally mediation has been described as an art. With the development of statistical risk analysis, game theory, behavioural economics and neuroscience it has to be asked is this really true any more (see **Chapter 18**).

- **Off the shelf v bespoke** As mediation becomes more mature as a product, so it can become commoditised. There is a growth in schemes, one hour telephone mediations and the new development: online dispute resolution where parties to the dispute will not into act with a life mediator but will interface with an algorithm-based decision process. (see **Chapter 6**).

This book

1.18   This book aims to help advocates and their clients get the best out of the mediation process in the UK. The core of the book is civil and commercial mediation. It does also refer to family, workplace and community mediation. The reason why they are given less prominence is that at the moment as these mediations are conducted in the UK there is less scope for advocates. Usually the parties are not represented at these types of mediations.

There is a chapter on self-advocacy (**Chapter 19**) to help unrepresented clients. There are also sections discussing what advocates can do in preparing their clients for mediation even if they are not going to represent them at the mediation itself.

The emphasis in this book is on the practical rather than theoretical. However, there is discussion about the competing philosophies and theories of mediation so that at least readers will be able to recognise waffle when they hear it.

Conclusion

1.19   An advocate who wants to help his clients get the best out of the mediation process needs to:

● feel confident in explaining the process and the concept of mediation to his clients (**Chapters 1** and **2**);

● know how to find and appoint a suitable mediator(**Chapters 3**);

● prepare himself and his client for mediation (**Chapters 5, 7, 10, 11** and **13**);

● be able to effectively participate in the mediation on the day and to work effectively with the mediator (**Chapters 6, 9, 14, 16** and **17**);

● be familiar with the attitudes towards mediation displayed by the courts and the most important legal provisions and current case law (**Chapters 8, 12** and **14**);

● know what the mediation process is, both in practice and theory (**Chapters 4, 9** and **10**);

● know what mediators do (**Chapters 1** and **9**);

● know what they do themselves when taking decisions, particularly in circumstance of stress and uncertainty (**Chapters 16, 17** and **18**);

● know the marketplace (**Chapter 3**); and

● minimise the risk to his client and himself (**Chapters 14** and **15**).

Advocates should self-audit their skills using the three self-audit checklists in **Chapters 6, 16** and **18**.

Chapter 2

What is Mediation?

In this chapter you will learn:

- What ADR is and go through the ADR menu
- What is different about mediation
- The pros and cons of the different ADR options to help advocates choose the most suitable one for their clients
- A brief overview of mediation's development over the last 40 years and current trends

---

What is ADR?

2.01   ADR is usually defined as Alternative Dispute Resolution. Alternative denotes that it is an alternative to a court process, ie litigation in a court or a tribunal. Other commonly used definitions are 'Appropriate Dispute Resolution' or 'Amicable Dispute Resolution' which is preferred by the International Chamber of Commerce (ICC).

There are dozens of varieties of ADR, of which 20 are listed with commentary in **paras 2.03–2.25** below.

What is mediation?

2.02   There is no single definition. A conventional, workable definition of mediation is:

> 'Mediation is a voluntary, confidential process in which the parties to a dispute can, with the help of a neutral intermediary meet to work out their own settlement.'

This definition is analysed at **para 2.27** below.

Here is a recent formulation of mediation in the context of modern commercial mediation, which illustrates the qualities needed to be an effective mediation advocate. It comes from the International Chamber of Commerce (ICC). As explained in **Chapter 1**, mediation is now an established part of the legal process and legal training in many jurisdictions. For example, the ICC runs an annual mediation competition for law students. In 2014, 66 teams from over 40 countries attended the competition in Paris.

In the *Guidelines For Judges* at the competition, the ICC said:

> 'Judges are asked to mark on the basis that they are looking *for the most effective dealmakers* who make best use of the mediation process. This will involve evidence of *skills such as flexibility, listening and empathy* to other competing teams showing that it is capable of *moving forward towards a collaborative outcome.*

> It is collaboration that is being marked because *collaboration is a true reflection of commercial mediation.* It involves *cooperation* but accepts that the Competing Teams may have *different business interests, which they should defend.* The skill is therefore demonstrated in the ability of the Competing Teams *to understand these differences and find a way through such differences to establish a new resolution while protecting their own commercial interests.*'

[Emphasis added]

The ADR menu

2.03   Mediation is not the only ADR technique but it is the most common formal one currently being used. It is not always the best choice for every dispute. Mediation advocates need to be aware of the options and to be able to select the best one for their particular case. Below is an alphabetical list of 20 of the main ADR processes, followed by a fuller list giving brief descriptions and comments on their pros and cons.

Arbitration	Fact finding
Adjudication	F D R
Advisory arbitration	JSMs
Arb/Med	Judicial mediation
Conciliation	Med/Arb
Con /Arb	MEDALOA
ENE	Mediation
E D	Negotiation
DRPs	Ombudsman
Facilitation	Time limited mediations

There are other techniques and new ones are being devised all the time. What are the differences? Are some better than others? Here is guidance on the various options.

Arbitration

2.04   This has been part of the legal system of many jurisdictions for centuries. Many regard it as simply privatised litigation. It has been described as litigation behind closed doors. In practice, arbitration is now more a mainstream than an alternative method of dispute resolution.

It is a process where the parties select their own arbitrator who then holds a hearing much like a court hearing except that is in private, at which he listens to their submissions and makes a decision. The arbitrator acts as a judge.

It is possible to have paper only arbitrations, which dispense with oral hearings.

Pros

- Well established and understood in many jurisdictions.
- Parties usually able to choose their arbitrator or the appointing body.
- Experts in the subject matter of the dispute can be appointed rather than generalist judges.
- The courts retain an overarching supervisory function.
- Limited rights of appeal so that finality can be achieved.
- International treaties providing that arbitral awards can be enforced in different jurisdictions.
- Arbitration of international disputes remains a popular method of resolving cross-border disputes.

Cons

- As expensive as litigation and can be more expensive because the parties pay the arbitrators' fees and the appointing body's charges which are usually higher than court fees.
- Arbitrators have a more limited range of powers than judges, eg injunctive relief, orders against third parties, power to commit to prison for defying court orders.
- Not necessarily speedier than court proceedings and, because of more limited case management powers of arbitrators, it can in practice be slower.
- Less quality control over the competence and impartiality of arbitrators than over judges.
- Absence of the deterrent of adverse publicity.
- More opportunity for parties to game the system by alleging misconduct and bias against arbitrators if they do not like the award.
- More risk of a power imbalance between a large big spending party and a smaller poorer one affecting the process and possibly the outcome.
- In many jurisdictions domestic arbitration has become less popular because it has become so similar to litigation.
- For many parties and their legal advisers it is not an obvious alternative choice to litigation.

Adjudication

2.05 In essence adjudication is a simplified form of arbitration. The parties chose a Third Party Neutral (TPN) to come to a decision (ie adjudicate) on their dispute.

It is often used in construction disputes where disputes arise during a project but it is essential that the project is not delayed as a result of the dispute. The parties want a relatively quick and cheap solution. This is to enable the project to continue pending a final resolution. An example is the Housing Grants, Construction and Regeneration Act 1996 (HGCRA).

Pros

- Cheaper than arbitration and litigation.
- Choice of adjudicator
- Can choose an expert in the area of the dispute.
- Court supervision.
- Can be set up and concluded quickly.

Cons

- Lack of finality – often the adjudication is not a final decision but a provisional one pending a final resolution of the dispute, which may be resolved at court or in arbitration as under the HGCRA.
- Less quality control over the competence and impartiality of adjudicators than over judges. Growing concern about quality of adjudicators and their decisions.
- Time pressures can be very oppressive on smaller less well-resourced parties.
- Parties can indulge in unreasonable conduct without costs sanctions.

Advisory arbitration

2.06 Advisory arbitration can be used in a conciliation if the conciliator decides. It is used in US labour disputes but not used much in the UK. The arbitrator conducts an arbitration hearing in the normal way. He publishes his award but it is not binding on the parties. It is more like a settlement proposal or recommendation.

Pros

- An additional tool for the conciliator to help focus the parties on settlement.

Cons

- Can be a comparatively expensive way of obtaining a third party indication.
- No finality.

Arb/Med

2.07   Arb/Med is a hybrid technique combining arbitration and mediation. It is intended to deal with what is seen as the biggest drawback in mediation, namely that there is no guarantee of a final outcome.

The parties choose the same TPN to act as both arbitrator and mediator. The TPN acting as arbitrator first holds an arbitration hearing in the usual way and makes his award. He does not publish the award but places it in a sealed envelope, which he retains. He then acts as a mediator. He knows what the award says but the parties do not. They can only guess what it might be depending on how well or badly they think their case went at the arbitration hearing.

The mediator conducts the mediation in the usual way. There is no procedural change because it is taking place after an arbitration. The parties know that if they do not achieve a settlement at mediation the arbitration award will be published. They know therefore that there will be a definite outcome. Each party takes a decision on whether or not it thinks that the settlement offers them a more favourable outcome than what they expect to receive in the award.

Pros

- It saves time and money by having the same neutral doing both jobs.

- It provides the parties with finality. They know that their dispute will be over, one way or the other.

- Practitioners acting as TPNs who have been correctly trained will be able to separate the different roles and also to control themselves during the mediation not to reveal anything about their award.

- If the mediator does not hold caucuses but conducts everything in joint sessions the risk of the parties trying to extract sensitive information out of the mediator will be reduced.

- A lot of the advocacy that goes on at mediation where the parties argue their legal case and predict outcomes at trial is rendered otiose. This reduces the down time before considerations of settlement proposals starts and makes positional negotiating less attractive.

Cons

- The parties will try and read the mediator for clues as to what is in the award.

- The mediator will not be able to avoid giving clues by his body language and tone of voice or type of questions.

- The power and possibly also the temptation of the mediator to manipulate the parties towards a proposal that accords with his award will be overwhelming.

- The mediator will not be able to be evaluative in any way without in fact revealing his decision in the award.

- The mindset of an arbitrator who is acting like a judge is fundamentally different from that of a mediator who is not acting like a judge.

There are mediators who practice Arb/Med but it is not widespread. The English courts have not been encouraging. In *Glencot Development and Design Co Ltd v Ben Barrett & Son (Contractors) Ltd* the decision of an mediator who, having conducted a failed mediation then sat as an adjudicator, not arbitrator, was set aside.

Lloyd J said:

> 'Mr T went to and fro between the parties. We do not know what he heard or learned… nor given that the content was "without prejudice" and confidential ought there to be an enquiry as to what happened. These private discussions could have conveyed material or impressions which subsequently influenced his decision. … In the adjudication Mr T was asked to decide certain points about which there was no documentary evidence. These are areas where unconscious or insidious bias may well be present.'

There is an alternative version, which is called Med/Arb (see below).

Conciliation

2.08   Conciliation has different definitions in different jurisdictions. In some jurisdictions, conciliation is seen as a sort of arbitration where the arbitrator suggests settlement options to the parties. In other jurisdictions it is used as a synonym for mediation.

In the UK it has many of the same features as mediation. The important difference is that in conciliation the conciliator takes a more proactive role in bringing his own expert knowledge to the process and in suggesting settlement solutions.

The procedure of joint meetings, caucuses, follow up sessions is much the same as in mediation. The techniques used by conciliators are similar to those used by mediators.

The types of dispute where conciliation rather than mediation is used tend to be group disputes, eg employment disputes that go to Acas, or where there is a desire or a need for the parties to preserve a relationship, eg where new working practices are being introduced into a series of workplaces or there is a new development with potentially adverse impact on the surrounding land.

Pros

● It shares all the advantages of mediation, with the possible exception for those who prefer the facilitative mediation model of giving more power to the conciliator.

Cons

● The same as for mediation namely the lack of a guarantee of finality.

Con/Arb

2.09   Con/Arb is another hybrid process. It is the same as Med/Arb, and is sometimes used synonymously. The difference is that the same TPN acts as a conciliator instead of as a mediator.

Disputes Review Panel (DRP)

2.10   A disputes review panel (DRP) is also known as a dispute board, dispute review board (DRB) or dispute adjudication board (DAB).

The key features are that:

- it is usually made up of three people who are appointed by the contracting parties at the start of the project before any disputes have arisen. They visit the site at agreed intervals and have an on-going involvement in the project, even sometimes after it has finished.

- all its powers and authority arise out of the contract. It is involved at the early stages of a dispute or potential dispute. It issues recommendations.

Pros

- It saves time, money and friction and allows projects to keep moving forward.

- It provides real time value by becoming part of the process of contract administration and can acquire a preventative role.

- The board is seen by the parties as part of the team and their findings are more likely to be accepted than those issued by a third party outsider.

- It has wider application than in the construction industry where it originated. Now used in shipping, long term projects and financial services.

- It is used internationally in different jurisdictions.

Cons

- Most contracts provide that the decision of the board, as with adjudication, can be reviewed in arbitration or the courts. So there is no absolute finality.

- The board members have to be paid even if they are never called up on to carry out any dispute resolution.

Early Neutral Evaluation (ENE)

2.11   With Early Neutral Evaluation (ENE), the parties appoint an expert who is often a retired judge to review the evidence and the submissions and give a non-binding opinion.

ENE offers the following key features:

- It is not much used in the UK, but it has been used in complex technical disputes in the financial sector.

- ENE is most useful where the outcome of the case in court or arbitration would not depend on contested factual evidence, which would have to be tested in cross-examination, but on evaluating legal arguments, established market practice or technical expert evidence.

- There is no fixed procedure. The parties agree to this process and choose the evaluator, which can be a source of disagreement. The evaluator usually decides what procedure to follow.

- Usually the parties submit written submissions and evidence. Sometimes there are oral hearings.
- The evaluator considers the material and produces a recommendation giving his assessment of the evidence, the legal arguments and the probable outcome at trial.
- The evaluator's recommendations are not binding on the parties.

2.12 ENE can be arranged through the court in the Commercial, Mercantile and Technology and Construction Courts. Details can be found in the court guides for these courts:

Technology and Construction Court – https://www.justice.gov.uk/downloads/courts/tech-court/tec-con-court-guide.pdf

Admiralty and Commercial Courts – https://www.justice.gov.uk/downloads/courts/admiralitycomm/admiralty-and-commercial-courts-guide.pdf

Mercantile Court – https://www.justice.gov.uk/downloads/courts/mercantile-court/mercantile-court-guide.pdf

Pros
- At an early stage in a dispute, potentially authoritative views can be obtained which can have a persuasive influence on the disputants.
- Although the recommendations are non-binding, the parties do decide to adopt the recommendations to settle the dispute
- It is cheaper than going to trial or arbitration.
- One party can ask for an ENE of its own case.

Cons
- Many think that this is an unsatisfactory procedure.
- Why would a party seek an ENE of its own case? That is why parties go to lawyers.
- Why have an ENE, which is a sort of miniaturised trial without the potentially entertaining and destructive parts such as cross-examination?
- There is an element of transferring responsibility for one's own decisions. The parties ask someone to tell them what the answer is but do not agree to accept it if they do like it.
- You might as well go to court if you want a definitive answer.
- A mediation with an evaluative mediator will deliver more value:
  — The parties will be more involved in the process;
  — they can make sure that issues or considerations which are not included in the pleading or submissions which will tend to be legal are taken into account in any settlement; and
  — it is much cheaper and quicker.

Expert Determination (ED)

2.13 This process is similar in some ways to arbitration. The parties select a TPN to decide who is right and who is wrong. However, there are significant differences:

- The courts do not exercise as much regulatory influence over an expert as they do over an arbitrator. There is no equivalent of the Arbitration Act.

- The rights and obligations of the expert are almost entirely a matter of the contract between the parties and the terms of the expert's appointment. There are very few implied terms. Great care has to be taken in drafting the contract and in making sure that the clients understand it. Many contracts do include provision for expert determination. Many decisions to go to ED are also taken ad hoc.

Pros

- The contract usually provides that the decision is final, ie no appeal and binding.

- The parties can choose their expert

- Anecdotally, there is evidence of concern about the level of expertise of some experts.

- It is quick and cheap compared with the other adjudicative options.

Cons

- There is no implied obligation to apply the principles of natural justice.

- There is no equivalent to the New York Convention so that a decision in one jurisdiction will not be enforceable in another.

- There is no implied obligation for the expert to give reasons for his decision.

- The expert cannot ask the court for help in carrying out a function, eg compelling witnesses to attend or that property should be inspected.

- There is no immunity for experts. Unlike the arbitrator who has the protection under s 29 of the Arbitration Act he can be sued for negligence or breach of contract.

- It is a less good choice than other procedures for general contract disputes.

- Care must be taken if the expert is going to be asked to determine questions of law with no appeal to the court if he makes an error.

ED is best suited for disputes where there are limited and clearly defined issues and where only an expert will be authoritiative.

Facilitation

2.14 Facilitation is a process where a facilitator helps all parties to work out a procedure or process for discussing settlement of the dispute. The facilitator usually then guides the agreed process.

Pros

- These appointments are often ad hoc. This allows the procedure to be tailored to the particular dispute.

Cons

- There has to be a degree of common ground between the parties about the need for a facilitator and the choice and powers of the facilitator to launch the process.

- Facilitation is not much used in the UK.

Fact finding

2.15   The parties appoint a TPN to investigate and possibly establish facts. He may be asked to reach a decision on those facts. He does not deal with questions of law or compensation or other remedies.

Pros

- As an ancillary exercise to settlement procedure it can be useful. The cost and time expended needs to be justified in the overall scheme of things.

Cons

- The TPN's findings are not usually binding.

Financial dispute resolution meeting (FDR)

2.16   A financial dispute resolution meeting (FDR) takes places before a family judge, but not the one who will hear the case if it is not settled. Such meetings are held at court.

The key features of a FDR are as follows:

- Before the FDR the parties will have exchanged a lot of financial information. They will both have filed a Form E. Issues arising out of further disclosure of financial information will have been dealt with.

- It is expected the parties will attend the FDR in possession of most if not all of the financial information they need.

- The parties attend court several hours before the appointed time for the FDR and engage in negotiations. The intention is to try and come to an agreed settlement to put before the judge at the FDR.

- If that is not possible the FDR hearing takes place before the judge. Each side briefly sets out their case and identifies the issues on which there has not been agreement.

- The judge asks questions and then gives an 'indication'. This is not a judgment or a decision.

- All discussions both inside and outside the court are without prejudice.

Pros

- When an FDR produces a settlement it is justified.

- Even when an FDR does not produce a settlement, it makes the parties and their advisers think about the issues, both legal and evidential.

- It is a reality check.

Cons

- The indications are not binding, so there is no finality.

- The FDR judge can give an 'indication' but the judge who hears the case is not bound by it. There is plenty of evidence that they may come to different decisions, sometimes diametrically opposite ones.

- Parties can feel exhausted and stressed and do not always appreciate that when a judge gives an indication that this is not necessarily the same as a judgment.

- A lot of explanation and expectation management is required.

The fact is that parties engaged in matrimonial proceedings in the English courts have no choice.

Joint settlement meetings (JSMs)

2.17   Joint settlement meetings (JSMs) are also known as round table meetings (RTMs) or three room meetings.

The key features of JSMs are as follows:

- There is nothing new about these procedures. The parties to the dispute meet to try and settle it.

- No third-party neutral is involved.

- They have been described as mediation without a mediator. This is more confusing than helpful. Mediation has been described as assisted negotiation. If that is correct then JSMs are unassisted negotiation. They have nothing to do with mediation.

- The use of JSMs has increased given the courts' encouragement to parties to try and settle. Some judges do regard them as a form of ADR. If they are at all, they are a very weak form of ADR.

- The three room meeting is a variation that proved very popular in personal injury cases. There is a joint session and then the parties break up into their private rooms. The barristers go into the third room and have private discussions in the absence of their clients. They come back and report what has being going on.

Pros

- JSMs are cheaper. You do not have to pay the mediator's fees.

- They can be quicker to arrange because you do not have to worry about the mediator' availability.

- They are more informal and do not generally last as long as mediations although they can go on for hours.

- They can provide more opportunity for the client to be heard. He has more of a voice than he does at mediation where he can be stifled because of the formality of the proceedings.

Cons

- JSMs are not significantly cheaper. The only difference in cost between a well-prepared JSM or RTM and mediation is the cost of the mediator. The advantages of having a third-party neutral present far outweigh the cost. A significant number of mediations take place after a JSM and or RTM has failed, which means that there is an extra layer of cost.

- There is no agreed procedure, which is monitored by a third-party neutral. This gives more scope for people to play games instead of attending to the job in hand which is to achieve a settlement.

- There is less reality checking so that parties maintain their positions longer.

- There is no external source of encouragement to keep the parties engaged and the momentum going when they reach 'the wall' at 3.30pm.

- Most lawyers at JSMs or RTMs cannot resist the forensic urge to argue their case. They see their job as demolition men to reduce the other side's case to rubble. They cannot easily resist the temptation to grandstand in front of their clients. To be fair, some of the clients demand a bravura forensic display on their behalf.

- They tend to be lawyer dominated and the clients do not have the same opportunity of being acknowledged by a new audience, ie the mediator.

- There is no one who actually has a duty to address any imbalance of power and to make sure that the powerful well resourced and represented party does not try and intimidate the other weaker and poorer party.

They sometimes work. Generally they do not work as well as mediation. If clients and advocates are serious about trying to settle they should choose meditation

Judicial mediation

2.18 Judicial mediation is practised in The Technology and Construction Court (TCC) and in the Employment Tribunals.

TCC process

The TCC process is known as the court settlement process (CSP). With the consent of the parties the case is assigned to another TCC judge who acts as mediator. The procedure is regulated by the court settlement order, which is set out in appendix G of the TCC Guide. The procedure is very similar to most mediations.

The key features are as follows:

- TCC is without prejudice, voluntary, confidential and non-binding.

- The judge who conducts the CSP can conduct it in any way he likes taking into account the parties own views, the circumstances of the case and the overriding objective in the Civil Procedure Rules.

- The judge holds a preliminary court settlement conference to decide the procedure, the duration and what disclosure shall be given.

- Unless the parties otherwise agree the judge can have separate or joint meetings or communications in which he can give opinions about the dispute. A party can ask for a private meeting with the judge.

- Confidential information given to the judge by one party is not disclosed to the other without consent.

- If there is no settlement parties can ask the judge to give a written assessment on some or all of the issues, the probable outcome at trial and his suggestions for a settlement.

- The parties' rights are fully preserved and nothing they say during the CSP prejudices any position they may wish to take in any subsequent litigation.

- Each side pays their own costs and splits the court costs unless otherwise agreed.

- The judge who has conducted the CSP takes no further part in the litigation.

Anecdotal evidence suggests that some people are very happy with the procedure and that it worked well. Others are less happy. The number of judicial mediations that are taking place is much lower than the number of mediations of the same sort of disputes that are taking place using non-judicial mediators.

Since one of the reasons parties like to go to mediation is to avoid a judge giving his opinion on their case when he gives a judgment at trial, why would they want to ask for his opinion in a CSP hearing?

Judicial time and resources are limited. They are better spent on judging.

Employment tribunals

2.19   Under the employment tribunal's judicial mediation scheme, the judge at case management discussion chooses suitable cases for judicial mediation. If all parties agree, the regional employment judge will decide whether or not the case should be referred to judicial mediation.

If there is a mediation it operates in much the same way as other mediations.

The key features of the scheme are as follows:

- The parties have to be committed to the idea.

- There is no continuing ACAS involvement.

- The length of the final hearing is at least three days.

- It is listed for a private hearing and all case management orders are suspended, but the final hearing date is kept.

- Originally limited to discrimination cases, it is now available to all types of cases,.

- The mediation style is now indicative, not facilitative as it was originally.
- The fee of £600 is paid by the respondent.
- They take place at the employment tribunal premises.

Pros

- It saves time money and stress.
- Non-judicial solutions can be devised.
- The parties potentially have a greater involvement in the process and influence on the outcome.
- It is successful but not much used. In 2013 there were 105,803 claims. There were 319 successful mediations and 154 unsuccessful ones.

Cons

- It has some of the features of a FDR in the family courts with much the same advantages and disadvantages.
- It tends to take place in a 'court' setting with a real judge so that the parties can be both confused about what is really going on and also intimidated.
- Not all employment tribunal judges have been trained in mediation and there is limited court time to devote to it.
- Anecdotal evidence from mediation trainers reveals that judges, whether sitting or recently retired, find the transition from *telling* people what is important to *asking* people what is important difficult.
- The shift from the facilitative model to the indicative model reflects the judicial mediators' proclivities. The distinction between being evaluative and being indicative is not entirely clear. It has been explained by the President of Employment Tribunals as:

  'the mediator identifying the barriers to success at the final hearing that each side will face, rather than predicting the outcome or telling the parties how he would decide the case if he was going to hear it, which of course he cannot.'

Mediation

2.20   This is examined in detail at **paras 2.26–2.35**.

Med/Arb

2.21   This is the opposite of Arb/Med: the mediation takes place first. If it produces a settlement that is the end of the matter. If there is no settlement the mediator then acts as an arbitrator. He conducts a hearing in the usual way and makes and publishes his award.

Pros

● The imminence of the arbitration might concentrate the parties focus on settlement.

● The Johnson effect. This can encourage parties to see the realities of their positions more clearly and to stop believing their own propaganda. The bluffing might stop earlier:

> 'Depend upon it, sir, when a man knows he is to be hanged in a fortnight, it concentrates his mind wonderfully.'

> Samuel Johnson, in James Boswell, *The Life of Samuel Johnson LL D* (Vol 3)

Cons

● The parties will try and game the mediator so as to influence him when he acts as arbitrator.

● They will withhold confidential information from him because it might influence him even unconsciously at the arbitration.

● They tell him, confidentially, of action that they intend to take, eg bring fraud charges against the other side in the hope that it has some influence on his view of the other side.

● An arbitrator cannot be certain that he has excluded information or impressions, which he gained in private confidential discussions with one of the parties during the mediation. As arbitrator he should take his decision based upon evidence that is put before him at the hearing by both parties in presence of each other.

● It could encourage mediators to be more evaluative, knowing that if it does not settle they will be entirely evaluative so that they might as well let the parties know how they provisionally see things.

Mediation after last offer arbitration (MEDALOA)

2.22 This is a technique derived from baseball arbitration in the United States.

The key features of MEDALOA are as follows:

● If at mediation the parties cannot achieve a settlement, the mediator acts as an arbitrator.

● His sole purpose is to decide which of the proposed rulings submitted to him by the parties he prefers as being the most reasonable.

● He picks one and that becomes the arbitral award.

● The idea is that each party will have the incentive to put forward the most reasonable proposal in the hope that the arbitrator will choose their proposal.

● The parties will have the benefit of having had discussions with the arbitrator during the mediation when he was acting as a mediator before formulation of their proposal for submission to the arbitrator. This can give them the opportunity to read his mind.

Pros

- It guarantees an outcome.

Cons

- There are no obvious ones, once the parties have decided that they would rather than have a Third Party tell them the answer than work it out for themselves.

- The parties have to be confident that they choose the right person to decide which of the competing proposals is the more reasonable.

Negotiation

2.23   This is the longest established and best-known technique for resolving disputes. It has been going on since the beginning of time.

This simple traditional process has developed into a science and industry of negotiation. This is not the subject matter of this book. There is a discussion in **Chapter 16** of some of the main points that are relevant to the practice of mediation as it is currently carried on in the 21st century.

In **Chapter 1**, three key points were identified:

- Not every negotiation is a mediation but every mediation is a negotiation.

- Every negotiation involves the recognition of reality: your own and the other side's.

- In negotiations, deals are not made by arguing about points but by discussing proposals.

Ombudsman

2.24   The ombudsman was originally set up as an independent representative of the public to investigate complaints against government departments.

The ombudsman's key features are as follow:

- It is a form of ADR where the ombudsman deals with complaints against various entities, both governmental and commercial.

- The ombudsman is usually a single person but there can be a panel or board.

- The ombudsman tries to resolve the complaint through conciliation, and sometimes mediation.

- In the end the ombudsman issues a decision. The decision can be either binding or non-binding.

- Usually the ombudsman does not hold a hearing but comes to a decision on the basis of written evidence and submissions.

Pros

- It is comparatively easy for the complainant to access the procedure.

- It is not confrontational.

- It is often free.

- In many schemes, the ombudsman's ruling is not binding on the complainant but it is binding on the party about whom the complaint is made.

Cons

- It can take an unexpectedly long time as the ombudsman investigates. Many services are under resourced and overloaded with cases, such as the Financial Ombudsman Service.

- You are dependant on a case handler with whom there is little direct contact.

- You have to be able to present information in written form in an intelligible way. Not everyone can. Many complaints seek some help with their written advocacy.

Time limited mediations

2.25 Most civil and commercial mediations are open-ended in duration. The mediator is usually booked for a certain number of hours. If the mediation continues beyond the stated time the parties are charged extra by the hour. There is an expectation that all parties and the mediator will stay beyond the allotted time if necessary to try and conclude a settlement.

In time limited mediations there is an absolute cut-off point.

Time limited mediation has various key features:

- The time limit is short. Scheme or court annexed mediation are often limited to two or three hours.

- There is no expectation that the parties or the mediator will stay beyond this time.

- Quite often there are no facilities to enable them to do that. For example, in the old Central London County Court mediation scheme which lasted from 16.30–19.30 it was not unknown for settlement agreements to be signed by the headlights on car bonnets.

Pros

- Time limited mediations are, through necessity, more streamlined.

- Having a time limit concentrates people's minds. A surprising number of mediations settle within the time limit on terms the parties can accept and which give them satisfaction.

- Time limited mediations cost less.

Cons

- The significance of the time limit cannot be exaggerated. Some parties can feel pressured to make a decision.

- Generally mediations expand the time available for the mediation so this can save time.

- Optimism bias leads people to underestimate the time it takes to complete any task. Parties who are working hard and in good faith to reach a settlement can find that they just run out of time.

The ADR spectrum: where does mediation fit in?

2.26   Below is a bar chart showing the different mediation procedures. It compares various ADR procedures by:

- degree of adjudication, ie litigation is the most adjudicative and negotiation the least;

- the length of time the procedure takes; and

- the cost of the procedure.

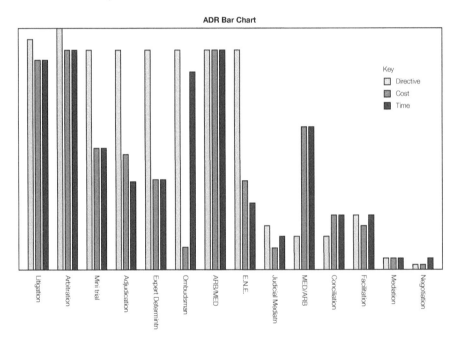

This shows that as the procedure becomes adjudicative it also becomes both longer and more expensive. The cheapest and quickest way of solving a dispute is by direct negotiation. The longest and most expensive is by litigation or arbitration. Mediation stands out as the best alternative to either of them.

What is different about mediation?

2.27   In the definition at **para 1.02** mediation is described as a voluntary and confidential process where a neutral Third Party helps the parties to the dispute to find their own settlement.

Voluntary

2.28   In some jurisdictions, mediation is now compulsory. This is discussed in more detail in **Chapter 8**.

Even in jurisdictions such as England and Wales, where the civil litigation rules do not make mediation mandatory, there is enormous pressure on parties to go to mediation before going to trial. Mediation clauses are also increasingly used in commercial contracts instead or as a supplement to arbitration clauses. The English courts as discussed in **Chapter 12** will uphold them. But there is still an essential voluntary element. The parties may be compelled to go to mediation but they cannot be compelled to reach a settlement. The parties only settle their dispute if they want to settle.

The terms on which they settle will be the terms that they have worked out themselves and agreed. Nobody will have imposed terms on the parties. This is the exact opposite of what happens at litigation, arbitration, adjudication and expert determination.

Dispute

2.29   When disputes go to court or arbitration they are framed as claims or defences in legal categories. The disputants' advisers tell them what their legal rights are and what remedies are available to them. Not every element of a dispute can form part of a legal claim. For example:

- The parties to a contract dispute cannot be ordered to re-negotiate, which might in fact be the sensible solution for both sides.

- In an employment dispute, the court cannot order the employer to provide a reference for the employee.

- In medical negligence cases, most claimants want an apology and an explanation of what went wrong. The explanation may emerge during the court hearing. But the judge can never order the doctor to give an apology.

- In boundary disputes, the court can decide the boundary line. It may order that a boundary fence be moved if it is in the wrong place. The best practical solution to the dispute may be for the neighbours to exchange land. The court cannot order this.

This ability for mediation to provide solutions, which the court cannot provide by way of legal remedies is the reason why the scope of discussions at mediation is often wider than the scope of argument at court or arbitration.

Mediation can take place where the parties are in dispute and before legal proceedings have been started. There is growing anecdotal evidence of there being more pre-litigation mediations taking place.

Confidential

2.30   This is discussed in detail in **Chapter 12**. There is a growing body of case law about this in England and Wales. The mediator and parties cannot assume as blithely as they used to that what is said and done at mediation can never be disclosed.

The key point is that mediation, like arbitration, takes place in private. However, unlike in arbitration, the parties in mediation can have private and confidential conversations with the mediator.

Process

2.31   What happens at mediation is discussed in more detail in **Chapters 9** and **10**. The three classic stages were described at **para 1.04** above:

- exploration;
- exchange; and
- formulation.

Sometimes all three stages are carried out jointly with the parties together at all times. More usually in civil and commercial mediation there are joint sessions, but also private sessions with just the mediator and one side. In some jurisdictions the mediation usually takes place within a day – this can be anything from 4 to 14 hours. In others there is a system of rolling mediations where a series of sessions of about two hours are held over a period of weeks or even months.

Family mediations

In family mediations, most and sometimes all of the discussion between the parties and the mediator takes place in joint sessions. Private sessions are being used more often. It is rare but not unknown for a family mediation to take place and be concluded either with or without a settlement within one day. The standard model assumes three to five sessions of about one to two hours spread over a number of weeks.

Community and workplace mediations

In community and workplace mediations, there are usually one or two rounds of private sessions before a joint session. Ideally mediations will be concluded within a day but more often than not they are spread over several days or weeks.

Mediation is a flexible process. Usually the parties and the mediator work out together the process that they want to adopt. Some mediators are more prescriptive than others and insist for example that they hold a Joint Opening Session. Generally the process is adapted to meet the needs of the parties without too much disagreement.

Neutral

2.32   There is a lot of debate about what neutrality means. Is it the same as impartiality? Much of this debate is academically interesting but is in practice of little relevance. In this book it is assumed that:

- Neutrality means that the mediator has no personal stake in the outcome.

- Impartiality means that the mediator is not prejudiced in favour of one party or the other and acts in an even-handed way.

There are mediators who have a reputation of being pro-claimant or pro-insurers, just as there are judges and arbitrators with similar reputations. However, there has been no reported case in England and Wales where lack of neutrality or impartiality has been alleged. In practice, if at a mediation anyone has doubts about the neutrality or impartiality of the mediator, they can raise them. If they remain doubtful they can leave.

Third Party

2.33   As has been said, all mediations are a negotiation. The key difference between a mediation and negotiation is the presence of a Third Party. In fact mediation is often described as assisted negotiation. The role of the Third Party is discussed in detail in **Chapter 4**.

The presence of a Third Party changes the dynamics of the discussions between the disputing parties. They behave differently in the presence of a stranger to the dispute. They may know the mediator personally but he is not part of their dispute. Just by being present the mediator lowers the temperature of the debate. It is a case of two's an argument and three's a conversation.

Mediators have different and sometimes distinctive styles. There is no settled view on how significant the mediator's style is to the outcome of the mediation. One can see how it could be crucial. It probably has more to do with the quality of the mediation experience than the outcome. How do the parties feel that they were treated? Did they have a chance of having their say or did they feel railroaded and sidetracked? Different mediator styles are discussed in **Chapter 4**.

The parties

2.34   Party autonomy has traditionally been promoted as a distinctive and attractive feature of mediation. The parties to mediation retain much greater control over both the process and the outcome than they do for example in litigation or arbitration. Parties can play a much bigger role in what actually happens at mediation than they can at court.

This is undeniably true but there are sceptics who doubt the extent of this freedom. They emphasise the pressure on parties that can be exerted at mediation to settle, in particular the desire of the mediator to achieve a settlement for his own professional satisfaction and reputation. Professor Heather Genn in particular has been vociferous, articulate and, in the author's opinion, wrong on this point and on mediation generally, as for example, when she says that: 'The outcome of mediation is not about just settlement – it is just about settlement.' It is investigated in more detail in **Chapter 6** when discussing the role of the advocate at mediation.

Own solution

2.35   There is a fundamental difference between mediation on the one hand and litigation or arbitration on the other. In litigation or arbitration, the judge or arbitrator imposes the solution. A mediator cannot impose any solution on the parties. The parties only agree what they want to agree. There is much more scope for the parties to devise their own creative solutions to their problems and disputes in a way in which a judge could never help them do even if he wanted to.

This is true in theory and also in practice to a degree. The question of to what degree is examined in **Chapters 5** and **7**, when discussing the importance of devising settlement options before attending mediation.

Which ADR method to choose?

2.36   The percentage choice, ie the one that will deliver the best outcome in the best way in most cases, is mediation. Others might be suited to a particular set of circumstances.

The ADR tick box list below shows why.

ADR Tick Box Chart

	1 Adjudicative	2 Party control	3 Choice of TPN	4 Choice of time	5 Choice of venue	6 Choice of process	7 Choice of duration	8 Choice of outcome	9 Clients participation
Litigation	✓								
Arbitration	✓		✓	✓	✓				
Mini trial	✓		✓	✓	✓	✓	✓		
Adjudication	✓		✓						
Expert Determination	✓		✓	✓	✓	✓	✓		
Ombudsman	✓								
ARB/MED	✓		✓	✓	✓	✓			
E.N.E.			✓	✓		✓	✓		
Judicial Mediation									
MED/ARB	✓		✓	✓	✓	✓			
Conciliation		✓	✓	✓	✓	✓	✓	✓	✓
Facilitation		✓	✓	✓	✓	✓	✓	✓	✓
Mediation		✓	✓	✓	✓	✓	✓	✓	✓
Negotiation		✓		✓	✓	✓	✓	✓	✓

Conclusion

2.37   To conclude:

- If the parties cannot solve their dispute themselves through direct negotiation, the next best way most of the time is assisted negotiation, ie mediation.

- There will be disputes where some adjudicative element is needed and another process such as ENE or ED could be appropriate.

- Clients and advocates should not just accept the propaganda of the mediation evangelists, but read this book to discover the reality of mediation.

- There is a crucial role for mediation advocates in trying to help their clients to get the best out of the process.

- This is much more obvious in civil and commercial mediations than in family, workplace or community, where the advocate's role is much more limited, and which in many ways are significantly different.

Chapter 3

Mediators – Who Are They?

This chapter asks:

- What sort of people are mediators?
- How can you find them?
- How would you choose one?

Who are mediators?

3.01   Typing this question into Google or any other search engine will not help much. Most of the sites tell you:

- what mediation is;
- what mediators do; or
- details of the mediators who are on their panels who provide mediation services.

It is difficult to find information on who mediators are as a breed. What are their backgrounds, experience, training and characteristics?

In **Chapter 2** the nature of mediation and other ADR methods was discussed. In **Chapter 4** the various models of mediation are discussed. This chapter looks at who mediators are in England and Wales.

Civil and commercial mediators

3.02   The most up-to-date information about civil and commercial mediators is contained in the Sixth Biennial Mediation Audit carried out by CEDR issued in May 2014.

Mediators' profile

3.03   The survey reveals that:

- Most mediators are aged 50 or over. The average female mediator is aged 50 and the average male mediator is 57.

- Most are men. Women comprise 26 per cent and men 74 per cent.
- Most are white – about 96 per cent.
- Most are lawyers – 52 per cent.
- Of the respondents, 22 per cent are novices. Novice mediators are those who are accredited but have no experience as a lead mediator.
- The percentage of respondents describing themselves as intermediate is 22 per cent. Intermediate mediators are those with some but limited experience as a lead mediator.
- The percentage of respondents describing themselves as advanced is 56 per cent. Advanced mediators are those who have reasonable or more experience as lead mediators.
- Nearly all those in the novice and intermediate categories carried out less than four mediations a year. Just over half the advanced mediators carried out more than 10 mediations in a year.

This is the position in 2014. Certain trends can be seen.

The number of women is increasing

3.04   The percentage of women mediators is:
- 2014: 26 per cent.
- 2012: 22 per cent.
- 2010: 19 per cent .

However, the percentage of women in the advanced group is increasing:
- 2014: 25 per cent.
- 2012: 18 per cent.

Some of the most successful commercial mediators are women.

The number of advanced mediators is increasing

3.05   It has been a pattern of civil and commercial mediations for many years that a small group of mediators dominates the market and carries out most of the civil and commercial mediations.
- In 2010 90 individuals held 85 per cent of the market.
- In 2012 100 individuals held 85 per cent of the market.
- In 2014 130 individuals held 85 per cent of the market.

In a period of four years the group of 90 has increased to 130. Clearly the monopoly enjoyed by the elite is under threat. This is part of the increasing diversity and maturity of the market referred to in **Chapter 1**.

The number of mediators who are not legally trained is growing

3.06   This is both as a percentage and in absolute numbers. The first wave of non-lawyer mediators came from the traditional professions such as surveying and accountancy. Now there is a much more diverse intake including HR professionals, management consultants, ship brokers, IT professionals, diplomats and actors. They need to work out how they will be able to bring a distinctive contribution to their practice as mediators from their professional experience.

However, most of the commercial mediators are still lawyers. Originally, when mediation was introduced into the UK 25 years ago, most were solicitors. Over the years barristers have qualified as mediators in increasing numbers. Now former judges have decided that mediation makes an attractive alternative retirement activity to golf. They have their own distinctive contribution to make.

Mediators' earnings are falling

3.07   As is clear from the statistics about how many mediations are carried out, it is unlikely that mediation could be a full-time job. It is difficult to make a living sufficient to pay the mortgage and bring up children on the average earnings from mediation.

The increase in the number of mediators has led to downward pressure on fees.

In 2010:

- 10 per cent of mediations were carried out for no fee.
- 57 per cent of mediations were carried out for a fee of less than £2,000 for a one-day mediation, ie eight hours.
- Average earnings for less experienced mediators for one-day mediations were £1,390 and for more experienced mediators £3,450.

In 2012:

- 7 per cent of mediations were carried out for no fee.
- 55 per cent of mediations were carried out for a fee of less than £2,000.
- The average fee for a less experienced mediator was £1,517 and for a more experienced mediator £4,279.

In 2014:

- 8 per cent of mediations were carried out for no fee.
- 51 per cent of mediations were carried out for a fee of less than £2,000.
- The average fee for less experienced mediators was £1,422 and for the more experienced mediators £3,820.

3.08   If the definition of an experienced mediator is one who carries out more than 10 mediations a year this means that the threshold is only £38,000 a year.

Those carrying out between 20–30 mediations a year are earning about £70,000 a year.

For a one-day mediation the average time spent working with clients on the day is about eight hours with seven hours before the mediation in preparation and client contact and 1.7 hours after the mediation – a total of just over 16.5 hours. In other words, for each day spent in mediation there is another day spent on related activities. Each one-day mediation therefore is a two-day job.

This means that for most mediators, mediation is not a full-time job. Amongst the most experienced group, 47 per cent now describe themselves as full-time mediators. In 2012 the figure was 39 per cent and in 2010 37 per cent.

The number of mediators is increasing

3.09   No one knows how many mediators there are, but the Director of Training at the ADR Group estimated in 2014 that there were about 6,000–7,000 mediators in England and Wales, with a further 900 being trained each year. This includes university students who complete a mediation module as part of their degree course, which leads to accreditation. This means that there are a great many mediators who do very few mediations.

These trends give rise to the following questions.

How many active mediators are there?

3.10   How active a mediator is one of the factors that must be taken into account when selecting a mediator. This topic is discussed in more detail at **para 3.24.**

Anyone who is not regularly practising their trade can quickly become deskilled. Many occasional mediators are aware of this and complain about it. The Civil Mediation Council (CMC) has recognised the problem. It now allows mediators who cannot undertake the minimum number of mediations a year, as provided in their rules, to observe or attend simulated mediations as a way of keeping their skills up to date.

On the other hand there are mediators who are too busy. The 2012 Commercial Mediation Group survey found that many of its members thought that mediators should raise their fees so that they would not take on so much work. They were concerned that the busy mediators had too much to do. Service levels were falling for reasons such as:

- they were not properly prepared;
- they had not really delved into the documents; and
- they turned up to mediations jaded and operated on autopilot.

These suggestions and observations were not welcomed by busy commercial mediators.

What sort of people are mediators?

3.11   There has been surprisingly little research into what sort of people become commercial mediators in the UK and in particular what sort become successful mediators.

To date there has been a myriad of subjective observational research allied to demographic data that informs the reader, but nothing in the qualitative field. However, there is currently research being undertaken by Aaron Hudson-Tyreman at Queen Mary College London into the personality traits of commercial mediators. This utilises a focus group identified by the two largest UK legal directories.

As far as one can tell, the sort of people who are successful commercial mediators exhibit consistent traits across the spectrum. The mediation community and its customers will have to await the final results which are expected to be published in 2015 to fully appreciate the outcomes and whether they will have an impact upon how mediators are selected and trained.

Family mediation

The latest statistics from the Ministry of Justice in December 2014 suggest that there were about 8,000 publicly funded mediations started between July 2013 and June 2014. Statistics for privately funded mediations are hard to come by but anecdotal evidence suggests that family mediators face the same problems as civil and commercial mediators in attracting work. There has been a fall in the number of family mediations because of the introduction of fees and the abolition of Legal Aid for family disputes.

There are more women as a proportion of family mediators than there are women as commercial mediators. A higher proportion of family mediators have a non-legal background than commercial mediators. Family law as practised by barristers or solicitors has a higher proportion of women practitioners than commercial litigation.

Community mediation

Many community mediators are provided by panels maintained by local authorities or by organisations with links to social services departments or the police. They are often funded by charitable donations and many mediators provide the services for no or reduced fees.

Novice mediators are often advised to do pro bono mediations for community organisations in order to acquire some training and practical experience.

Can anyone be a mediator?

3.12   Another and more provocative answer to the question 'Who are mediators?' is 'Whoever wants to call themselves a mediator'. Anybody in England and Wales can call themselves a mediator. There is no restriction on the use of the term 'mediator' as there is, for example, with architects or solicitors.

There is no central unified regulatory body for mediators as there is, for example, for doctors with the British Medical Association or the Bar Council for barristers or the Royal Institute of British Architects (RIBA) for architects. The Civil Mediation Council is gradually assuming a central role, but slowly and with reluctance. It now maintains a register of mediators who have applied to join. There are minimum standards for entry onto the register. These can be found at the CMC website (www.civilmediation.org).

3.13 There are several mediation training organisations but not all are accredited by the CMC. Accredited trainers agree to provide minimum standards training, for example 40 hours' training, of which at least 50 per cent must be spent in role-play and the assessment must be carried out by someone who has not been involved in the training. Details of accredited trainers can be found on the CMC website.

This does not apply to family mediators who have their own regime. Details can be found on the FMC website (www.familymediationcouncil.org.uk).

The standard training consists of:

- 52 hours' training to acquire core mediation skills;
- a course of six days, run over two three-day modules;
- the first three days of intensive training is followed by a written assignment; then
- the second three days is followed by two written assignments and one video assignment.

On successful completion, trainees can begin to co-mediate.

In the cases of both civil and commercial and family mediations, the newly trained mediator has to undertake observations with experienced mediators before being accredited. Details can be found on the CMC and the FMC websites.

3.14 Within the mediation community there has been for several years a debate about whether or not there should be central regulation. The arguments in favour focus on:

- quality assurance;
- public confidence; and
- inevitability.

In the end all new activities and markets end up being regulated. Sometimes the regulation is self-regulation and voluntary. Usually some degree of compulsory regulation is introduced. It has been a feature over the last 40 years in the UK that industries providing services to the public have become regulated. Professionals in all sorts of sectors habitually complain about the amount of regulation that has been introduced. In the end they recognise that it is inevitable and a reflection of the rise of consumerism.

Those who are against regulation argue that:

- it is unnecessary – the market regulates itself;
- it will introduce an extra layer of costs; and

- it will stifle commercial creativity.

Most successful mediators are in fact accredited in some way. This usually means that they have received training that is recognised by the CMC because it has been provided by a CMC accredited trainer. Most also join the CMC as a member and agree to be bound by its Code of Conduct and Rules. These provide that:

- they have professional indemnity insurance in place;
- they will carry out and minimum of three mediations a year; and
- they will keep up-to-date with good practice by undergoing continuing professional development (CPD).

3.15   As part of the regulatory regime there is a limited system of accountability. The question of mediators' legal liability is discussed in more detail in **Chapter 12.** Leaving aside more narrowly legal questions of negligence or breach of contract, there can be complaints about poor service. The CMC and its affiliated mediation providers operate a complaints system. The redress is usually limited to a rebate of fees and/or the removal of the offending mediator from a panel.

Mediators who are also members of other professional bodies such as the Law Society/Solicitors Regulation Authority, the Bar Council, or RIBA are also liable under those organisations and systems to make redress for poor service. Some mediators who practice as solicitors as well as mediators, for example, complain about this double jeopardy.

The International Mediation Institute (IMI) at an international level is also trying to bring in some degree of standardised accreditation. Details can be found on their website (www.imimediation.org). One of the advantages of this scheme is that it will allow users of mediation to have access to a panel of mediators who they can be reasonably confident meet a minimum acceptable standard of experience and competence irrespective of where they originally trained or now practice.

Is mediation a profession?

3.16   At gatherings of mediators there is always reference to mediators being a profession. Those who think that it is do so mainly reason by analogy. They point to the main characteristics of a profession:

- training;
- codes of conduct;
- accountability;
- professional standards; and
- the nature of the activity.

In practice, however, they seem to rely upon the fact that most mediators belong to another professional body such as solicitors, architects, doctors, etc who have their own professional standards, which the mediators import into their practice as mediators. There is a lot of truth in this assertion. But it overlooks the fact that:

- different professions have different norms;
- some professions are closely regulated on an individual level, whilst others are not;
- most professions have mandatory requirements, but mediators do not; and
- there is little effective redress, unlike most other recognised professions – mediators cannot be banned from practicing.

3.17   Most mediators are self-employed. Some are in paid employment for their main job, for example, solicitors or accountants in private practice. They may provide their mediation services through their firm or they may do it with permission of the firm as an outside activity.

Nearly all mediators provide their services on a direct access basis. In other words they can be booked direct. Others provide their services through mediation providers, for example the ADR Group, CEDR, the Academy of Experts, Clerksroom, or JAMS. They do this by being on a panel. As discussed above that means that they have to comply with certain requirements about training, experience, PI insurance, etc.

Others form marketing groups, for example In Place of Strife or the Panel of Independent Mediators. More and more of these groupings are being formed as mediators try and secure work.

In many ways mediation at the moment in the UK is not so much a profession as a cottage industry. This is not necessarily a bad thing as one of the characteristics of the increasing sophistication of the mediation market is that it is in danger of becoming institutionalised. This has been the subject of recent criticism from academic commentators, for example, Professor Debbie Di Girolamo of Queen Mary's College in *The Fugitive Identity of Mediation: Negotiations, Shift Changes and Allusionary Action* (Routledge, 2013) and Penny Brooker in *Mediation Law: Journey through Institutionalism to Juridification* (Routledge, 2013).

How to find a mediator

3.18   Most people use all the following methods or a combination of them to find a mediator.

Previous experience

If a mediator has mediated a dispute for you before and has done a good job then why not use him again? There are a number of advantages of using someone you have used before:

- You know what to expect from them and in particular you will know their style of mediation and their personality. That will make it easier to find a match with your client. Often the most important factor is how well will the mediator get on with the client, in particular the decision-makers.
- You know that they can do a good job.
- You know what they will charge.

There are of course also disadvantages:

- Familiarity can start to develop and breed discontent. Both sides start to take each other for granted. The mediator may think that he does not have to try so hard. The instructing solicitor may think that he can cut corners on the preparation because the mediator will not complain and will be able to fill in the gaps himself.

- Some solicitors and clients become very sensitive if they think that there is a prior course of dealing between the mediator and the other side. They think there might be bias. In practice there is no more risk of bias than if counsel who are habitually instructed in a matter or if an arbitrator or judge has previously acted for all the parties provided of course that there is proper disclosure.

Go with their choice of mediator

3.19   If one party suggests a mediator in whom they have confidence it is a good idea to accept their suggestion. They are likely to pay attention to what the mediator says. He will have some influence with them based upon the fact that they have confidence in him. This does not mean that neutrality or impartiality will be compromised. It just means that there is a working relationship ready to start work.

It is also a matter of personal preference. There are some solicitors including, for example, the Head of Dispute Resolution at a large international firm, who never use the same mediator twice. Other members of his department, which is over 200 strong in London alone, do.

Recommendations

Apart from personal prior experience of the mediator this is the second most used way finding a mediator. In many firms e-mails are circulated asking for suggestions or comments on names that have been proposed. It is not just colleagues that can provide useful recommendations. Counsel, other mediators and clients may have their own ideas.

Other factors come into play when deciding what sort of mediator to choose and these are discussed in more detail at **para 3.24.**

Talent spotting

3.20   Mediators seem to be everywhere. There are more and more of them. Just listening to them at book launches, seminars and conferences can provide useful information on what they might be like as a mediator.

Some lawyers who regularly instruct mediators attend mediation gatherings such as the Breakfast Club, which meets in the Punch Tavern in Fleet Street London (dwo@pengaron.co.uk). They meet lots of mediators and take note of those that impress.

Directories

In a survey carried out in 2012 by the Commercial Mediation Group, 40 per cent of respondents said they use directories. The two most widely used are *Chambers* and the *Legal 500*. They have to be used with an intelligent appreciation. There can be startling discrepancies. The descriptions have to be decoded.

The internet

Going onto the internet and searching for mediators will produce pages and pages of individuals and organisations. It is important to bear in mind several features of the internet:

● On the internet anyone can be a dog. In other words you have to check what is behind the web page.

● People can pay for the names to appear as adverts. Some mediation organisations and individual mediators do that.

● Optimisation techniques are employed to drive searchers to particular websites.

Registers

3.21   The CMC maintains a list of its members who have asked to be put on the register. They do not recommend any particular mediator. They simply provide details. The FMC does the same.

Panels

These are similar but different from the registers operated by the CMC and the FMC, etc. They are operated by mediation service providers, for example, the ADR Group, CEDR, or JAMS. Most of them are also training organisations. Members of their panel would usually have trained with them. Others are operated by professional bodies such as the Law Society, Academy of Experts, or RICS. Most charge their members a fee to be included on the panel. They also charge the users a fee for organising and administering the mediation.

Most but not all mediation service providers who operate panels are members of the CMC. If they are, some comfort can be derived from the fact that they operate according to the CMC guidelines.

Many mediators appear on multiple panels. So to some extent the cornucopia of choice is illusory.

Marketing groups

Some mediators band together for marketing purposes. They are not attached to a training company or a professional body. They are together for administration and marketing. Examples are In Place of Strife or The Panel of Independent Mediators. They are independent mediators who share some common facilities. More and more marketing groups are being formed.

Barristers' chambers and firms of solicitors

3.22   Barristers who are working at the Bar in chambers will have a clerk. When acting as a mediator they are usually clerked in the same way by their clerks. Some chambers identify specialist ADR groups within their set and offer mediation suites. Some firms of solicitors offer similar facilities and have set up specific mediation arms distinct from their litigation and/or dispute resolution services.

Family mediators also operate through chambers and firms of solicitors. A recent example is the family mediation service start-up in Middlesbrough called Divorce Puzzle. It offers lawyer-supported mediation at fixed fees. The intention is to fill a gap in representation met by the government's cuts being laid for private family work. They will be competing with solicitors.

Individuals/independents

These are people who practice as mediators. Some may also be panel members or work in professional firms. Many are not associated or affiliated with anyone.

The little black book

Many firms, especially as part of quality control programmes, have databases listing approved suppliers. These will include barristers, forensic experts and now mediators. Many practitioners after a few years develop their individual little black book of favoured and trusted professionals who they can call upon. The difficulty is that the list needs constantly updating and refreshing.

Mediation providers

3.23   The advantages of using mediation providers are as follows:

● It can save time. One telephone call or e-mail and they supply a list of names for consideration.

● The names from their panel will be mediators who have received proper training and have kept their experience up to date.

● They will attend to the logistics of arranging rooms and dates.

● There is likely to be a complaints procedure and their members will have professional indemnity insurance.

There are also disadvantages:

● They can charge more than a mediator who is approached on direct access basis.

● They tend to only put names forward who are drawn from their list of members.

In the 2012 Commercial Mediation Group (CMG) survey, 56 per cent of respondents said that they used specialist providers and 40 per cent said that they used directories. As the 2014 CEDR Survey reported:

'There seems also to have been a halt in long-term trend towards commercial clients and advisers making referrals directly to their chosen mediators rather than working through providers.'

Weighing up the mediator

3.24   Anyone appointing a mediator should ask themselves and the mediator the following questions.

How is he accredited?

For civil and commercial mediations, it can be dangerous to appoint someone who is not accredited either directly or indirectly by the CMC. For family mediators, the FMC plays a similar role to the CMC.

How is he regulated?

This is a similar point to the one above. The limited scope of regulation was discussed at **para 3.12.** Why chose someone who is not regulated at all?

Does he have professional indemnity insurance?

So far there have been relatively few claims against mediators in the UK. There will be more. Mediator liability is discussed in **Chapter 11**. PI insurance for mediators is cheap and if a mediator does not have it, it suggests either overweening self-confidence or carelessness.

How many mediations has he actually carried out?

There is no agreed definition of experienced or advanced mediator. Within the mediation community a rule of thumb is that mediators who have carried out fewer than 10 mediations cannot call themselves experienced. Some providers such as Clerksroom have a category of elite mediators who have carried out in excess of 50 mediations.

What you need to know is how many mediations he has carried out as the lead mediator. This does not include observations, acting as an assistant or co-mediator or even being a representative at a mediation.

Most mediators say in their CV or profile how many mediations they have done as a mediator. If the CV is silent it is a safe inference that they have not done very many. It is worth specifically asking as some mediators claim to have very busy mediation practices, when in fact, upon closer enquiry, they have done very few mediations.

How many mediations has he done that week?

3.25   Very busy mediators can find themselves with back-to-back mediations. Some refuse to do more than two a week. Without a gap they cannot recharge from the previous one or prepare for the next one. Being offered a mediator on a Friday when he had already done three that week is not attractive. Drooping eyelids, heavy yawning and lapses of concentration do not impress clients. Solicitors are judged by those they choose, whether barristers or mediators.

The best day of the week for a mediation is Tuesday, followed by Wednesday or Thursday. Friday is the worst because people are tired and want to go home for the weekend. Monday can be a bit soon after the lull of the weekend for many people. Tuesday gives maximum post mediation time for tying up loose ends or for further negotiation if a final settlement has not been reached.

What is his CV or website like?

If the mediator does not have a website the question has to be asked as to whether he is really sufficiently up-to-date about the 21st-century. Not to have a website these days is an affectation. People with affectations tend to have a well-developed sense of their own uniqueness. This is not always a valuable quality in a mediator.

Can I talk to the mediator?

Most mediators are only too happy to receive enquiries for their services. They do not mind talking about themselves and their experience. If there is a reluctance to do that the question must be asked: Is he the man for the job?

What are his charges?

3.26   This topic is discussed in more detail in the section about Mediation Agreements at **Chapter 13**. Surveys show that mediators think that the level of charges is less important than their clients do.

In the 2012 CEDR Fifth Mediation Audit, fees was listed as second out of 17 factors that influence the respondents' selection of mediators. In the 2014 Sixth Mediation Audit it was listed as fifth. In both audits the mediators ranked it as 5 or 6.

It may be that the level of charges is less significant as a criterion because the level of charges is falling.

Is he available?

In the Sixth CEDR Audit, availability was numbered 2 in the list of factors, which mediators thought was important and number 1 by the lawyers. In practice availability is often the deciding factor. A mediator may be the best mediator in the world but if the mediation has to take place on 1 May and he is not available then he is not appointed. Some of the most successful full-time mediators have very full diaries and it can take three or more months to book them for a mediation.

What sort of mediator do I want?

3.27   As well as applying the criteria listed above it is important to consider the type of mediator that is best suited to the dispute. The following are key considerations.

Lawyer or non-lawyer?

Who makes the best mediators – lawyers or non-lawyers? This is a question that is routinely debated on the mediation conference circuit. Usually the vote is evenly split. Non-lawyers appear to be more interested in the question than lawyers. They know that the market for civil and commercial mediations prefers to appoint lawyers rather than non-lawyers but they rail against this trend.

Advantages of lawyer mediators

3.28   The advantages of lawyer mediators are as follows:

- If, as has often been said, mediation takes place in the shadow of the law, lawyers are better able to work in the shadow. They know the law better than non-lawyers.

- They are familiar with litigation procedure. They will not be confused by the language of litigation and references to Part 36, Tomlin Orders, counterclaims and Part 18 requests, etc

- They are better able to interpret what the lawyers at the mediation are actually saying about their prospects at trial and the merits of their case.

- There are used to assimilating large amount of facts at short notice and to identifying the key points from a legal point of view.

- They are better able to reality test and challenge the lawyers about the weak points in their case, both legal and evidential.

- One of the obstacles to settlement at mediation is often the question of costs. Lawyers are much more familiar than non-lawyers with costs. They have a better idea of the likely level of costs and the way in which the court applies the cost rules.

- They can speak to the lawyers on both sides at the mediation on a lawyer -to-lawyer basis with mutual understanding. There is an instinctive understanding, which is not present with a non-lawyer mediator.

- Most civil and commercial mediations are initiated by lawyers. It is lawyers who instruct the mediator. They frankly admit that they are nervous about instructing non-lawyer mediators, especially in disputes which have already become legal ones, because they do not want to be criticised by their clients.

Disadvantages of lawyer mediators

- They are lawyers. They are brought up to analyse facts in terms of legal categories and to argue their client's case. This is especially true of litigation lawyers. It is less true of transaction lawyers who are more inclined to be dealmakers.

- Lawyers are trained to analyse and advise. They find it difficult when given a set of papers to read not to form an opinion. It is second nature to them. This tendency is particularly pronounced in mediators who are senior barristers or former judges. Indeed they often use a closing technique based upon their eminence.

- Even if they are not adopting an overtly evaluative approach to mediation they let it be known that they have views on the merits and unless forcibly stopped will express those views throughout the day.

- Lawyers have a tendency to believe that mediation will be resolved by a balancing of the legal arguments. Whoever ends up ahead on points will in some way be able to dictate the terms of settlement. The problem is that there is no one at the mediation to mark the score card.

- They overlook the fact that most disputes even civil and commercial are not settled as a result of legal arguments. Personal and commercial considerations prevail. Non-lawyers understand this more readily.

Advantages of non-lawyer mediators

3.29   There are a number of advantages to using non-lawyer mediators:

- Not being lawyers they can sidestep the legal debate. They can simply speak directly to the non-lawyer decision-makers and say: 'I am like you. I am not a lawyer. I have sat in your position. I have negotiated commercial settlements which is what we are here to do today.'

- Although lawyers may not feel able to speak to the non-lawyer mediator in the same way that they can speak to a lawyer mediator. Their clients may feel more comfortable in speaking to a non-lawyer mediator.

- When both sets of barristers or solicitors are saying that their client has a very good chance of settling cases even as high as 80 per cent on both sides the non-lawyer mediator can say: 'I do not know which of you is right but I do know something that is 100 per cent right. One of you is wrong.'

- Having been in the client's shoes themselves they will probably be able to have a better insight into what is going on in the client's head.

- They also have a wider range of commercial experience. If they have not been in business but have worked in the medical profession or as a psychotherapist or social worker or in HR they will have a wide range of experience in dealing with people under stress in a non-legal context.

Disadvantages of non-lawyer mediators

- There is a distinctive school of non-lawyers who become mediators because really at some time in their life they wanted to be a lawyer. This is their chance. They make full use of it by engaging in what they call reality therapy and other people would call amateurish cross-examination.

- They underestimate the influence which the litigation default position has on decision-makers. While it is true that personal and commercial considerations prevail at mediation, legal considerations are not entirely ignored. At the very least the decision maker may have to justify his decision to settle when he returns home either to his wife or to his Board of Directors. He needs to be able to answer the question: 'Why did you settle at that figure when the lawyers told us that we could expect to get twice that at trial.'

- Even experienced non-lawyer mediators cannot have an instinctive and up-to-date feel for how cases turn out at trial. This makes it more difficult for them to challenge the predictions given by legal representatives.

- Very few have a good working knowledge of costs. Some consciously try to keep up-to-date. Most do not. There was a change in the law as from 1 April

2013 about the recoverability of After the Event ('ATE') insurance premiums and success fees. Quite a few non-lawyer mediators were not familiar with this.

- They are not as skilled as lawyers in making sure that the legal requirements for an enforceable settlement are in the settlement documents.

- They are not as useful as a lawyer mediator in resolving drafting difficulties in the settlement agreement, which is usually some sort of Tomlin Order in civil and commercial litigation and mediation.

If the mediation is about the dispute in a sector in which the non-lawyer mediator is an expert, for example, dilapidations or property valuation many of the disadvantages listed above do not apply. They are much more like a lawyer mediator in these circumstances. This leads to the question of whether mediators should be generalists or specialists.

Generalist or specialist?

3.30   Is it better to have an expert in mediation rather than a sector expert? This question overlaps with the lawyer or non-lawyer debate.

A specialist for these purposes is someone who has sector experience. In other words he has, as a lawyer, advised or, as a non-lawyer, practised in the area of the dispute, for example hotels, IT procurement contracts, pension advice, etc.

Advantages of a sector specialist

3.31   Using a sector specialist has both advantages and disadvantages:

- Parties think that a specialist will more quickly understand what the dispute is about. There will be less learning time. He will be familiar with the concepts and vocabulary of the sector. This will save time and therefore be cheaper.

- His prior knowledge means that he understands the dispute the better. In practice, what parties who say this mean is that the more that the mediator understands the dispute the more likely he is to agree with us and disagree with the other side. This view is more prevalent amongst potential paying parties. In professional negligence actions for example the defendants often want somebody who has practised in the same area so they will understand why the defendant did what he did and why it is not negligent.

- He will be able to engage with any expert evidence much better and more quickly than the generalist. He will be better able to reality test what the expert says.

- He will be better at generating ideas for a settlement based on his own technical experience.

Disadvantages of a sector specialist

- Like the lawyer mediator, the specialist mediator finds it difficult to keep his opinions to himself.

- Like the lawyer mediator, the specialist may think the settlement revolves around technical points rather than broader personal or commercial considerations.

- The saving in time and costs of briefing a specialist rather than a generalist mediator are exaggerated. Lawyers in particular are used to having to get up to speed on a subject quickly. Many mediators include their reading-in time in their fee with no additional charge.

- Sector specialists because of their specialism think that they are worth more and can be more expensive.

Advantages of a generalist

3.32   Likewise, using a generalist brings both advantages and disadvantages:

- Generalists who are trained in mediation and have mediation rather than sector experience will concentrate more on the process than the substance of the dispute.

- At court the judge concentrates on the substance of the dispute, ie the legal and evidential issue. At mediation the mediator does not act as a judge. He is there to find out what the obstacles of settlement are, how much common ground there is in fact between the parties and what the real goals of the parties are. As is repeatedly said, it is practical, personal and commercial considerations not legal and evidential ones which drive settlements.

- He is less likely than the specialist to allow himself to become a participant in the debate about the merits and the technical issues.

- Having no specialist knowledge gives the generalist licence to ask simple questions which a specialist may think beneath them. These simple questions can cause the parties to widen their focus and field of vision.

- He is less prone to the cognitive biases such as the curse of information (this is where so much knowledge is known about a subject that it prevents people from thinking about it), authority bias, the hammer tendency (aka déformation professionnelle), or false consensus effect (for more information on this vital topic see **Chapter 18)**.

Disadvantages of a generalist

- It takes them longer to bring themselves up to speed on the technical issues in the dispute.

- The technical experts on each side try to blind the generalist with science.

- Where a party has simply misunderstood the technical issues and his lawyers have misunderstood the legal ones it can be easier for a specialist and a specialist lawyer to correct these misunderstandings. This is where former judges can have an advantage. In practice this total misunderstanding is very rare.

The last word

Perhaps Rolf Dobelli sums up the dilemma best when he says:

'If you take your problem to an expert don't expect the overall best solution. Expect an approach that can be solved with the expert's tool kit.'

Insider or outsider?

3.33   This dualism is less debated or even acknowledged. There is a great deal of discussion on the mediation circuit about diversity and cultural awareness. This is often interpreted as meaning people from different religious or ethnic backgrounds and the need for mediators to be aware of their different norms. It is in fact wider than this and includes generational and gender differences.

There will be disputes in which serious consideration has to be given as to whether a man or a woman would be a more appropriate choice as mediator.

A selling point of the mediation that is often emphasised is that it provides a safe environment or place in which the parties can do dangerous things such as think the unthinkable and test ideas on the mediator or the other side knowing that it is confidential and without prejudice.

In other words mediation is a place where the disputants can feel comfortable. Putting the parties at their ease and establishing rapport is an essential skill for all mediators. Some parties may feel more comfortable if they think that the mediator is one of them. In other words an insider. An insider can be seen as someone who will instinctively understand the dynamics of a particular party and their team and will be better able to interpret what is actually taking place rather than what appears to be taking place.

Other parties feel exactly the opposite. They want somebody from outside. They think that outsiders will bring a fresh viewpoint and will not be influenced by the shared norms. They will be free from the expectations of the group and are less likely to have any links with the group. Being an outsider can be seen as aiding neutrality and impartiality.

Co-mediation

One common solution to this problem is to have co-mediation. One mediator can be an insider and the other an outsider. Usually the outsider is the one who is most experienced in mediation as a process. The insider is the one who has various shared assumptions and norms with one or all of the parties. A co-mediator is not a party appointed mediator. This is not like having a panel of arbitrators where each party can appoint its own arbitrator and for them to appoint a third arbitrator as umpire. Apart from community mediation, co-mediation, although actively promoted by some mediators and trainers, has not really taken off yet in the UK. The main reasons seem to be:

- the perceived extra cost which is not really justified except in big -ticket multi-party mediations;

- lack of familiarity;

- the present sole mediator model works well enough most of the time, so why change it; and

- a perception that it is really a job-creation scheme for under-employed mediators.

In practice:

- the charges for co-mediations are often competitively priced and it is not double the cost;

- the benefits of having two mediators to meet the different requirements of the dispute, eg technical/legal, or of the parties, eg linguistic/ cultural, easily justify any additional costs; and

- downtime is a problem in all mediations. This is where parties are sitting by themselves in their room while the mediator is with the other party. They can feel side-lined and become disengaged. With multi-party mediations the problem is much greater. Co-mediation can be an effective solution.

The author's prediction is that co-mediation will become more popular, but mediators will have to charge less so that the clients are not paying double.

Selection criteria

3.34   What is it that most parties look for when choosing a mediator?

Useful information can be derived from three surveys: the Commercial Mediation Group Survey of 2012, the CEDR 2014 Sixth Mediation Audit and the IMI 2013 Survey of In-House Counsel.

In the CEDR survey, the lawyers ranked the factors influencing selection as follows:

(1) Availability

(2) Professional reputation–mediation style

(3) Professional reputation–experience/status

(4) Fees

(5) Sector experience

The CMC survey ranked the following factors:

(1) Personal recommendation of the mediator

(2) Personal experience of the mediator

(3) Sector expertise

(4) Bedside manner

(5) Legal expertise

The IMI survey ranked the following factors:

(1) Experience as a mediator

(2) Past experience with a particular mediator

(3) Mediator's personality and attitude

(4) Independently verified feedback from other users

(5) Expertise in the core issue of the case

(6) Evidence that the mediators competency has been independently assessed

As can be seen from the results of the surveys, an important factor when choosing a mediator is what their style of mediation is. It is not just a matter of their own personality and how they behave towards people but their approach to mediation. This is discussed in more detail at **Chapter 4.**

Conclusion

3.35   To conclude:

- not all mediators are the same in terms of experience, style, expertise or personality;

- for most mediations, mediation experience is much more important than sector experience;

- many years' practice as a lawyer or surveyor or psychiatrist do not make an experienced mediator;

- ask around when selecting a mediator and talk to the mediator before making your final choice; and

- on the internet anyone can be a dog. Check if the mediator has PI cover, who accredits him and how many mediations he has actually mediated.

Chapter 4

Mediation Styles: What Mediators Do and Why

This chapter discusses:

- The different mediation styles and models
- The Big Four
- The mediation process
- What mediators try and do:
- What mediators actually do
- Mediators' tricks

The paradox of choice

4.01   One of the less helpful results of the increasing sophistication and maturity of the mediation market is the proliferation of mediation styles. A recent literature review identified 25 different models of mediation (Wall and Dunne, 'Mediation Research: A Current Review' (2012) 28 *Negotiation Journal* 217–24). Many seem to be examples of repackaging and putting old wine into new bottles. The working mediation advocate does not need to have a deep knowledge of them of all. A familiarity with the most important ones and an ability to recognise the others is enough.

One of the problems of this proliferation is that the terms used to describe the different approaches and styles are used almost interchangeably. For example, almost from the birth of mediation there has been a distinction drawn between evaluative and facilitative mediation. These terms were coined in 1976 by Professor Leonard Riskin. He has now said that they are obsolete and has coined the words elicitive and directive as up-to-date replacements. In practice these new coinages have not caught on and 'evaluative' and 'facilitative' are the terms still widely used. Therefore, they are used in this book. These distinctions are discussed at **paras 4.07–4.14**

Most mediators and commentators accept that facilitative mediation was the original variety and evaluative developed later. Not all welcome the development. Some mediation gurus say that evaluative mediation is an oxymoron. This is countered by others saying that facilitative mediation is an oxymoron.

The busy practitioner looking to try and arrange a mediation might find this all confusing. His client who has been told about mediation and decides to investigate it on the internet will come across this distinction and many more. He might ask his adviser for clarification. Here are some of the labels that anyone looking on the internet will come across.

Mediation styles: a vocabulary list (this is in alphabetical not relevance order)	
Bargaining	Narrative
Directive	Norm generating
Elicitive	Norm educating
Evaluative	Social emotional
Facilitative	Strategic
Indicative	Task orientated
Insight framework	Therapeutic
Integrated	Trashing bashing and hashing
Interventionist	

4.02   On closer examination some of these appear to be distinctions without a difference. However, some underlying distinctions may be drawn for example those outlined below.

Settlement based v relationship based

- The settlers are mediators who want to try and help the parties to solve the dispute that has been referred to them.
- The healers are mediators who want to change the way in which the parties will behave towards each other in the future.

Solution seeking v resolution seeking

This distinction is similar to the above. They share a premise: behind every dispute there is a broken relationship. Once the reasons for the breakdown in the relationship are identified it becomes possible to find ways of restoring it to some degree of functionality for the future.

In practice not every dispute arises from a broken relationship. Not every dealing between people that gives rise to dispute can be called a relationship. Some are a transaction or interaction. Buying a pair of trainers, which turn out to be defective is not a relationship. The purchase of a house, which gives rise to a negligence claim against the conveyancing solicitor is not a relationship in any useful sense. It is a transaction. It would be different if the solicitor were the family solicitor who over several years acted on all purchases, drew up wills and advised start-ups.

- The resolvers says that if all the mediator does, for example, in a boundary dispute is to achieve agreement on where to put the fence he is only doing half the job. He will not resolve the underlying feelings that the neighbours have towards each other that gave rise to the disagreement over the boundary post in the first place. There are likely to be future disputes over something else because the underlying tension between the parties remains. The underlying and fundamental causes of the conflict have not been identified and dealt with. They should be.

- The solvers say that they are not counsellors or therapists. They have neither the training nor the time. Nor do their customers want them to be counsellors or therapists. They come for objective third party neutral intervention into a dispute, which they cannot solve themselves. The parties are usually in or facing a legal dispute and they want the issues identified and dealt with quickly and cheaply. They do not want an encounter group. They do not want a series of sessions dragging on over several weeks or months. They want certainty and finality now.

Giving opinions v giving support

4.03   This underpins the distinction between facilitative and evaluative mediators.

- Facilitative mediators say that they consciously avoid doing anything to indicate their own views on the merits of the case or give indications of the likely outcome at trial. They are only there to try and help the parties work out their own solution.

- Evaluative mediators by contrast give opinions – sometimes whether asked for or not. They make it clear that they have their own views on the strengths of the argument being put forward and on what the court is likely to do at trial. They also not only help the parties generate options for settlement but suggest their own and advocate them.

The self-indulgence of endlessly elaborating competing styles and the vehemence of the arguments between their proponents is reminiscent of *Gulliver's Travels* and the wars between the big enders and the small enders. Cracking eggs might be trivial. Cracking disputes and getting deals done is not. How has this unhappy state of affair come about? Part of the answer lies, as with all disputes, in history.

Development of mediation

4.04   Some commentators trace mediation back to ancient civilisations, including Sumerian, Greek and Roman, or to ancient ethical systems such as Confucianism. This may be of some historical interest and reassure those still sceptical about this new-fangled idea of mediation that it has a long tradition.

In practice mediation as it is understood and carried out in the 21st century started in the 1970s. The speech by Frank Sander of Harvard at the 1976 Pound

Conference on 'The Causes of Popular Dissatisfaction with the Administration of Justice' is seen as the Big Bang moment for ADR when the universe of modern mediation was created. Before then there had been developments towards non-court based systems of resolving disputes. In the 1960s in the United States, there was a move to empower local communities who felt unprotected by the American court system. It had become overloaded as it tried to cope with the demands of an increasingly litigious society. Court annexed mediation schemes were developed. Mediation had a counter-culture flavour and still does for many devotees.

In the 1980s mediation was imported into the United Kingdom, Canada and Australia and in the next decade into Europe and South Africa. Now in the 21st century it has been introduced globally and embraced, even by the European Union. There are now three EU directives and regulations about mediation, which for some is a beacon of progress and for others is the kiss of death.

For some practitioners and commentators mediation is an ideology as much as it is a process. They refer to mediation as a calling rather than a profession or a business. For them mediation is a way of 'doing good 'in the world. At the 2014 ADR Group Conference held in Thessaloniki, Prof L Kotsiris, the President of the Greek Accreditation Committee for Mediation, said that 'Mediation was good for mankind'

4.05   In 2012 at the ADR Group Conference in Oxford, Peter Adler, the distinguished and pioneering American mediator (who is not a lawyer), explained that for many of his generation mediation had lost its way. They felt that its original values had been lost. These were:

- empowering people so they did not have to seek advice from experts on what to do;
- the ability to repair broken relationships;
- having the choice as to whether to go to mediation and who to appoint as the mediator; and
- the idea of parties creating their own negotiated solutions.

Instead, for them mediation has become an institutionalised, solution-driven process mainly used as a way of reducing pressure on overcrowded courts – hence, perhaps, the EU Directives.

This philosophical dissatisfaction is reflected in a more practical sense in the way that mediation is currently carried out in the 21st century. During the development of mediation techniques in the United States in the 1970s and 1980s, the dominant theory emerged that mediation helps people find their own solution to their own problem. It does this by concentrating on the future, not by reliving the past. This applies even to family mediations. The legendary American family mediator and trainer John Haynes proclaimed this message frequently and forcefully.

In the 1990s the Harvard Negotiation Project was established. This has been hugely influential on the way in which mediators still go about their work. The key text is the book *Getting To Yes* by Fisher and Ury (Random Hose Business, 2012). They developed the model of Principled Negotiation and introduced the world to BATNA (Best Alternative to a Negotiated Agreement) and WATNA (Worst Alternative to a

Negotiated Agreement). Their method focuses on peoples' interests and the future. This is discussed in more detail in **Chapter 16.**

4.06   Inevitably there has been a reaction to this problem-solving/ solution-focused approach. As described in **Chapter 1** there is a division between those mediators who want to problem solve and achieve a settlement and those who want to change the way people behave towards each other and achieve a resolution.

This resolution seeking approach led to the development of transformative mediation. It uses the therapeutic techniques of examining un-recognised and unresolved conflicts in peoples' pasts. This is turn has given rise to narrative mediation. Both are more frequently applied in family, workplace or community mediations than in civil and commercial mediations.

By sifting through the multiple models of mediation four main ones can be identified:

● facilitative;

● evaluative;

● transformative; and

● narrative.

There are others. But this is the core material that is discussed in this chapter. They are the ones that the advocate needs to know about so that he is well placed to make an informed choice on not only which ADR procedure to use but also what type of mediation and what style of mediator to choose.

The scope of mediation keeps on expanding. Different styles fit different needs. Mediation is becoming much more widespread as a technique for resolving conflict. It is used by organisations such as, for example, the United Nations, who are trying to help neighbouring countries settle land disputes, large utility companies trying to resolve problems with local populations about land use and schools who want to teach pupils how to get along without fighting and local councils who want to try and put an end to anti-social behaviour.

Mediation models: the Big Four

Facilitative

4.07   Facilitative mediation is the classic model. It is still widely taught by mediation trainers in the United States and Europe. It underpins the conventional definition of mediation given in the introduction, namely:

> 'an informal, voluntary, confidential process in which parties to a dispute can with the help of independent meet to work out their own solution.'

The key elements are as follows:

63

- The mediator helps the parties to find their own solution by taking them through a process. He does not in any way evaluate their dispute, their case or even the proposed settlements.

- The facts are not as important to him as they are to them. He does not require a lot of detailed background information. He may not want any documents at all.

- He is in charge of the process but the dispute and the solution remain the property of the parties. There are some facilitative mediators, however, who are so devoted to the idea of party autonomy that they tell the parties that the mediation day belongs to them and he will do what they wish.

- He is not a judge and will not say who is right and who is wrong in general or on any particular point.

- He will play Devil's Advocate and engage in reality therapy. This is not because he is taking sides. He is merely testing the parties' expressed positions. He will do the same in both rooms. Sometimes this is described as having challenging conversations.

- By asking open questions he will encourage the parties to tell him what is important in the dispute for them, why is it important and how they would like to see it achieved.

- He will not devise solutions or settlement proposals but he will help generate them.

- He will not give legal advice on anything.

- If asked he will help draft of the settlement agreement but prefers to leave that to the parties' lawyers.

- In order to achieve this the mediator follows the three-stage process: exploration, exchange and formulation – see below.

4.08   In practice, facilitative mediators are seen by some commentators and also by some clients and their lawyers as purists or even wimps. They say:

- they bring no value to the process beyond making sure that people do not swear at each other and acting as postmen taking messages from one room to another.

- they provide no direction or guidance on how to close a deal.

- they are disingenuous because in fact when acting as Devil's Advocate or applying reality therapy they are being evaluative without acknowledging it. Even if they are not giving opinions they disclose their view by the way in which they frame questions or by their body language when receiving answers.

This is why it is said that facilitative mediation is an oxymoron. It is simply impossible not to be evaluative to some extent. In any case, as the mediation day wears on, all mediators tend to become more evaluative. This happen for various reasons:

- The parties encourage them to.

- The mediator feels more confident about his knowledge of the facts and the dynamics of the dispute.

- The mediator has got to know the parties better and feels that he can express an opinion without causing offence. He has built up some intellectual and social capital with them and he can now spend it.

Some types of dispute lend themselves to a more evaluative approach even if the mediator is expressly and consciously adopting the facilitative approach. It is often said that commercial disputes which are about money with limited personal involvement for the people present at the mediation fall into this category. They are contrasted with a workplace mediation, for example, between two warring employees, both of whom want to remain in employment.

The three stages

These were outlined at **para 1.04** above.

Exploration

4.09   In this stage the mediator wants to find out what each party regards as important in the dispute and what it thinks the other party regards as important. He is looking for answers to three questions:

● What is important?

● Why is it important ?

● How do you want to achieve it?

He does this through a combination of open questions and active listening (see **Chapters 6** and **9**).

Exchange

The mediator is now finding out what each side needs to know about the other's position. As previously explained in **para 1.13**, he is trying to fill in gaps in each side's information and understanding. If people have different information they are more likely to have different opinions. The more shared information they have the less scope there is for differing opinions. In this way the mediator is already trying to expand the common ground.

By the time most parties come to mediation they are not communicating directly with each other. They are usually doing it through third parties and in particular through lawyers. In any dispute there is always a large element of misunderstanding arising out of poor communication. In this stage the mediator is able to correct misunderstandings.

At all times the mediator respects the confidentiality of the process and only discloses to each party what he has been authorised to disclose.

Formulation

4.10   In this stage the mediator is working with each party to formulate proposals for settlement. Remember Core Principle 5 in **Chapter 1**: settlements are achieved not by the parties arguing points of evidence or law but by discussing proposals. The sooner the parties can put proposals on the table that can be discussed the more chance they are giving themselves of achieving a settlement on the day. It is for this reason that **Chapter 7** emphasises the importance of parties formulating potential settlement proposals before they attend the mediation as part of their preparation.

In both the exchange and formulation stages, the parties are negotiating. In the facilitative model of mediation the theory of negotiation which is most often used is the Harvard Negotiation Project model of Principled Negotiation.

Fisher and Ury, in their book *Getting to Yes,* set out five principles:

- separate the people from the problem;
- focus on interests not positions;
- invent options for mutual gain;
- insist on using objective criteria; and
- know your BATNA.

This model emphasises the primacy of people's interests not their legal rights and the need for parties to collaborate to achieve an outcome which is beneficial to both sides rather than trying to win something at the other party's expense. In other words every dispute can be a win-win situation not a zero sum game.

It is based on trying to achieve a solution, which is workable for the future. It is not trying to change people or their behaviour. This is discussed in more detail in **Chapter 16**.

As previously mentioned there is a growing tendency for facilitative mediators to be regarded as purists or even wimps and for evaluative mediators to be regarded as tough-minded realists. In the academic-training complex, many still teach the facilitative model not the evaluative one. They still refer to evaluative mediation as an oxymoron.

Others, however, are now beginning to teach the evaluative model. They recognise that in many civil and commercial mediations the mediator during the course of the mediation day will be evaluative to some extent.

Evaluative

4.11   Evaluative mediators say:

- Parties want an opinion on both the drags and merits of their cases and the likely outcome at court and also on settlement proposals.

- As experienced lawyers or specialists (or sometimes both), they are well placed to know when clients and lawyers are bluffing.

- It is useful for the parties to have an independent third party give their view up this on the merits of their case and their prospects at trial. It helps them concentrate on the realities of their situation.

- they only give their views on the merits of the case if the parties ask them to.

- They are addressing the big weakness of mediation: that there is no guaranteed outcome. The parties may work hard all day trying to reach a settlement. If they do not succeed, the dispute or the case continues. This is the opposite of what happens in an adjudicative process such as arbitration. There will be an outcome and the dispute will end even if the parties do not like the result. At least there is finality and certainty, which they prize.

- They admit that they are driving the process and the parties towards settlement but they say that is what the parties want them to do. That is why they hired them.

In practice, evaluative mediators tend to give their opinions whether they are asked for them or not. QCs and former judges are particularly prone to do this.

Clients who think that they might like to appoint an evaluative mediator should ask themselves how they will feel if their solicitor is taken on one side by the mediator after the Joint Opening Session and told: 'Your man is bang to rights isn't he?' Or how they would feel to be on the receiving of the opinion of an evaluative mediator's opinion that their case was rubbish.

4.12   Not all evaluative mediators are quite so open in what they do. Some have been known to tell the parties in the first private session before the mediation has even started and while the mediation agreement is being signed that they have their own views on the issues in the case. Some say that they see their job as to spread alarm.

Self-proclaimed and self-confident evaluative mediators can almost end up becoming Early Neutral Evaluators. But they carry out their evaluations:

- as they go along rather than in a considered fashion away from the parties; and

- on a partial understanding of the issues and the evidence. Professor Di Girlomo quotes an anonymous CEDR mediator as saying:

  'I meet them at the knees, ie will bring them down to size … I have a roadmap that I tell the parties: 60% of their time is spent with the mediator; that leaves 2 hours for bargaining and 2 hours for drafting the agreement. Also, all mediators have to be somewhat evaluative. The parties expect it.'

Are evaluative mediators correct in what they say?

Do clients really wish to hear the advice of someone who has spent a few hours over the weekend 'reviewing', not 'studying' or 'working through', the documents. Do they prefer this to the advice of their own lawyers including counsel, who will have spent considerable time on their case and know it much better.

Do clients and their advocates really welcome a mediator saying after he has been invited to give an opinion on the case that they are going to lose?

In practice what they want is for the mediator to go to the other side and tell them that they are going to lose. As Richard Moran advises: 'Beware those who ask for feedback. They are really asking for validation'.

An advocate who really does want a second opinion from the mediator should ask for it in private. Having received it he can then discuss with the mediator how to share it with the client. Sometimes the advocate who has a recalcitrant client will really be seeking the help of the mediator. He wants the mediator to confirm his own view of the merits of the case. These are often less favourable than his client's own view.

4.13   But what happens if the mediator gives an opinion which the advocate was not expecting and does not share? What is the advocate to do? Is he to tell his client? Or should he seek the help of the mediator in gently breaking the bad news?

In practice many advocates will in fact feel defensive and want to justify their own opinion. What happens at mediations when conflicts of interest develop is discussed in more detail in **Chapter 5**.

Some clients want mediators to issue recommendations. Some mediators are happy to do this. Others are not. This is discussed in more detail in **Chapter 9**.

There is no doubt that in some jurisdictions, including the UK, the market for civil and commercial mediation services increasingly wants evaluative mediators.

What is evaluative?

There is, of course, disagreement about precisely what evaluative means. For example:

- Is it evaluative to give an opinion on the likelihood of the other side accepting a settlement proposal?

- Is it evaluative to identify the legal obstacles which a party will have to overcome at trial?

- Is it evaluative to give an opinion on what is likely to happen at trial?

- Is it evaluative to give an opinion on whether a settlement proposal should be accepted?

Many mediators would say:

- It is not evaluative to give an opinion about whether a settlement is likely to be accepted.

- It is probably evaluative to identify legal obstacles to be overcome at the trial, although some now would say that it was 'indicative' rather than evaluative.

- It is definitely evaluative to give an opinion on how the judge will decide the case or whether a party should accept an offer.

Many commentators now say that the distinction between facilitative and evaluative is old-fashioned and redundant. The distinction between 'evaluative' and 'facilitative' has recently been described by one of the UK's leading mediators as 'undoubtedly mediation's most boring and misconceived issue' (Bill Marsh, in 'Who's Running the Show?' (2 January 2015) at http://kluwermediationblog.com/2015/01/02/whos-running-the-show/). In fact there is a spectrum of intervention by the mediator. The words evaluative and facilitative are redundant.

The current ones are directive and elicitive. Types of intervention and what mediators in practice do are discussed at **paras 4.18–4.20**.

Theoretically this change of name may make a difference but in practice it does not. In the end each mediator decides what he should do based on his own experience and the dispute in front of him. It is for the parties and their representatives to decide what sort of intervention they want from the mediator.

Transformative

4.14   Transformative mediation, developed by Robert Baruch Bush and Roger Folger in 1994, is part of the reaction against problem-solving mediations. It is consistent with facilitative mediation in emphasising the parties' freedom to choose. The big difference is that the job of the transformative mediator is to help the parties learn from their past experience and develop new skills for use in the future with an improved and better sense of control over their own lives. It is more about changing how people see the world and each other than about finding a settlement or solution.

In other words the parties are being encouraged to examine their past, identify problems and work through them for the future. For some commentators, such as Boulle and Nesic, transformative mediation is the same as therapeutic mediation. Its primary objective is not a settlement.

It is not widely used in the UK outside community and workplace mediation.

Narrative

4.15   This also draws on the therapeutic tradition. It has its origins in the work of Michael White and David Epston in Australia in the 1990s, who pioneered narrative family therapy. They have applied those techniques to mediation. Its main features are:

● It has a post-modernist flavour with its insistence that there is no such thing as objective truth. One's point of view is necessarily subjective not objective and is derived from one's socio-cultural context.

● It assumes that people see the world in terms of stories or narratives: their own and other peoples. The role of the mediator is to encourage the parties to tell their own narratives and then to try and understand the other side's narrative. The mediator tries to unsettle and destabilise each party's belief in their own narrative and to try and adopt a new collaborative one for the future.

● It prioritises relational over substantive issues.

● It adheres to the post-modernist view that language creates reality and that language is a socio-economic construct, which betrays the power structure in the society in which it is used. This has led to it being used by mediators working with marginalised groups.

The three stages in narrative mediation are described differently from the stages described at **paras 4.09–4.10**. Instead of exploration, exchange and formulation there is:

● engagement;

● deconstructing the conflict saturated story; and

● constructing an alternative story.

In practice the engagement phase is much like the exploration stage. In it the mediator tries to establish a rapport with the parties and once it is established encourages them to tell their stories. In the deconstructing phase the mediator tries to deconstruct the stories and externalise them. What this means is to show a party that there is another way of looking at things and that his view is not necessarily more correct, authentic or valid than the other party's point of view.

4.16 The mediator also challenges the party's stated reasons for having a particular point of view. This is done not by attacking the party when he is explaining his story but by persuading the party to imagine that the conflict is someone else's and asking him to look at it through the eyes of an outsider or third party.

In the third phase the mediator having helped a party to externalise the conflict now works with the party to co-author a new narrative. This is a narrative in which the parties work together against a common problem. At this point there can be overlap between the narrative technique and the problem-solving approach. As Prof Toran Hansen said:

'Narrative mediation is thus interested in resolutions that go beyond simple settlement to consider the effects of the mediation on society at large and, like transformative mediation, considers mediation as a means for conflict parties to achieve a higher moral self'.

Both therapeutic and narrative are much more ambitious than the standard evaluative and facilitative models. They both draw heavily on the techniques of psychotherapy. As Professor G Neil Martin says, this is 'usually called the "talking cure" (although it rarely cures)', hence the considerable scepticism about these techniques amongst civil and commercial mediators.

They doubt the value of unrestricted and undirected talk, which tends to be repetitive and self-serving. They and their clients doubt the relevance of this technique to what they do. Its application to conflicts involving parties with on-going and deep relationships is more obvious. But whether it is more effective is a different matter.

Son of evaluative mediation

Indicative

4.17 This is a relative newcomer to the mediation scene. It is a term adopted by the employment judges who conduct judicial mediations in the employment tribunals in England and Wales. When the scheme was first established they said that they would follow the facilitative model. In 2014 they decided to adopt the indicative model. They emphasise that this is not the same as the evaluative model:

- They do not say what they think the merits of the case are or how one of their fellow judges will decide the case.

- They identify the hurdles that each side is going to have to overcome in order to win.

Apparently this causes both sides to focus on the realities of their legal positions. The settlement rate for the 2013 calendar year was 75 per cent, with 319 of the 473 mediations undertaken in England and Wales being successful.

In practice:

- An indicative mediator could easily become evaluative.

- Many facilitative mediators do identify issues that the court will consider at trial and invite to the parties to say how confident they are they will overcome them. They may do this in specific terms by addressing particular issues or more globally by simply asking what the overall confidence factor is. They are usually at pains to say that they do not know how the court will decide the case.

- The indicative model is probably less of a stand-alone model and more of an advanced technique used by both facilitative and evaluative mediators.

Interventions

4.18   As Bill Marsh said (see **para 4.13** above) the current emerging orthodoxy is that what mediators actually do is not really evaluate or facilitate. They make interventions. In practice there is nothing current or emerging about this. It is what mediators have actually been doing since the start of mediation. For these purposes an intervention can be defined as:

> 'an identifiable piece of verbal and non-verbal behaviour that is part of the practitioner service to the client.'

This definition comes from John Heron who was a pioneer of cooperative enquiry in the social sciences. He developed his Six Category Intervention Analysis.

The Heron model

4.19   There are two basic categories of style: authoritative and facilitative. A mediator making an authoritative intervention is giving information, challenging the other person and suggesting what the other person should do. A facilitative intervention is one designed to help draw out ideas and solutions from another person and generally give encouragement. The two basic categories subdivide into six styles.

Authoritative

Prescriptive

- Give advice and guidance.
- Tell the person what they should do.
- Tell them how to behave.

Examples

- 'I think that you need to reconsider …'
- 'Being adversarial is not going to help …'

Informative

- Give your view and experience.
- Explain the background and principles.
- Help the person acquire a better understanding.

Examples

- 'If you look at it from their point of view then you can …'
- 'When I was a solicitor I used to take this sort of case to trial and …'

Confronting

- Challenging the person's thinking.
- Repeat exactly what the person has said or done.
- Tell them what you think the obstacle is.

Examples

- 'What message do you think you are sending when you say that what message you think is being received?'
- How have you calculated your risk/reward?'

Facilitiative

Cathartic

- Help the other person express their feelings and emotions.
- Empathise with them.

Examples

- 'How do you feel about this?'
- 'Most people feel annoyed if that happens to them.'

Catalytic

- Ask questions to encourage new thinking or generate new proposals.

- Listen and summarise.

Examples

- 'What would happen if you …?'
- 'From what you say it sounds as though you really want revenge.'

Supportive

- Give praise and recognition.

Examples

- 'That's a very helpful suggestion.'
- 'Thank you for that. We are making progress.'

4.20   Advocates will find it useful if they can recognise the different sorts of interventions that mediators make. The impact of the intervention will be influenced by the timing and the manner in which it is made. It is perfectly possible for a mediator to smile and nod and be friendly while asking the most challenging and confrontational question.

The more authoritative the interventions the more the mediator is likely to be regarded as evaluative or directive. The more facilitative the interventions the more he is likely to be regarded as facilitative and elicitive.

Of course, during mediation day advocates make interventions themselves. They do this when talking to their clients in private as well as when talking with the mediator in a caucus. A knowledge of Heron's Six Categories Model will help make it clearer what they are trying to achieve with their questions.

In practice mediators do not confine themselves to asking open questions. They use other techniques. Some advocates regard them as mediators' tricks. Undoubtedly there are some highly manipulative mediators. To regard these techniques as tricks is probably being unduly suspicious. This might prove to be an obstacle to the advocate fully engaging in the process. As has been said elsewhere the two main reasons why settlements are not achieved on the day of the mediation are:

- lack of preparation, both physical and mental, in advance; and
- lack of engagement in the process on the on the day.

Knowing what mediators are trying to do with these different types of questions will help advocates to prepare themselves and their clients for them and to avoid being over defensive towards any sort of questioning. It willl also help the advocate work with rather than against the mediator on the day, as he recognises the different approaches and can respond appropriately.

To help advocates and their clients prepare themselves mentally for what the mediation may do there is a list of some of the main techniques with commentary in **Chapter 9**.

Conclusion

4.21   To conclude:

- In civil and commercial mediations, the distinction between facilitative and evaluative styles is less stark or significant than it was.

- The distinction between problem-solving mediators and resolution seekers is alive.

- Remember it is much easier to argue about the legal merits than to craft a commercial solution.

- If the client wants therapy, do not take him to mediation.

- If the client wants an end to his dispute, take him to mediation

- Think twice before dismissing co-mediation.

Chapter 5

What Does The Client Want?

In this chapter, the following issues are discussed:

- Does everybody at mediation want the same thing?
- What clients want
- What clients really want
- How to find out what clients really want

Do clients, advocates and mediators want the same thing?

5.01 Clients come to mediation saying that they want a settlement. They sign Mediation Agreements in which they confirm that:

- they have agreed to submit the dispute to mediation; and
- they will negotiate in good faith and confirm that they have authority to settle on the day.

Advocates also sign the agreement, although not as a party. They are duty bound to carry out their client's instructions and to give their best effort to carry out their clients' wishes. They must therefore want settlement as well.

The parties and their advocates hire mediators to help them achieve a settlement. It goes further because mediators are often judged by their settlement rates. A measure of success is how many mediations that they mediate end in a settlement. So mediators must want settlement as well.

Is this true?

Client and representatives

5.02 Many responses to this question depend on individual experience and anecdotal evidence of others' experience. Fortunately, so far as the United Kingdom is concerned, help is provided by a recent survey.

As part of the increasing maturity and sophistication of the UK mediation scene more research is being undertaken as to what clients actually want. The results of the most recent survey undertaken on 29 October 2014 illustrate the third of the themes identified in the introduction : asymmetry.

City of London 2014 Survey

The survey was undertaken at an international convention held by the Corporation of the City of London. It was sponsored and supported by many of the major law firms and players on the international mediation scene. It was called 'Shaping the future of international dispute resolution.'

More than 150 delegates from over 20 countries attended. Using digital devices they were able to express their opinion on core issues. There were also able to chat. The full results can be accessed on the IMI website. The headline results are:

- 66 per cent of end users ranked achieving certainty and containing costs as the two key factors for choosing ADR. They rank them equally.

- Only 13 per cent of end users ranked focusing on the key issues, ie the legal issues in the dispute as an important factor.

- By contrast representatives ranked focusing on key issues as more important than achieving certainty.

- 77 per cent of end users thought that mediation should be conducted as early as possible and if possible before proceedings are commenced. By contrast, only 44 per cent of advisers thought this.

- 38 per cent of advisers thought that ADR should only be attempted 'when issues are sufficiently developed, whenever that may be'. Only 15 per cent of end users thought this.

- 75 per cent of end users would use mediators as dealmakers even if there were no dispute between the parties. Only 38 per cent of advisers would.

- 66 per cent of end users favoured the use of a cooling-off period during arbitration before the award is made, to allow the parties to mediate. Only 33 per cent of advisers were of this view.

5.03   What this survey does is confirm what many mediators say that they have found in practice when talking to clients at mediations: What they want above all is certainty.

- *Businesses need to manage risk*

    If the cannot measure risk they cannot manage it. They want to cap their downside. This is also true of civil mediations where individual as opposed to corporate clients say how much they dislike uncertainty. This is a well-known phenomenon known as aversion bias and is described in more detail in **Chapter 18**.

- *End users want to control costs and contain them*

    This applies in both commercial and civil mediations, but especially in civil mediation, where individuals are paying legal fees out of their own pockets and the prospect of adverse costs orders terrifies them. They often say that if they had realised what they now face – namely the prospect of not only not collecting the money that they think is due to them but also having to pay their own legal costs and the other side's costs – they would not started proceedings. This realisation only usually comes home in stark form when Precedent H costs budgets are exchanged.

- *They want to settle as soon as possible*

  End users do not think that it is necessary for legal proceedings to be started and the pleadings to be exchanged and issues in cases developed in order for there be a negotiation leading to settlement.

Given the fact that most civil and commercial mediations in England and Wales are conducted after proceedings have been commenced, it does not look as though representatives are giving effect to their clients' wishes.

Representatives and mediators

5.04   There is a well-developed school of thought amongst solicitors and barristers that they want something different from what the mediators want. They have a client. Mediators do not, or at least not a physical client. As one barrister who is also a mediator, said: 'At mediation my client is settlement.' It came as no surprise to learn that although he had been qualified as a mediator for 10 years he had only carried out three mediations.

The same point has been developed with great skill and panache by a well-known commercial solicitor Craig Pollack in an essay published by the Chartered Institute of Arbitrators in 2014 in a collection of article from their magazine *Arbitration* entitled 'ADR, Arbitration, and Mediation'. His primary thesis is that mediation advocates should see mediators as settlement junkies who are prepared to feed their habit of settlement by almost any means. He goes on to say that the mediator's sole ambition is settlement. By contrast, the mediation advocates' interest is settlement on the best possible terms for the client and he concludes by saying, 'the difference is critical and therein lies the conflict between them'.

The conflict of interest may not be a real one but only a perceived one. However, as mediators frequently tell parties and their representatives: perception is reality.

The question therefore arises: is the client's interpretation of the best possible settlement the same as his representatives? What is clear to many mediators is that as part of the preparation for the mediation there has been inadequate and insufficient exploration of what the client really wants. This can be for several reasons.

The advocates have not asked the right questions

5.05   Advocates assume that the best possible terms means as close an approximation to a 100 per cent victory at trial as can be negotiated. This is because they look at settlement in terms of achieving an outcome for the legal dispute, ie the case. They try to predict what the court could order and hope to achieve as much of that as possible by consent.

Representatives do consider this but they fail to consider what might be in the interests of the client, which the court could not order. Several examples are given in this book including the classic ones of:

- exchanging parcels of land in a boundary dispute;

- giving an apology in a medical negligence action; and

- providing a supportive reference in an employment dispute.

These are simple examples. Very often a settlement is done on a basis which could not be used by the court.

Example 5.1

There was a shareholder dispute in which the departing directors were also shareholders. The remaining directors accused the leavers of trying to divert commercial opportunities from the company and misuse of confidential information. They were desperate to prevent the leavers from trying to win the crown jewel of their most lucrative contract.

It was a feature of the litigation that many of the documents that might have been expected were never put in place. This included any document requiring the departing shareholders to dispose of their shares.

As it turned out the two sides were able to agree a retrospective severance agreement. It included limited non-compete clauses but allowed the departing shareholders the opportunity of bidding for some of the company's contracts at renewal. There was no real loss to the company because with the departure of the directors they lost those members of the company who had had a relationship with the client and who were the ones who had in fact the expertise and experience to perform the contract. Without them, they had been told by the client, that the contract would not be renewed.

As part of the settlement the leavers agreed to sell their shares to the stayers. The vendors were happy because otherwise they were locked into a private company with no exit route at a time when they needed to raise capital for their new venture. The purchasers were delighted to have regained complete control of the company and not be put in the invidious position of working hard for the benefit of shareholders who were also competitors.

The remedies that could have been obtained at court would have been limited to damages, an account of profits and possibly a restraint on dealing with former customers for a limited time.

Exploring what the client wants

5.06   In practice many clients find it difficult to crystallise their instructions to their lawyers about what they really want. One of the reasons is that they are not really sure themselves. They do not sit down and in a systematic way work through what their requirements are. The use of the neutral umbrella word 'requirements 'is deliberate because the language of investigating requirement is complicated and possibly misleading.

The PIN paradigm

It is conventional to draw a distinction between positions, needs and interests. Mediators are trained not to ask parties what they *want* but what they *need*.

- 'Position 'is regarded as a statement of legal rights combined with an expression of determination to achieve them.

- 'Interests 'are what will in fact benefit the client and may be, and often are, not expressed in any legal documents.

- 'Needs' are said to be those things which the client has to have.

'Wants' therefore are an amalgam of positions and interests.

Using the triangular or iceberg paradigm of PIN, ie positions, interests and needs, mediators try to move the parties from considering positions to exploring the interests and concluding by securing their needs. Through the techniques of opening questions, reframing, summarising, etc, they penetrate beneath the surface where just the positions are visible and plunge the depths of reality. Uncovering interests and needs is what the HNP model enjoins mediators to do. Mediators try and encourage the parties and their representatives to join in and cooperate with them in doing this.

The PIN paradigm is more of a teaching aid than a technique for use at mediations. In practice, the process of moving beyond stated positions is more like the unpeeling of the layers of the proverbial onion – something that can induce tears of frustration in the participants.

Goals

A more focused and less complex way to analyse 'wants' is to simply identify the client's goals. These will be a combination of position, interests and needs shot through with psychological imperatives and economic demands. The more specifically the goal can be stated the more likely it is to be achieved. For example there is a difference between saying, 'my goal is to travel to Europe,' and, 'my goal is to stay in the Plaza Hotel on Duke Street, London'.

Once it has been specified, the client can then be asked to analyse how each element can be achieved. What substitutes could he accept for some elements? Would for example, the Crown Hotel be acceptable instead of the Plaza? He can consider how realistic his expectations are and his ability to achieve a particular element.

Once the goal has been established it gives the negotiation process conducted at the mediation shape and focus. Everything that is said or done at the mediation is governed by whether or not it helps achieve the goal. Anything that does not try and achieve the goal should be abandoned. Trying to ascertain the client's goals helps the client work through a systematic thought process before going to the mediation.

The three key questions lawyers must ask themselves

What does my client need?

5.07   The emphasis is on the word '*need*'. The question is not about what a client is entitled to or what are his legal rights are. It is about what are his interests and needs. A lawyer who approaches the mediation intending to persuade the other side that they must satisfy his client's rights is going to have a difficult time. That sort of approach is more suitable for what happens in litigation. The problem about this approach is that the arguments cannot be decided. All the lawyers can do is argue. There can be no end to the argument. The other side's lawyer is not going to publicly change his mind. The mediator cannot decide whose argument is stronger and which side wins. That is what happens at trial.

There are two different types of need:

- psychological
- financial

Psychological needs

There are two basic human needs that need to be satisfied in any mediation if there is to be settlement:

- acknowledgment
- fairness

Acknowledgment

5.08   Any party attending a mediation wants to feel that they have been heard. This means both being able to:

- express their version of the dispute and their feelings about what has happened; and
- see that they have been acknowledged.

They do not expect that the other side will agree with them but they want to see that they have been listened to with respect and proper attention. Lawyers at mediations can help achieve this in various ways:

- They can explain the client's view of the dispute in a way that the other side will not reject out of hand. This means not presenting it in an aggressive, insulting and personalised way (see **Chapter 6**).

- They can acknowledge that the other side has their own point of view. If one side does this it is more likely than the other side will do the same. Reciprocity is vital at mediations.

- They can allow clients to speak – both to the other side and to the mediator. It is dangerous if lawyers insist on exclusively speaking for their clients. Admittedly there is a risk that the client may say something that he may regret and would have been well advised not to say. But there is a much greater risk that clients who are prevented from speaking may not be able to think constructively about settlement because they feel frustrated and unacknowledged.

Fairness

5.09   Research now shows that humans are motivated by a sense of fairness. This seems to be universal and to apply across different cultures, social and economic groupings, age ranges and times. It may have evolutionary origins as a component of the impulse towards co-operation, which humans needed to have in order to survive. Evidence for this has been obtained from experiments such as the Ultimatum Game.

Example 5.2

There are two participants: the Giver and the Receiver. The Giver has a fixed amount of money, say €100. He gives some of that to the Receiver. He decides how much to give. If the Receiver accepts what he is given, both participants keep what they have. If the Receiver rejects the amount, neither participant keeps anything.

It might be thought that it is in the Giver's interests to give as little as possible and keep as much of the money for himself as he can, and it is in the Receiver's interests to accept any amount that he is given. After all something is better than nothing. But the results show that this is not what happens. Instead:

● Receivers reject amounts that they think are too small.

● If their perception is that the allocation between Giver and Receiver is unfair they will reject it so that the Receiver does not profit by his unfairness.

● For a Receiver to be confident that the amount that he gives will be accepted he has to give at least 30 per cent.

This bias helps explain why at mediations a party will refuse to accept a proposal, which his lawyers advise him is a good offer in the sense that it is a reasonable commercial alternative to what could be achieved at court.

Of course the definition of fairness is not the same for everyone. Some may call a proposal unfair for self-serving reasons. This is why it can be so important to establish some objective criteria for fairness, for example, in a shareholders' dispute having an independent third party value the company.

What about my rights?

5.10   However, be warned: do not ignore rights. As we have explained in **Chapter 4**, mediators encourage parties to focus on their interests and needs not their rights. But advocates at mediation must exercise some caution. Rights cannot be entirely ignored for the following reasons:

● Parties at mediation often have a strong belief that they are correct If they think that their rights are being ignored they can feel tempted to take a chance at court and to try and convince the judge to decide the case in their favour.

- At mediation, clients have to compare any proposals put forward with what might be the outcome at court. If they accept the proposal they might regard this as giving up their rights. They have to decide whether the value of settlement is worth this sacrifice.

- The concept of fairness discussed above. Many people who feel that their rights have been ignored will regard this as unfair. This can easily happen if there is an imbalance of power or resources between the parties. A party will be reluctant to settle if it thinks that it is being pressured into agreeing because it does not have as much money as the other side. Such a party may well prefer to go to trial and at least have the opportunity of persuading a judge that their rights have been infringed and they are entitled to a remedy.

Example 5.3

This view was expressed to the author by a shareholder and director in a mediation of a shareholder's dispute. After the mediation, which resulted in a settlement far more favourable than could have been achieved at court he wrote saying:

> 'I believe the intent of mediation to be a fine and noble thing that will produce results but not necessarily fair, reasonable or honest.'

If one party is significantly more powerful or financially stronger than the other then the process still allows the weaker to be bullied into acceptance, particularly as it would appear the mediator (no personal offence meant in any way) constantly reminds the parties of their deficiency/shortcomings. Given that any correct arguments or strong documentation supporting a case can be safely ignored, because ignoring them will not affect the trial, the process (I assume) will always eventually default to horse trading which will normally benefit the richer, stronger risktaker rather than the financially weaker, cautious party. In this way a settlement is achieved but not necessarily a just one, in which case the law is brought into disrepute to the average man on the street who cannot afford litigation.

In essence all evidence, advice, legal argument and witness statements have absolutely no standing in the process.

I could understand why an individual undertaking mediation could be most aggrieved as there appears to be no mechanisms to uphold an honest case. I appreciate that to do this is basically a trial but some effort should be made in the process to have 'fair' points recognised in any settlement, in a way the adjudications we have undertaken were better, as the 'rightness' of each case was at least assessed by an independent third party, which one assumes would be suitably qualified.

Some suggestions for the mediation process could be:

- face-to-face meeting to be mandatory. In this way guilt pressure is usually built up on the 'guilty' party;

- the mediator at certain points could give an opinion on the arguments presented;

- the mediator should provide a written report to the judge for consideration. In the report he could comment on any intransigence, bullying, consideration given by parties of others' arguments, etc; and

- the mediator to be the only one to be able to close a session either to avoid a party being held to ransom or apply pressure on an unreasonable party.

Of the two I would prefer an adjudication (perhaps with a face-to-face meeting) as it is more likely to recognise the rights of the case and provide an independent opinion which could be presented to the parties to agree: if they do not, then they go to trial, with the report going to the judge.

5.11   To put this into context, these remarks, although thoughtful and heartfelt, were made by someone:

- whose views on settlement were not shared by his co-director or shareholders;
- who was advised by his counsel and solicitor that:
  - the chances of defeating the whole of the petitioner's claim at trial were slim;
  - his valuation was more accurate and realistic than the petitioner's; and
  - the petitioner had also acted unreasonably;
- whose conduct in dealing with the minority shareholder had led to the unfair prejudice petition; and
- who had the drive, self-confidence and perseverance characteristic of those who build successful businesses.

In other words this person felt a strong need for acknowledgment and vindication as well as more than a dash of revenge.

Sacred values

Apart from acknowledgment and fairness clients often have other non-financial needs eg to protect their reputation, to preserve their sense of identify and self-worth, not to lose face with the other side, their family, community and even with their lawyers.

Sometimes there are sacred values. These are not necessarily of a religious or spiritual nature. They are some sense of loss or grievance that no amount of money, however much is offered, can cure. Indeed the offer of money might make matters worse because it is perceived as an insult. When this happens a final settlement is not possible. A conditional or provisional settlement may be achieved under which the sense of grievance that is the origin of the dispute or conflict is managed by an agreed protocol.

Mediators confirm that these situations do arise but that they are rare As one leading international mediator said: 'Never underestimate the healing power of money.'

Financial needs

5.12   Advocates must analyse these in detail with their clients. In **Chapter 7** there is a discussion of how to carry out a Pre-Mediation Analysis (PMA). There is nearly always a significant difference between what a client says that he wants and what he actually needs. Clients tend to exaggerate their losses. Lawyers tend to claim every possible type of claim and loss, knowing that they will not succeed on everything.

Useful questions to ask a client are:

- What will happen to you, or your business if you do not receive the amount that you are claiming?
- Can you survive loosing either by not collecting any money or by having to pay out money?
- What do you want to be doing in two years' time? What do you need in order to be able to do it?

Sometimes clients are in a desperate position where unless they receive a certain minimum amount of money they will become insolvent and go into liquidation or bankruptcy. More usually by the time the mediation is taking place they have absorbed the loss. The receiving party may have not received the money that they are claiming as damages but they have still survived. The paying party will probably have provided for the potential payout in their accounts or reserves. If they have to pay they should be able to do so out of their provision.

Ask a client: what do you want to do in the future? This can be particularly relevant to individuals rather than to corporate clients.

Example 5.4

Take the example of someone who has been dismissed and is arguing over compensation for breach of contract or their entitlement to commission or the value of their share options. The client may say that he wants to establish a new business in a different part of the country. Asking him for his business plan and working out how much is actually required to finance the project will provider reliable and more realistic information on what the client needs.

What does the other side need?

5.13   Lawyers involved in any sort of negotiation need to learn how to see the situation form the other side's perspective. Advocates and clients at mediation especially need to develop this skill, a skill Stuart Diamond calls seeing the pictures in the other side's head.

Clients can tell their advisers what they need but are not always able to say what they think that the other side needs. Asking them to consider what the other side might need stimulates thinking about how a settlement might be structured. Once parties and their advisers start thinking about how to structure settlements rather than how to win cases they are making real progress. This sort of analysis will also reveal what one party may be able give to the other party, at limited cost to itself. This opens up the discussion about trading, which after all is the essence of negotiation.

It is inaccurate to say that negotiation is all about compromise. Rather it is all about trading, ie exchanging something that I have that you need for something you have that I need. As Donald Trump says: ' If you have what the other guy wants, you have a deal.'

Therefore effective advocates try and find out what the other side wants. This can be done before the mediation, either by asking the other side or by imaginative reconstruction with the client. It is much easier to do at the mediation because the mediator will only be too happy to ask each side what they want and what they need. He will encourage each side to give him permission to disclose their responses.

What can we give the other side?

5.14   Nobody is suggesting that in the interests of principled negotiation a party should be contemplating making unilateral donations to the other side. What it means is to identify things which one side can do for the other in exchange for something from them.

There are a number of benefits of doing this:

- It encourages the client to prioritise. Not all things are equal. Different things have different values at different times. It is useful to review what is valuable now. It is often different from what is valuable when the dispute started or what might be valuable when the dispute finishes. Circumstances, over which a client has no control, change and that in turn can change the perception of the value of settlement.

Example 5.5

A corporate client at mediation was engaged in litigation with a longstanding supplier. The clients felt strongly that they had been let down. Their lawyers advised that they had a very strong case that was likely to succeed at trial. Shortly before the mediation the clients received an unexpected but welcome offer for their business. They knew that due diligence would be carried out. They did not want to have to disclose the existence of the litigation with a longstanding supplier. The value now of settlement was much greater. In the actual mediation on which this example is based the value of settlement suddenly became much greater than the value of recovering compensation.

The clients instructed their solicitor that, no matter what, the case would be settled that day. He was flabbergasted. It was settled and the terms were reasonable if not brilliant, but the result was just what the clients needed and they were delighted and much better off.

- It generates thought about how settlements can actually be structured. It is not always possible to work out in advance precisely how the settlement will be structured. A prototype can be created. At mediation other variations, variables and permutations will be introduced. Make the prototype flexible enough to accommodate them. The more this has been thought about and anticipated the easier it will be to do at the mediation.

- Mediators often say in their opening statement that it is important for the parties to be flexible in their thinking and sometimes even to think the unthinkable.

Example 5.6

In a shareholders' dispute the goal of the minority shareholder seeking redress may be to be bought out at the earliest possible opportunity for the highest price.

A real problem is that the money is simply not available to buy the shares, even if the price can be agreed without too much difficulty. Usually the remaining shareholders' capital is tied up in the company.

To release value from the company to generate cash in order to buy the shares it is often necessary for the company to raise further finance. If the shareholders do that individually they often need to use the collateral of their shareholding as security. This requires the cooperation of the other shareholders.

It is not unknown for shareholders:

- to agree to a truce and to cooperate to work for the sale of the company over the next two or three years;

- to structure the disposal of the shares by instalments; and

- to appoint an independent third party chairman to act as referee between the shareholder groups during the truce.

It is essential to have the names of some suitable nominees ready, willing and able to take on this role, before making the suggestion at mediation If these alternatives have been contemplated and thought through before the mediation, it will be the easier for the client to take an informed decision and for the advocate to give informed advice**.**

5.15   Since no disputants contemplate making unilateral donations the question arises: What can the other side give in exchange? Once the clients are thinking about what they can exchange in order to get a deal done real progress is being made, both psychologically by getting into the problem-solving, peacekeeping mindset, and practically by focusing on what is in practice doable.

When the parties are looking at the same problem and seeing what building blocks they have available to them with which to construct a settlement, the process of mediation is really underway. When they are doing it at the same time, ie on the mediation day, then business can be done.

Linking what the clients have identified as being significant factors in choosing ADR as recorded in the City of London 2014 Survey, described at **para 5.02** above with these questions leads the advocate to consider with the client both the costs of settlement and also the benefits of settlement.

Costs of settlement

5.16   On one level, calculating the cost of settlement is quite straightforward. It is legal costs plus whatever has to be paid or given up from the 100 per cent claim.

It is more difficult if some of the things that are being given up or acquired are intangible. If an actual price cannot be placed on them, a value for the purpose of settlement can be ascribed. It may only be a notional value rather than one that can actually be achieved in the open market, but it will still help the client to carry out an informed cost/benefit or risk/reward calculation.

What do clients really want deep down?

5.17   No solicitor has ever said that his client has come into his office and said what they want is two years of litigation with an uncertain outcome and a large bill plus a unquantifiable level of risk, anxiety and wasted time. What they say is that they want revenge, justice, or money. That is at the beginning of the dispute. But after the initial expression of outrage, as the City of London Survey results show, they just want an early solution that brings certainty.

When contemplating the benefits of settlement, remember that no one's last words were: 'I wish I'd spent more time in court.'

Conclusion

5.18   To conclude:

- Find out what clients need even though they may be reluctant or unable to say.

- What clients need is more important than what their legal rights entitle them to.

- Emotions and legal rights both influence clients but they can conflict.

- People make decisions for their reasons not yours, so find out what makes them tick.

Chapter 6

What is Mediation Advocacy?

This chapter discusses:

- The meaning of mediation advocacy
- What representation clients need at mediation
- The role of the advocate at mediation
- The new things that the advocate must learn

What is mediation advocacy?

A misnomer

6.01 Mediation advocacy is a misleading term. A better term is mediation representation but, as explained in **Chapter 1**, the phrase 'mediation advocacy' is too well established. What it does not mean is that the person who represents a client at mediation has to be legally qualified. In some countries and jurisdictions the word 'advocate' is confined to those people who are legally qualified.

Even if it does not have a legal connotation, the words 'advocate' and 'advocacy' imply a person putting forward an argument on behalf of somebody. Traditionally an advocate set out his client's case and marshals the arguments and evidence in favour of it. He then turns to his opponent's case and tries to demolish it by identifying all the weak points in it and marshalling the arguments and evidence against it. This is what advocates do in courts, tribunals, the Houses of Parliament and TV debates. The process is essentially one of attack, defence and counter-attack. The goal is not agreement or settlement. It is submission or judgment.

Non-adversarial

Cross-examination is an essential part of advocacy in court proceedings in many jurisdictions. This is particularly so in jurisdictions that have based their legal procedures on the English model. Barristers are taught cross-examination in their Bar courses. The inquisitorial questioning undertaken by the examining magistrate in civil law jurisdiction is not the same as the adversarial cross-examination in the common law jurisdictions.

This sort of advocacy has no place in mediation. As has been previously mentioned, mediation has been referred to as assisted negotiation. The point of any negotiation is to reach an agreement or a deal. As stated at Principle 5 in **para 1.08**, deals are not achieved by people arguing about legal or evidential points. They are achieved by people discussing proposals. A successful outcome is not achieved by exchanging criticism but by sharing explanations and trading concessions.

This means that an advocate at mediation has to adopt a different mindset and different skills from an advocate at a trial or arbitration. Instead of confrontation there is cooperation. Cooperation is not the same as capitulation. Parties will have different priorities and interests but they have enough shared assumptions, values and goals to want to try and achieve a deal. They look for the common ground not the battleground. Most negotiations, and certainly most mediations, are in fact an exploration of the boundaries of the common ground. The more common ground there is the more chance there is of a deal. Exploration of the extent of the common ground is not undertaken by cross-examination but by shared explanation.

Common ground or battleground?

Parties to the dispute and their representatives, particularly if their representatives are legally qualified, can find it difficult not to present their position in an adversarial way. They believe that attack is the best form of defence and that they must get their retaliation in first. They turn the common ground into a battleground. The fog of war obscures the realties of the situation.

At many mediations, much energy and time is spent first in the parties attacking each other then in remedial works. If people are under attack they are not in a frame of mind to consider settlement. Traditionally the first four hours in mediation are spent in this sort of activity and the next two hours spent in trying to bring the parties round to a settlement mindset. The last two hours are spent in bargaining and agreeing a settlement document. This is the wrong way round. Too much time, energy and goodwill is spent on the wrong thing.

A specialism?

There is a growing tendency to regard mediation advocacy as a specialist skill and activity. Two of the most experienced and respected practitioners, Henry Brown and Arthur Marriott conclude at p 406 of their standard work *ADR Principles and Practice* 3rd Edn (Sweet & Maxwell, 2011) that: 'Mediation Advocacy has become a specialist skill attracting a body of specialist practitioners.'

Standing Conference of Mediation Advocates (SCMA)

6.02 In the UK, the champion of this view has been the eccentrically named Standing Conference of Mediation Advocates (SCMA). It was established:

- to promote mediation awareness amongst the public at large including the judiciary, lawyers and businessmen;

- to provide training for those wanting to be mediation advocates; and

- to disseminate research findings and statements of good practice.

It now also provides training for mediators.

International Mediation Institute (IMI)

6.03   IMI have added to their certification for mediators a certification for mediation advocates. This was introduced in 2013. Details can be found on their website (http://www.imimediation.org).

As further evidence of the sophistication and maturity of the market, their requirements for a mediation advocate comprise two Annexes. These contain the areas of practical skills that are required for effective mediation advocacy:

- Annex 1 – 'Mediation Advocacy General Knowledge Requirements' – contains 24 separate headings.

- Annex 2 – 'Mediation Advocacy Practical Skills Requirements' – contains 110 items.

Although this may sound comprehensive and even daunting, IMI expressly says: 'The list is not necessarily exhaustive or mandatory and is offered as guidance.'

These competency criteria are the ones identified by an IMI committee of experienced international mediators drawn from several jurisdictions as being required by competent mediation advocates. In the introduction to the competency criteria IMI states that:

> 'Mediation is most successful when the parties' advocates/advisers are knowledgeable and skilled in the principles of the mediation process and negotiation theories. Mediations can fail when party representatives act as if they were in a court room rather than in a negotiation.'

This rather assumes that parties need representation. Is this in fact the case?

Can the client represent himself?

6.04   In civil and commercial mediation the client is usually represented. In most family, workplace and community mediations the parties are not represented at all. This does not mean that they do not have access to legal advice if they want it. But it does mean that they speak for themselves during the mediation. They put forward their own points of view and respond to those from the other side.

Why is civil and commercial mediation different?

6.05   There are several reasons for the difference between civil and commercial mediation:

- In family workplace and community mediation the parties are personally involved in a way that they are not in a civil and commercial mediation.

- The outcomes directly impact upon the parties in an individual and personal way.

- They are more concerned with managing or repairing the breakdown of a personal relationship, ie marriage or civil partnership, employment, or between neighbours.

- Legal proceedings have usually not actually been commenced. They may be in the offing or started, for example, in divorce proceedings, but at the time of the mediation they have not usually started or progressed very far.

- The nature of the disputes means that a solution or even a resolution depends upon people modifying their behaviour towards each other. This is often the principal remedy rather than just a sum of money being paid. This is less true of divorce mediations.

- In divorce mediations, the financial aspects of the break-up have to be dealt with. If children are involved as they often are there will be a need for the spouses to remain in some sort of relationship even if it is only that they are parents. For example, decisions of schooling and arrangements for contact will have to be modified and agreed as time passes.

- The nature of these disputes are ones which courts might find it difficult to deal with in the sense of finding adequate remedies. For example, it is much better if workplace colleagues can agree conflicting holiday arrangements and flexible working times between them. A court or tribunal could not impose an arrangement on them.

- It has been said of family disputes that the parties themselves are their own experts in their dispute. The same is also true of workplace mediations. It is perhaps less true in disputes about boundaries, rights of way, noise or parking arrangements. This sense of the disputants being their own experts in what the dispute is about would not be true in the same way, for example, in a professional negligence action against an architect or a complaint about defective workmanship.

- With the exception of some divorce mediations, the sums of money involved are usually much less than in civil and commercial mediations.

- Parties feel more confident about expressing themselves in matters where they are the subject of the dispute in some way, for example, with a neighbour, with a work colleague, or with a spouse or partner. They feel that they know what they are talking about in a way that they do not feel so confident in other types of civil and commercial disputes, and think, not always correctly, that there is less law involved.

- Lawyers are more closely involved; as mentioned above, the legal colonisation of mediation is a prominent characteristics of the current mediation scene.

Self-representation

Advantages

6.06   Some commentators and clients think that there are advantages if the client is not represented at the mediation:

- They save money – they do not have to pay the fees of the representative.

- They can speak more directly both to the other side and to the mediator.

- They can approach the mediation as a process like that of a commercial contract negotiation, of which they usually have experience. The lawyers are not there with their legal interpretation of events.

- There are no lawyers present to further their own interests, which may not coincide with those of their clients. It has to be acknowledged that many clients suspect that their lawyers prefer to take matters to trial because they make more money doing so.

- Lawyers who tend to engage in quasi-courtroom behaviour and feel that they have to put on a show for their clients are not present.

- A tactical advantage of not having lawyers present is that a party can slow down the process if they want and say that they need to take legal advice. They may even arrive at an agreement in principle with everything in place except their signature and say they want to run it past their lawyer before signing. This means that they do have a cooling-off period and are not at risk of succumbing to settlement fever.

Disadvantages

There are disadvantages:

- The main disadvantage is a variation of the adage that 'a lawyer who represents itself has a fool for a client.' It is in fact much harder than people imagine to do yourself justice and represent yourself well. There are lots of reasons for this, but the main ones are the difficulty in understanding what is relevant, seeing the wood for the trees, stepping back and seeing the bigger picture and being afflicted by tunnel vision.

- Clients become overconfident. They think that all they have to do is tell their story. They do not prepare properly. They perform badly in joint sessions and therefore give encouragement to the other side. If they do not present well at mediation what will they be like in court?

- They lose confidence. They have underestimated how lonely it can be at mediation. The client is having to deal with the mediator, who is an unknown quantity, receive information from him and from the other side, and respond to offers without being able to discuss them with his adviser. It can all become too much.

- They do not understand what can happen at trial. Before they came to mediation they were told by their lawyer what all their options were, but they have only listened to what they wanted to hear, which is the strong points in their case. They underestimate the weaknesses.

- They find themselves in a stressful situation and become prone to a wide range of cognitive biases which they can fail to recognise. There is no one to act as a corrective (see **Chapter 18**).

For these reasons most commercial clients choose to be represented.

Minimising the disadvantages

6.07   In fact, many of the potential dangers of being unrepresented can be ameliorated by careful preparation. The problem is that it costs money. Either the client spends the time himself doing it all or, if he asks for help from his lawyers, who charge for their time and work. The costs advantage of not been represented is therefore much reduced.

Some clients, as part of their normal daily life, are used to making presentations and appearing before strangers to argue their case. Some are experienced litigators, such as insurance representatives. For these clients, self-representation may be a more realistic alternative. For other clients it is just the opposite. They have no experience of anything like this and the thought of speaking to a room full of strangers induces anxiety attacks. Others may not be naturally articulate or may not have English as a first language. This can put them at a disadvantage

Supporters

Even those clients who are confident about being able to perform well at mediation without legal representation usually want to take someone along with them.

This person can provide:

● moral support and encouragement especially when the going gets tough as the day drags on;

● a second pair of ears and eyes to collect information that can be shared with the client about what is going on;

● a sounding board for proposals; and

● company, because being in a mediation can be lonely, especially when the mediator is in the other room and the clients are on their own.

There can be disadvantages:

● if the supporter is personally involved in some way with the dispute or its outcome. If so they can have their own agenda and influence the client in a way, which a legal representative would not. That influence may not be to the client's benefit;

● if the supporter ends up colluding with the client by encouraging him to think that he is right and not encouraging him to critically review his opinions and positions; and

● if all the supporter does is echo what the client thinks, he is not really helping the client's decision-making process.

Who should represent a client?

6.08 In civil and commercial mediations most clients, once they have decided that they want representation, choose legal representation.

Usually someone from the solicitors attends. This is not always the fee earner who has the conduct of the case. Sometimes a trainee is sent along with counsel. Sometimes the partner who has overall charge of the matter or the relationship with the client attends. Increasingly there is a tendency for counsel to attend with no solicitors. This is especially true if the solicitors are acting for legal expenses insurers and there are cost constraints.

Key requirements

What the client needs in practice is someone as a representative who:

- knows enough about the details of the case or dispute to be able to advise him on whether the settlement agreement deals with all the relevant issues;

- has carried out or is able to carry out on the day an informed pre-mediation analysis so that the client can be aware of his option if the case does not settle and is therefore able to benchmark any proposal that is put forward;

- enjoys the confidence of the client or, if they have not met, can establish rapport and engender confidence. This is essential. Leaving aside providing legal analysis and advice, the advocate is there to provide psychological support. It is not easy being the client at mediation. The client is being asked to take important decisions under pressure of time, and absorb new information and advice in unfamiliar surroundings. The more preparation that has been carried out as described in **Chapter 5** and **7** the easier he will find it to cope with all this;

- must help the client to stay engaged in the process and focused on what he has to decide. That is much easier to do if the adviser has himself been well prepared, even if he is not the actual fee earner running the case and has discussed the case and the mediation with the client beforehand;

- have the authority to sign settlement documents. Of course the client often has to sign them but sometimes the solicitor's signature is also required, as described in **Chapter 14**; and

- have the authority to negotiate and agree costs. This is particularly important when insurers and third-party funders are also involved.

The lawyer's role

How do lawyers perform these activities in the context of mediation? In debates about lawyers and mediation it is generally assumed that the lawyers will be barristers or litigators. Is this a safe assumption?

The lawyer's essential roles of analysis, advice and advocacy described in **Chapter 1** have to be performed at mediation. The key feature of mediation as described in **Chapter 1**, ie making peace not war, requires a different mindset and skill set from what is necessary for conducting litigation.

It is not very different from what transaction lawyers employ when negotiating deals on behalf of their clients. This is why it is sometimes said that transaction lawyers make better mediation advocates than litigation lawyers. Is this true?

The advantages of transaction lawyers

6.09   Transaction lawyers bring with them both advantages and disadvantages:

- They are experienced in negotiation

- Their success is measured by making deals not breaking deals

- They discuss with their clients what their clients' commercial interests are.

- They are used to comparing one proposal with another to evaluate which are more likely to be in their clients' interests.

- They understand that to reach a commercial deal the parties have to cooperate and a degree of mutual trust has to be developed.

- They understand that deals are more easily achieved amongst people who like each other.

- Their big advantage is the commercial context in which they work as dealmakers. People enter into commercial negotiations because they think that they can make a profit from making a deal. In other words both parties think that they will be better off as result of coming to an agreement. There is something in it for both of them. The chances of there being a win–win situation rather than a win–loose situation are greater. As explained in the discussion of Principled and Positional Negotiation in **Chapter 16** the aim at mediation is to try and achieve a win-win situation.

The disadvantage of transaction lawyers

- They are unfamiliar with court proceedings.

- They are not as good at predicting the outcomes of a trial.

- They do not like confrontation.

- They may be too inclined to compromise in order to preserve relations.

- They may under – estimate the extent to which clients who feel aggrieved want to have their day in court. **See Chapter 5**.

- Non-contentious lawyers may not be as experienced or as good at articulating a client's legal rights as litigation lawyers.

The advantage of litigation lawyers

6.10   Likewise, there are both advantages and disadvantages to using litigation lawyers:

- They are familiar with court proceedings and are better than non-contentious lawyers at predicting the outcome of a trial.

- They are more experienced in evaluating a client's claim. Clients often have exaggerated expectations. They think that their cases are stronger than they are and their estimates of the level of damages that may be awarded by the court are often unrealistic.

- They are not afraid of confrontation and in dealing with aggression from the other side or the expression of emotion by their own clients. These things happen in court all the time.

- They understand about the economics of litigation and the impact of legal costs.

- They are more experienced in drawing up agreements or court orders that will be enforceable if the other side defaults.

The disadvantage of litigation lawyers

- They like fighting cases. They love the drama and theatre of courts.

- They see the negotiation of a claim as primarily a matter of overwhelming the other side's objections by forensic argument.

- At mediations they find it difficult to move out of advocacy mode.

- They are often worried that they are allowing their clients to settle on terms which are not as good as the ones they could achieve for a client at trial. It is a matter of professional pride.

Should barristers attend mediation?

6.11   There are many solicitors and mediators who think that barristers are a barrier to mediation. The main complaints are:

- they cannot make the transition from the courtroom to the negotiating table;

- they carry on making forensic points as though they were trying to persuade a judge but there case stronger banned their opponent's;

- they indulge in histrionics and prolonged displays of legal knowledge and self-advertisement; and

- in short they talk too much, over focus on legal arguments, are insufficiently commercial and do not understand that the centre of gravity has shifted away from them.

There is no doubt that many barristers behave in this way at mediations. With the growing maturity and sophistication of mediation as described in **Chapter 1** more barristers are becoming more familiar with mediation. They are realising that it is essentially different from arbitration, adjudication or litigation. The way in which an advocate sets out to persuade a judge is nothing like the way in which an advocate seeks to persuade the other side or the mediator. Put simply it is that litigation is about making war and mediation is about making peace.

The reasons for this growing familiarity are the following:

- Barristers are now taught about mediation advocacy on the Bar courses as part of their advocacy training modules. In this sense they are ahead of solicitors who receive no such training but nevertheless consider that they themselves better qualified to act as mediation advocates.

- The work of bodies like the SCMA.

- The greater exposure to mediation. More barristers have now attended more mediations as representatives. They see how the process works and recognise for themselves the differences between making peace and making war and the limited scope for traditional forensic advocacy.

- The number of trials continues to fall. The phenomenon of the disappearing trial has been much commented upon in the mediation literature. It means that if barristers want to represent clients in a capacity other than purely advisory they have to be familiar with the opportunities that mediation offers.

Hence the development of mediation advocacy as a separate and allegedly specialist skill which some barristers are now selling.

Why are barristers sometimes barriers?

6.12   What are the reasons that barristers find it difficult to engage in the peace process?

- **Habit and training** These are two of the main reasons. As described above, training is changing but not all barristers are receiving it especially those who were called to the Bar some years ago. Habits are hard to break. Even now at mediation, barristers still refer to making submissions, cite authorities and ask for directions. Their Mediation Statements (or Position Papers) read like Statements of Case or case summaries for a hearing at court. Many admit that they draft them to inform the mediator in the same way as they try to inform the judge.

- **The day job** As the former Lord Chancellor, Charles Falcolner, set out at the Chartered Institute of Arbitrators Mediation Day in 2012, it can be very difficult to switch from being a commercial silk arguing cases in court to being a mediator. The same is true for switching to being a representative or mediation advocate.

- **Distaste** Barristers would prefer to be in court not at mediation. Courts are where their reputations are made. It is where they enjoy exercising their skills and experience that they have acquired. They like the theatre and ritual of court. They know their role there. They do not know their role at mediation.

- **Fear** Barristers are uncertain what they are meant to do at mediation. Is there, in fact, a role for them at all? This applies to lawyers generally at mediation but it is particularly acute for barristers. Barristers are afraid that they do not have much to contribute apart from what they would do at court anyway. They are not the central figure at mediation as they are in court. The hard work is not done by them – it is done by the client. They find it difficult to let go of the leadership role. In litigation, counsel is the team leader. This is not as true at mediations.

Are barristers needed at all?

Barristers are not essential. Many mediations are successfully concluded with a settlement agreement without them being present or being involved by telephone or e-mail, but having barristers present at the mediation can help.

The value of barristers

6.13   Barristers are needed for the following reasons:

- **Specialist knowledge** Barristers may be instructed because they have specialist knowledge and experience in the area of the dispute. This can be very helpful at the mediation if, for example, a settlement has to be structured which changes existing legal arrangements, for example an exchange of land or a restructuring of shares holdings, the mediator or the other party wants to raise legal points – either ones arising from the pleadings of the evidence or just more generally discuss legal points or principles that might arise at trial.

- **Reassurance** Even if proceedings have not actually been started, counsel may have already given advice. The client has heard it and has paid for it. If he is being told at mediation either directly by the other side or through the mediator that his case is not as strong as he thought, he will want to know whether or not they are right.

  As has been explained above, being a client at mediation can be a lonely and stressful experience. Clients can draw comfort and support from having all the legal team around. This is especially true if the client is going to be asked to make decisions based upon new information or a different assessment of the legal merits.

- **Detachment** The relationship between a solicitor and client is closer and longer than that between a client and his barrister. There is a danger that solicitors can become too close to the case and to their clients. This is for the best motives. They want to do the best job they can for their client. An added complication can arise where the client is sharing the risk of litigation with the solicitor, for example where there is a conditional fee arrangement (CFA) or damages based arrangement (DBA). It can be easier for the barrister to tell the client bad news.

- **Co-pilot** It can be useful not just for the client but also for his solicitor to have another pair of ears and eyes. This is especially true if the other side have counsel present. There is no doubt that barristers find it easier to talk to other barristers. It might be useful at some stage in the mediation for there to be a back channel of communication between the two barristers. This is especially true if it comes to technical legal points in the structuring of the settlement.

- **Drafting** There can be no doubt that most barristers are better than most solicitors and most non-lawyers in drafting legal documents. Many solicitors can competently draft a Tomlin Order. Sometimes the provision of the Schedule to a Tomlin Order can be complicated. Also there can be ancillary documents required for example a form of charge over shares, a guarantee, an amended employment contract or licence agreement.

  Even where competent and experienced solicitors are at the mediation it helps in the difficult period between concluding the settlement in principle and signing the settlement agreement if counsel is also present. Counsel can be involved in the drafting and the solicitor can be providing assurance and stimulation to the client so they do not become completely disengaged from the process or decide that they have changed their mind and want to walk out

- **Deal with the unexpected** Barristers are often are more experienced and adept at thinking on their feet because this is often what they have to do in court. And very often the unexpected does happen in mediation. They can also help to defuse any legal landmines which the other side try to lay.

- **Liaising with funders and insurers** The involvement of third-party funders or insurers is increasingly common at mediations. They are not usually present. They rely on updates from the solicitors or counsel. Barristers carry more weight with them than solicitors do. Often funding or cover has only been provided because counsel has given a favourable opinion. If a settlement is going to be recommended, particularly one which is not entirely consonant with that opinion, it is helpful if the barrister who wrote it is on hand to provide an explanation to the funders.

- **Fees** Traditionally counsel have delegated agreeing fees to their clerks. These days they are increasingly personally involved in settling the final amount. This is especially true when they are also on some sort of risk-sharing arrangement such as a CFA.

- **Eyeball the mediator**: A lot of bluffing takes place at mediations. Much of it is about the parties' estimates of their chances of winning a trial. Mediators are routinely told by clients and their solicitors that counsel has advised that they have got an extremely strong case or have at least an 80 per cent chance of winning. More often than not when the mediator looks counsel in the eye, a more nuanced and even realistic appraisal of what counsel has actually advised is given.

The bottom line

6.14   If the client can afford to have his barrister as well as his solicitor present at the mediation it is worth it. If the barrister follows the advice in this book or the general guidance given by SCMA he will be of great value. If he does not he might make settlement more difficult and in the worst cases actually prevent it. In practice, although that is not unknown if an experienced mediator is appointed, it is extremely rare.

In-house counsel

6.15   In-house counsel can either be barristers or solicitors and can exhibit all or some of the strength and weaknesses of both. It might be thought that there was a greater danger of them being excessively invested in the case because they are part of one of the disputants and may be protecting their own position. In other words they might be too partisan.

There is also sometimes the danger of a powerful and self-confident director overruling his in-house legal adviser who may not feel able to stand up to him in front of others from the company. There may be a hidden political background, which is not apparent to the mediator but which is influential.

In practice in-house counsel often seem to be able to combine commercial awareness with legal analysis and enjoying the confidence of their client, namely the director who will have to sign off the settlement. This may simply be because in-house counsel are used to having to take decisions and give advice in a fast-changing commercial environment with competing priorities to colleagues who need fast practical legal solutions.

The seven deadly sins of barristers

6.16   Barristers may be guilty of any of the following 'deadly sins':

- They may draft for court rather than mediation. Their mediation statement or position paper reads like a case summary or a court hearing, not a framework for settlement negotiations, citing cases and explaining how the other side have simply got the law wrong.

- They may dominate their team, not realising that the centre of gravity has moved away from them. The client has a much more influential part to play in the mediation than at trial. Barristers may sit at the head of the table in their team's room and do all the talking, seeking to censor what the client says.

- They may grandstand at every opportunity. This is not just limited to the Joint Opening Session where they may act as though they were in court. It can also happen in a caucus with the mediator when they make life difficult for their client by egging them on with extended riffs on fairness and justice. It raises the temperature when cool reflection is required.

- They may be guilty of ego enhancement, ie telling everyone who will listen that in their experience the court would never do such thing or that they have never heard of case like this resulting in a costs order against the client. In other words they make it difficult for the client to accept a proposal from the other side without seeming to distrust his own adviser.

- They may be guilty of point-scoring, taking every opportunity to score a point off the other side. Barristers may feel they have to try and demonstrate that they are the cleverest most articulate and best lawyer in the whole building, not realising that settlements are not reached and deals not done by arguing but by discussing proposals

- Bringing works of authority and copies of cases.

- They may leave the client at the altar. Barristers are aware of the three functions of legal advisers namely analysis, advice and advocacy. Having spent most of the day in advocacy with some underpinning analysis at the psychological moment, they may say to the client: 'This is monstrous. All sense of fairness and justice has gone out of the window. There is of course mediation. It has to be your decision.'

The seven deadly sins of solicitors

6.17   For their part, solicitors too may be guilty of their own 'deadly sins':

- **Over involvement** Solicitors are closer to their clients than barristers as has already been discussed at **para 6.06**. They can find it difficult to stand back and take a wider view when they have been discussing the case regularly and frequently with their clients. They are immersed in the detail.

- **Unbalanced interests** The interests of the client and his legal advisers are not always aligned. It is true that just because people may have different interests there is not necessarily a conflict of interests. However, many clients have harboured unworthy thoughts that their lawyers wanted to keep the litigation running to generate fees. Some solicitors, it has to be admitted, do this, as do some barristers.

The problem has been aggravated by risk-sharing funding arrangements. If the solicitors are on a CFA, whether old-style or new style, they want to be paid their success fee. Under old style CFAs, where the success fee was recoverable, the paying party at the mediation often made it clear that they would pay a contribution towards basic costs but not towards the success fees. There was often a subsidiary mediation between the client and his solicitor. The client might want to settle but the solicitor would not give up his success fee and would rather go to trial and have the benefit of a costs order in his client's favour.

Under new style CFAs or DBAs, where the success fees are not recoverable, it can be a case of the lawyers wanting to settle and collect some fees rather than go to trial and risk getting nothing at all. Clients at mediations have expressed their suspicion to mediators in private that the solicitors in reality just want to be out of the case.

- **Ducking costs** Many solicitors do not explain fully and frankly to their clients what the cost implications of their case are. They may have given them general advice at some earlier stage, but they have failed to provide updated figures and in particular do not come to the mediation with up-to-date costs figures either for costs already incurred or for costs going forward to trial. This applies even under the new costs budget regime and where a Precedent H has been filed. Even when they have supplied figures to their clients they have not worked out with them what it means for the client in net terms.

- **Guerrilla warfare** During litigation the parties often conduct a sniping campaign in correspondence. There is no point continuing this at mediation. It does not promote movement towards settlement, and it is much better to declare a truce.

- **Over compensating** Some solicitors, although not barristers, like advocacy. Some clearly wish that they were barristers. At mediation they have a chance to be advocates. They act in an even more forensic and adversarial way than barristers. They often present their case extremely well and professionally. It would work well in court. It does not work well at mediation.

- **Avoiding the figures** Frequently figures are not available before the mediation and are cobbled together during the mediation. This takes time and the figures often lack credibility because of the obvious haste with which they have been completed.

- **Losing their nerve** Solicitors sometimes decide not to involve counsel in the mediation. Then they change their mind. This can happen shortly before the mediation. Counsel is instructed in a hurry. He has probably not met his client for sometime, if at all. Early morning conferences are arranged. People arrive late for the mediation and ask for extra time. The mediation does not get underway for an hour or two. Time and energy are lost, momentum is delayed and negative messages are received by the other side.

The alternative is that counsel is consulted during the mediation by telephone or email. He is usually In the middle of something else and is called upon to advise at short notice and in a vacuum. There is more loss of time, energy and momentum. Clients are rarely impressed when this happens.

Should representatives always be lawyers?

6.18 This is an offshoot of the perennial question on the mediation conference circuit: who makes the best mediators – lawyers or non-lawyers? Two points are always made in both contexts:

- Settlements at mediations are achieved by personal and commercial considerations, not legal ones. Non-lawyers are better at understanding this and not becoming bogged down in legal detail.

- In disputes that are essentially about technical issues, an expert can be the best person explain them to the mediator.

Non-lawyers

6.19   Provided that the representative has the minimum qualities and experience required, there is no reason why a self-confident articulate representative cannot do a good job for the client at mediation. However, there are certain core qualities or competencies that he must have, for example:

- be experienced in mediation and realise that the whole process is designed to make peace not war;

- have the detailed knowledge of the factual and legal points that might arise during the negotiation' and

- enjoy the confidence of the client.

Whatever particular interpretation of the advocate's role he chooses, an advocate must also meet the five key requirements listed here:

(1) **Stay on top** The advocate is not just there to parrot what his clients says and repeat his client's best points the whole day. He has to be proactive in defining and developing his client's position. There is no value in just being reactive to what the other side or the mediator said. This ability to stay in control depends on self-confidence, which in turn comes from experience and preparation.

(2) **Remain calm and professional** All sorts of emotions are generated at mediations. Sometimes they are brought to the mediation by one of the parties. Anger, greed and guilt are the three most common. Some arise out of the process: frustration, irritation and anxiety are the three most common. The advocate has to remain the calm centre of the emotional whirlpool.

    The absolute requirement is that the applicant must never lose his temper with his client, himself, the mediator or anybody on the other side. Once that happens the ability to think ahead, where options will need to be weighed up and decisions taken, the future is lost, as is the moral high ground, which is always a useful location to occupy in any negotiation.

(3) **Be restrained** Since at least1649 when Torriano published his *Commonplace of Italian Proverbs*, people have been advised that 'you catch more flies with honey than you do with vinegar.'

    The temptations and pressures to be extreme in language and conduct will be present at mediations. The advocate will know from experience that courtesy costs nothing. Rudeness and discourtesy can have a disproportionately negative effect. Just speak to others as you like to be spoken to.

    Advocates who call the other side liars and fraudsters, whether in mediation statements or in the opening statement at the joint session, do nothing but inflame and alienate the person they are trying to influence.

(4) **Keep up energy levels** Mediations are usually an intense experience for all concerned. They are particularly intense for the clients, who are centre

stage. Civil and commercial mediations usually last for at least eight hours. That is a long time for someone to be sitting in room without exercise with the same people concentrating on one topic. When that is combined with having to absorb new information, juggle priorities and take decisions under time pressure and perhaps also financial pressure people become tired and drained.

It is essential that the advocate maintains and tops up during the day his mental and physical energy levels.

(5) **Always be open to talks** This may sound either cringingly obvious or incomprehensible. After all mediation is all about talk. But it is surprising how relations between the advocates can deteriorate to such an extent but they can no longer communicate with each other. Sometimes this has happened before the mediation even starts, during the guerrilla warfare carried on in correspondence. Other times it happens because of the way people behave towards each other at the mediation.

More distressingly, but more frequently than might be imagined, advocates fall out with the mediator and find it impossible to conduct constructive conversations with him. When this happens there is a danger that the advocate will commit the cardinal sin of all mediation advocates: becoming a barrier to settlement. When the advocate becomes part of the problem not a part of the solution he is acting against his client's best interests.

6.20 There are two areas where non-lawyers may be less able to cope:

- litigation procedure – this is particularly important if proceedings are already underway.

- legal costs – surprisingly many of the lawyers, particularly transaction lawyers and barristers, are not always up to date on legal costs. They frequently do not know the rates allowed in different courts, or different grades of fee earner, or what the practice of particular cause is in allowing extensions to cost budgets. They are not as good at predicting future legal costs and recovery rates.

Both the client and the non-legal advocate can always take advice on these issues.

Lawyer advocates

6.21 A lot of the criticism directed at lawyers in mediation is mainly because they are prone to act like lawyers. There is some truth in the assertion that they find it difficult to leave legal analysis on one side while commercial proposals are discussed.

As Robert Townsend, the co-author of the universal bestseller *Up the Organization: How to Stop the Corporation from Stifling People and Strangling Profits*, who was also a director of American Express and President and Chairman of Avis, said:

'I don't know how much time and effort I wasted before discovering that deals aren't usually blown by principals they are blown by lawyers and accountants trying to prove how valuable they are.'

It still has to be recognised in defence of lawyers that:

- the reason why non-lawyers down play the importance of the law in mediation is that they do not know the law – lawyers do;

- the law cannot be completely discounted at mediation, especially if the dispute has already turned into a legal case with proceedings issued. As has been repeatedly said by senior members of the judiciary, mediation takes place in the shadow of the law;

- lawyers have experience of all sorts of disputes during their professional life. This gives them the ability to put to one side emotional and personal aspects of the dispute;

- barristers by training, inclination and experience are not dealmakers. Most lawyers and especially transaction lawyers are. However, no lawyer can practice commercial law whether contentious or non-contentious with any degree of success without being able to set aside legal issues and concentrate on the commercial ones;

- they are experienced and often very competent in getting on top of a new subject and absorbing fresh information quickly and in an organised way; and

- they are used to being flexible. In one case they will be representing the defendant and in another similar case they will represent the claimant. They do become accustomed to seeing both sides of any dispute – and there are at least three sides to any dispute.

6.22 In a previous book the author described the three classic roles of advocates at mediation as those of bodyguard, hired gun and coach. In summary:

- **Hired guns** see their role as destroying the other side through a combination of forceful and persuasive presentation of their client's best points and sustained and destructive attack on the other side's weak points. Barristers and solicitors with higher court advocacy rights particularly like this role.

- **Bodyguards** see their role as protecting their clients from themselves and bad deals. They can be reluctant to allow clients to speak or even have a joint opening session in which they give speaking and have been heard to say to the clients 'it is my professional duty not to allow you to enter into this settlement'.

- **Coaches** see their job as one of providing support, whichever way the client needs it on his journey towards settlement. They may be proactive but they don't feel the need to dominate or to be seen to be taking the lead all the time.

To some extent during the course of the mediation an advocate may switch from one role to another. Much depends upon the requirements of the day and client but also on the advocate's self-confidence and flexibility. Coaches tend to be more self-confident and flexible than bodyguards and hired guns.

Stress ball

In addition to whatever role the advocate takes, he will be required to be a stress ball and to absorb the frustration, pressure and sometimes even anger that clients can feel and express at mediations. Advocates have to have the professional personal maturity to absorb this. This is why it can be important for the advocate at mediation to have a significant degree of life experience. If a relatively junior solicitor, for example, is leading the mediation, it is a good idea to team up with a more seasoned barrister.

Essential skills for mediation advocates

6.23 There are three essential skills for mediation advocates:

- talking;
- listening; and
- smiling.

Most advocates think that their job is to advocate, ie talk on behalf of their client. In fact listening and smiling is just as, if not more, important. Most people prefer to talk than listen. They talk even more if feeling under stress. Talking can relieve tension. If you want to learn what the other side wants and is prepared to offer, it is better to listen to what they say either directly at any joint meetings or through the mediator. Listening and hearing are not the same thing. Lawyers often use the phrase 'I hear what you say'. Decoded it means 'I don't agree and I'm not going to change my opinion'.

Mediators are trained in active listening. This is more than just nodding and smiling to encourage people to keep talking. It is paying close attention to what is being said and letting the talker know that you are absorbing what is being said. Most lawyers and most advocates will think that they are good listeners anyway. A self-audit checklist is set out below.

Self-audit checklist

Active listening

6.24 Do you:

- Think about what you're going to ask next for the talker has finished?
- Talk over the talker?
- Finish their sentence?
- Interrupt?
- Nod?
- Smile?
- Paraphrase (aka reframing)?
- Say nothing?
- Fill the silence?
- Make notes?
- Have a pen in your hand?

Or do you:

- Maintain eye contact ?

- Encourage the talker to say more?

- Clarify that you understood what has been said?

- Use phrases such as:

  'I understand'

  'It must have been awful for you'

  'I know how you feel'

  'Tell me more'

  'What Happened next?'

  'What did you do then?'

  'How do you feel about it?'

  'Anything more?'

An advocate would not use these questions in talking to the mediator in the private session during a mediation. Some questions that he might use are:

  'How is it going in the other room?'

  'What was their reaction to?'

  'What they say is wrong with our proposal is ...'

  'How do they see this matter being sorted out?'

  'What is your impression of ...?'

  'How do you see the progress so far?'

  'What do you think we're going to need to do to get things moving/unblocked?'

Talking

6.25   Most advocates spend most of their time making statements or assertions rather than asking questions. Don't they? Listening helps advocates learn about the other side. Asking questions does the same thing. Questioning is essential and fundamental to any sort of successful communication. We are all asked and ask questions when engaging in conversation. It is important to note that questions can be used for different purposes.

Why do we ask questions?

Questions are asked for the following reasons:

- to obtain information;

- to engage with or show the other person that we are interested in them – this is important for rapport building and empathy;

- to clarify a point ;
- to find out what they feel the about an issue – this is very important in mediations where each side is trying to find out what the real problems are for the other side;
- to test knowledge – our own and theirs;
- to encourage further thought; and
- to show acknowledgment by asking for an opinion or reaction – in groups, this helps people feel engaged in a group activity and to keep attention.

There are several different types of questions that everybody knows.

OPEN QUESTIONS

6.26   These are used a lot in mediation both by the mediator and by skilled advocates. They are questions, which cannot be answered with a yes or no. The usual open questions are ones that begin with:

- Who
- What
- How
- Why
- When

They are used to open up discussion, thought or lines of enquiry.

CLOSED QUESTIONS

Closed questions are:

- those which can be answered with a short, often one word, answer, usually yes or no, for example: 'Do you drink coffee?'
- to make a choice from a list of options, for example: 'Would you like tea or coffee?'
- to confirm a certain piece of information for example: 'Where did you study law?'

They are used at mediations, usually to clarify or confirm something, eg: 'You would accept £500,000, yes?'

These are used to close down discussion, thought or lines of enquiry. They are a staple of cross- examination.

LEADING QUESTIONS

6.27   These are also known as loaded questions. Trainee barristers spend a lot of time learning how to use them and how to avoid using them. The golden rule being that in examination in chief you cannot ask a leading question, but in cross-examination you can. The distinguishing characteristic is that a leading or loaded question points the respondent to answer in a certain direction. It suggests the answer. Sometimes it is done subtly. Sometimes it is not done subtly at all eg: 'You are a dishonest man aren't you?'

RECALL QUESTIONS

These are used to prompt the respondent to remember something, eg: 'What did you do last Wednesday?'

PROCESS QUESTIONS

These require the respondent to give some more thoughts or analysis eg: 'What is the most important priority for you in this settlement?'

RHETORICAL QUESTIONS

These are usually used to highlight a point or attract the listeners' attention. They are sometimes used as humour, eg: 'Who wouldn't want to win at trial?' or 'Everybody thinks that they are going to win at trial, don't they?'

FUNNELLING

Interviewers and sometimes advocates in court use this technique. It is a series of questions that become more or less restrictive at each step. We start with narrow questions and open up to more general ones.

Listen to the response

6.28   Different types of questions produce different answers. It is worth being familiar with the main types of response. These have been analysed into the following main categories.

DIRECT AND HONEST RESPONSE

This is what most questioners hope to receive.

A LIE

Everyone knows what a lie is. Don't they? In adversarial negotiation, let alone in court, many responses are characterised as lies. Sometimes they are untrue. Sometimes they are just wrong. Sometimes they are just an alternative version or recollection.

In fact, research has established that most people overestimate their ability to tell when somebody is lying. Skilled questioners listen to both the words used and watch how the respondent speaks. Any discrepancies between what is being said, ie the verbal language, and what is being shown, ie the body language, can be very revealing. This is the area of cognitive dissonance.

A great deal of specialist training and practice is required to be able to reliably spot when someone is lying. People attending mediations rarely possess this expertise.

OUT OF CONTEXT

The respondent provides information or comment that has nothing to do with the question or the subject matter of the question. He may try and change the question. In these circumstances reword the question.

PARTIAL ANSWER

The respondent ignores part of the question and is selective.

AVOIDING THE QUESTION

Politicians and those who have received media training are extremely skilled in this. They deflect the question by reinterpreting it, restating it in a more positive way for them to answer or answer a question with a question.

STALLING

This is when people buy time to work out an answer. A common way of doing this is to answer a question with a question.

DISTORTION

This is a species of lying in the sense that the respondent is knowingly exaggerating what it suits him to say, for example about how strongly he feels about the case or even the amount of his salary.

REFUSAL

A simple non-response, ie silence itself, or by a statement, eg: 'I will not answer that.'

ATTACK

Sometimes the respondent can be aggressive, eg: 'That is a stupid question.' The question and the questioner are attacked on the basis that the respondent believes that attack is the best form of defence.

During the training, mediators are told to be aware that when these types of responses are given that there is another story that they are not being told. They are advised not to give up but to return to it later. This is why the mediation day can drag on. If you want to move forward be straightforward.

Smiling

6.29   In negotiation progress is made if trust is developed which is another name for rapport building and people start to like each other more. The simplest way of starting this process and maintaining it is to smile. However, remember that there are two types of smile: the genuine and the fake. There has been a lot of research into this.

- A genuine smile is both voluntary and involves the contraction of two sets of muscles: the zygomatic major, (raising the corners of the mouth) and the orbicularis oculi (raising the cheeks and producing crows feet around the eyes). This genuine smile is known as the Duchenne smile after the French physician Guillaume Duchenne, who studied the physiology of facial expressions in the 19th century.

- The fake smile is known as the Say Cheese or Polite Smile. It has been discovered that the Say Cheese smile is all controlled by the motor cortex in the brain's left hemisphere, while the emotion related to the Duchenne smile is controlled by the limbic system (the emotional centre of the brain).

The conventional wisdom is that you cannot voluntarily engage the orbicularis oculi but you can voluntarily engage the zygomatic major. Recent research has cast doubt on this. It suggests that people can fake a genuine smile. It is, however, far from clear whether in a real life situation, as opposed to a neutral laboratory situation, in the heat of an interaction people can actually fake a Duchenne smile.

Smiling is really a shorthand form of engaging in empathetic behaviour. As the key principles identified in **Chapter 1**, negotiation is the mutual recognition of reality and that an important skill of any advocate is to be able to see the pictures in someone else's head, ie see the position from their point of view. Remember Principle 8: people do not make decisions for your reasons – they make them for their own reasons.

Telephone technique

6.30 With the increase in the use of email for business communication, the amount of telephone communication has decreased, but there has been a growth in telephone mediation. There are several County Court schemes to deal with small claims. In addition there is a projected growth in online dispute resolution. At the moment this is a hybrid of techniques. The common factors are:

- there is no physical meeting;

- the communication is by telephone link, either through a conventional telephone line or via the internet;

- sometimes there is also a visual connection through, for example, Skype;

- the end result is that the human interaction is reduced. There is much less opportunity to observe how people react in a non-verbal way. Some of the technologies do allow for full room views but quite often all you can see is the head and shoulders of the speaker; and

- anecdotal evidence from mediators who carried out online dispute resolution supports the view that the technology is not robust. Often the visuals disappear and in fact mediation is conducted by voice only.

What this means is that advocates have to sharpen up their telephone technique. They will not be able to rely on their body language to the same extent to help them convey their message. Nor will they be able to rely on observing the other person's body language to interpret the messages that they are receiving. There is a more detailed discussion about body language in the next section.

What is telephone advocacy?

6.31 An advocate who has to rely upon his voice alone without any support from body language has to work much harder. The basic elements of telephone advocacy are:

- choice of words;
- timing;
- tone of voice;
- volume;
- rate of speaking; and
- emotion;

This is sometimes referred to as paralanguage.

Remember the well-established ratios about the impact of a message received:

- 55 per cent of the impact is non-verbal or visual;
- 38 per cent is vocal such as voice tone and inflection; and
- 7 per cent is verbal, ie the meaning of the words actually used.

This means that the scope of effective communication during telephone and on-line mediations is much reduced and the risk of miscommunication much increased. Therefore, the advocate must at all times be actively and consciously aware of what he is doing.

In practice, therefore, the *rate of speaking* becomes more important. It is not only a question of speaking too fast for people to understand or too slowly to retain people's attention. It is also the question of matching the rate of speaking to that of the other side. This is because the ability to engage in matching body language is not available.

Tone, which includes pitch and inflection, is important. Where the emphasis is placed in a sentence can radically change its meaning, for example:

'He is asking me to leave?'

'He is asking *me* to leave!'

'*He* is asking *me* to leave!'

Persuasion has been defined as a combination of empathy and sincerity. It is easier to convey both empathy and sincerity with words using body language and gesture. On the telephone it is more difficult. One way of doing it is to return to smiling.

Facial expressions

6.32 Here is a test. Put a big cheesy grin on your face. Pick up the telephone and pretend to have an angry conversation.

Difficult?

It cannot be done. Research has shown that facial expressions not only follow emotions but emotions follow facial expressions. In other words people can make themselves feel happy by smiling.

Observations of skilled telephone negotiators show that they use a lot of facial and hand gestures while speaking on the telephone. They do this even though the listener cannot see them. It still helps them convey the emotional content of the message. Less experienced telephone negotiators may feel self-conscious doing this.

Conversations

If, as many experienced mediators say, the best mediations are like a conversation it is worth remembering that conversations cannot be conducted in a deadpan monotone. Advocates who use a deadpan monotone may think that it sounds authoritative and makes it difficult the other side to read them: in practice, because it is boring, they lose the listener's attention and fail to generate any rapport.

Body language

6.33 People communicate whether they want to or not. As stated above, research shows 55 per cent of a message is contained in the visual body language of the speaker, 45 per cent in the verbal part of the message (38 per cent by the way the words are used and 7 per cent by the actual words used).

Other people's body language

Body language is seen as a tool for finding out what people really feel and think. It is not possible or wise to always believe what people say. By using body language the listener is able to double-check what they are being told. There is a mass of material about interpreting body language available on the internet. Much of it is highly entertaining and interesting. The question is how much use is it in practice in a mediation.

The difficulties are:

- Anybody who wants to be able to reliably interpret body language has to undergo a great deal of training and practice. If there is any doubt about this, take one of the tests available on YouTube. Just interpreting facial expression is much more difficult than might be thought.

- Signals are ambiguous. People may scratch their nose because they have a spot on it not because they are telling an untruth.

- Different people interpret the same signals differently – a tendency made worse by confirmation bias (see **Chapter 18**).

Your own body language

Despite the difficulties, it can be useful to have some guidance on one's own body language so that you do not send out unintended negative signals.

It is often said that body language is not a science. Dr Harry Witchel, at the Medical School of the University of Sussex is engaged in trying to establish the science behind body language. At the ADR Group Conference in Oxford in 2014, he gave his Six top tips for body language in mediation. They are:

- be engaging during private caucuses;
- be authoritative in joint negotiation;
- keep hands above table;
- use palm up batoning to encourage;
- lean forward to encourage; and
- lean back during drama.

Conclusion

6.34   To conclude:

- Reading body language is fun but it is difficult and of limited practical use in most mediations.
- Sharpen up your telephone technique.
- Forget about being adversarial.
- It is much easier to criticise than create but mediation is about creating solutions.
- Self-audit your active listening skills.
- Re-read the seven deadly sins for solicitors and barristers.
- Remember Core Principle1: You go to mediation to make peace not war.

Chapter 7

Risk/Benefit Assessment

This chapter discusses:

- Carrying out a pre-mediation analysis (PMA), including reviewing the risk/reward and cost/benefit ratios
- Working out who should attend from the client and other stakeholders such as insurers or mortgagees
- Risk profiles
- Structuring settlements

Risk and uncertainty: the evil twins

7.01 Risk and uncertainty are often confused. They are not the same thing. Risk can be measured. Uncertainty cannot be. Risk is the estimated likelihood of a known event happening. Uncertainty is not knowing what will happen.

A client's appetite for risk can be measured. A client's tolerance of uncertainty is much harder to measure. Generally people find it easier to cope with risk, once it has been quantified, than they do with uncertainty. There is a predilection or bias towards avoiding uncertainty. This is discussed in more detail in **Chapter 18.**

It is important for advocates and their clients when carrying out at pre-mediation analysis to be clear whether they are discussing risk or uncertainty.

Pre-mediation analysis

7.02 A pre–mediation analysis (PMA) is more than just working out what might happen at trial. It includes:

- establishing with the client specifically what his goal is by way of settlement;
- how bad it will be for him if he does not achieve this;
- how he can fund ongoing litigation;
- how he can fund a settlement;
- what are the obstacles to settlement;

- how they can be overcome;
- what is the client's appetite for risk;
- what is the client's capacity for sustaining a loss at trial;
- what is the impact of loss at trial on the client;
- what is the impact of settlement now on the client;
- what is the client's net cash position after trial compared with what it would be after settlement;
- what are the client's BATNAs, WATNAs, PATNAs (Probable Alternative to a Negotiated Settlement) or RATNAs (Realistic Alternative to a Negotiated Settlement); and
- reviewing the strengths and weaknesses of the client's case and the other side's case.

In essence there are three elements:

- risk analysis for own client;
- benefit analysis for own client; and
- risk/benefit analysis for other side

Risk analysis

7.03   Litigation lawyers do this in any event with their clients. They are used to calculating litigation risk. In the context of mediation there are three simple approaches that can be used with a client when discussing what might be a sensible commercial alternative to carry on fighting litigation to trial. These are:

- litigation risk;
- net cash position; and
- summing the differences.

Litigation risk

7.04   Lawyers routinely carry out an analysis of litigation risk. It is an essential, but not a sufficient, element of a PMA. Both lawyers and their clients are often inaccurate when calculating litigation risk. This is for a variety of reasons:

- The operation of optimism bias. This is explained in more detail in **Chapter 18** but both claimants and defendants habitually overestimate their chances of securing a favourable result at trial.

- The claimant's lawyers always give themselves a higher chance of winning than the defendant's lawyers.

- The reluctance to quantify risk. At mediations, when asked what their chances of succeeding at trial are, the most often used phrases include those such as, 'we have a strong case,' or 'it's at the top of the range,' or 'we are more likely to win than lose'.

116

- A reluctance to recognise reality. Verbal descriptions of risk can be more comforting than numerical ones. It is easy for the client to receive a rosier impression of their chances.

- Lack of familiarity with some simple techniques of quantifying risk.

Here's an example of a simple quantification based on probabilities.

Example 7.1

First identify the uncertainties. The more uncertainties there are, the lower the odds of winning at trial.

Take a professional negligence case. The claimant has to prove breach of duty, ie liability, causation and loss, ie quantum.

If the chance of proving breach of duty are 90% causation 70% and loss 100% the overall chance of proving all three elements is:

$$90\% \times 70\% \times 100\% = 63\%.$$

If the defendants made a Part 36 offer of £250,000, the probability of beating that has to be factored in as well. If there is a 90% chance of beating an offer option of £250,000 the chances of beating the Part 36 offer are $63\% \times 90\% = 58\%$

What starts off in verbal descriptions as a case near the top of the range is now one that is more likely to win than lose.

Doing this sort of quantitative calculation makes it easier to double check whether a qualitative assessment is too optimistic they usually are.

Net cash position

7.05 This is a simple calculation to do. Take the expected ranges of compensation if the client wins, the interest calculation and the level of costs expended and recoverable from the other side. Here is a worked example. It compares the net cash positions in three different trial scenarios:

- a good day in court;

- a bad day in court; and

- a middling day in court.

The first two are simple to calculate. The third is not but it is often the actual outcome at trial with neither party winning 100% nor losing 100%. Of course there can be several permutations for this scenario.

Example 7.2

Assumptions

In this example it is assumed that it is a contract claim for £200,000. The legal costs for each party at the time of the mediation are £30,000. Total costs of going to trial are £50,000 per party, ie an additional £20,000. Interest at the time of the mediation is £10,000 and at trial £12,000. The percentage of costs to be recovered by the winning party from the losing party is 70 per cent.

Scenario A: a good day in court

	Money received in (£)	Money paid out (£)
Damages	200,000	
Interest	12,000	
Total	212,000	
Net before costs recovery	162,000	
Costs	35,000	(50,000)
Final net figure (C)	197,000	
Final net figure (D)	(247,000)	

Scenario B: bad day

	Money received in (£)	Money paid out (£)
Damages	nil	
Interest	nil	
Total	nil	
Net before costs recovery		(50,000)
Costs		(35,500)
Final Net Position (C)	(85,000)	
Final Net Position(D)	(35,000)	

Scenario C(i): middle day

Assumption: the claimant wins 60% of his claim and costs

	Money paid in (£)	Money paid out (£)
Damages	120,000	
Interest	7,200	
Total	127,200	
Net before costs recovery	77, 200	

Costs	30,000	(50,000)
Final Net Figure (C)	107,200	
Final Net Figure (D)	(207,000)	

Scenario C(ii): middle day

Assumption: the claimant wins 50% of his claim and costs.

	Money paid in (£)	Money paid in (£)
Damages	100,000	
Interest	6,000	
Total	106,000	
Net before costs recovery	(56,000)	
Costs	25,000	(50,000)
Final net figure (C)	81,000	
Final Net Figure (D)	(181,000)	

7.06   In these examples the risk-reward ratio can easily be seen. It is difficult to believe that parties attend a mediation without having carried out this sort of calculation, but they do more often than not. They have several disadvantages:

- When the mediator suggests that they do the calculation the clients are often shocked at the outcome, particularly when they realise what their best case in court will produce for them net if they do not settle.

- This unwelcome and unexpected realisation often causes clients to change their attitude to settlement and to their lawyers.

- Parties often arrive with unrealistic expectations. They make an early offer to settle which is in excess of what they would receive on their best-case scenario. These sorts of proposals are a waste of time and goodwill and send the wrong signals.

Summing the differences

7.07   This is a simple way of encouraging clients to think about their cases and their prospects in a monetary way. See the following example:

Example 7.3

Take the same assumptions as used in the Net Cash Position example.

The claimant has a claim for £200,000. His legal costs are £50,000 and he can expect to recover £35,000 (70%) if he wins and to pay that if loses. Interest is left out of this calculation for simplicity.

If he has a 60% chance of winning the calculation looks like this:

$$200.000 \times 0.6 + 35,000 \times .6 + (15,000) \times 1 = £126,000$$

$$+$$

$$(35,000) \times 0.4 + (35.000) \times 0.4 + (15,000) \times 1 = (£43,000)$$

So the value of the claim is £126,000 – £43,000 = £83,000

Even if you assume an 80% chance of winning the figures are:

$$200.000 \times 0.8 + 35,000 \times 0.8 + (15,000) \times 1 = £173,000$$

$$+$$

$$(35,000) \times 0.2 + (35,000) \times 0.2 + (15,000) \times 1 = £30,000$$

So the value of the claim is £173,000 – £30,00 = £143,000

Confidence and risk factors

7.08   What all these examples show is that most claims are worth less than the claimants think. When this is combined with optimism bias (see **Chapter 18**) it explains the mindset often displayed by clients, which their advocates have to try and adjust.

Advocates can begin by asking their clients what their confidence factor or expectation is that they will end up in any particular scenario. In practice, even the most optimistic lawyers never tell their clients that they have more than a 80 per cent chance of winning.

If the client is asked if they want to spend £50,000 to gain £126,000 for with a 60 per cent of achieving this and a 40 per cent chance of losing £94,000 they always pause for thought. It is the advocate's duty to make sure that they have given their client the opportunity to think about risk and reward in an informed way.

Appetite for risk

7.09   The client's appetite for risk can be easily and quickly assessed by taking them through this sequence.

Example 7.4

The client is presented with two Scenarios A and B.

In Scenario A the client has £1,000. He is offered two options: a 100% chance of winning an additional £500 or a 50/50 chance of winning £1,000. Which would he chose?

Most people choose the first option and are certain of receiving the additional £500. They prefer to secure their upside.

In Scenario B the client has £2,000. He is again offered two options: a 100% chance of losing £500 or a 50/50 chance of losing £1,000 or nothing.

Which would he chose?

Most people chose the second option and take a chance on losing £1,000 or nothing. They prefer not to secure their downside.

Of course this is inconsistent. A client who is a risk taker should take option 2 in both scenarios. A client who is not a risk taker should take option 1 in both Scenarios. The end result is the same: the net cash position is that you have £1,500. If £1,500 was sufficient in scenario A then why was it not sufficient in scenario B?

A risk taker should take option 2 in both scenarios and end up with either £1,000 or £2,000.

This example is also an illustration of one of the influences that are identified in **Chapter 18** in the discussion on heuristics and cognitive biases. That is the tendency of people to be loss adverse. People find it harder to give up something that they already own than to give up the prospect of acquiring something that they do not already own.

This explains the different approach to offers and settlement negotiation between the receiving and paying parties. Advocates advising defendants who are usually the paying party have to be alert to protect their clients from the consequences of this tendency. They must also be alert of course to the danger that they may be exhibiting the same tendency themselves. When it is combined with optimism bias the outcome can be disastrous.

Impact and value of losing

7.10   Clients need to understand that having a 70 per cent chance of winning at trial does not mean that they will receive 70 per cent of what they are claiming. It means that if the case were tried 10 times they would win on seven days and lose on three.

Clients must be asked how they could withstand the impact of losing. The answers are often revealing. Of course the impact of having to pay out £200,000 is often more serious than failing to receive £200,000. This is not always so. Some parties may be relying on receiving the money that they are claiming, for example because they have persuaded another creditor not to sue for the money that he is owed because of the prospect of a favourable judgment in this case.

Impact and value of settlement

7.11   Calculating risk factors and net cash positions is only half of the pre-mediation analysis that the client must carry out. They also need to calculate the value and impact of settlement. This is not just limited to the financial savings that they can be achieved by not having to pay any further legal fees.

Non-monetary factors

7.12   Parties often tell their lawyers that they are prepared to fight the case as a matter of principle and it is not just about the money. As discussed in **Chapter 5**, the concept of fairness is very important for most people. Settlement therefore can have value if it satisfies other non-monetary criteria such as:

Heal wounds:	An acknowledgment of liability or an apology is often very valuable to the recipient. It is vindication.
Reduce stress:	Litigation is a stressful activity for most people. This does not apply, for example, to repeat litigators such as insurance claim handlers. But for most people it is. It also places strain on relationships. In many mediations, the claimant's wife has come along with her husband and has told him that she has had enough and wants the dispute settled today.
Give certainty:	Most people prefer certainty to uncertainty. This is as true in our business lives as well as private. Businesses do not like surprises. Uncertainty makes planning more difficult.
Save reputation:	There is always the risk that if the dispute goes to court that the judge can make adverse comments about the parties, even if he decides the case in their favour.
Confidentiality:	Many disputants prefer to keep the details of their dispute private for as long as they can. This is impossible once the trial starts. Details of the settlement can also be kept private.
Free up time:	Disputes are time consuming. Most people could be do something better with their time. Nobody's last words are 'I wish that I had spent more time litigating.'
Reduce distraction:	Many businesses find that they spend time and effort on litigation when they could have been spending it on their business. Litigation for most businesses is down time.
Relationships:	Many relationships, both personal and commercial, do not survive a court trial. Too many harsh words are said in public.
Protect third parties:	Litigation does not just affect the disputants. Innocent bystanders can be injured. If a company loses at trial its creditors and shareholders may suffer.
Contain the dispute:	Disputes have a tendency to escalate. They not only become more expensive. The scope of the dispute expands. More issues and evidence are uncovered. Parties often come to regret this.

Some of these non-monetary considerations are intangible and difficult to quantify in monetary terms. In practice when clients start to carry out a cost-benefit analysis they find that they can put a value expressed in money terms on most of the factors listed above. It is not an exact science. But it does allow clients to prioritise and define what they really need.

Value can change

7.13   All lawyers are familiar with the way in which cases can change and develop over time. They become stronger or weaker in some respects. New issues emerge. Experts change their opinions. Vary rarely is a case the same on the first day of the trial as it was on the day that proceedings were first issued.

The same happens with settlement. The value of a settlement can increase or decline as time passes. This has been discussed **in Chapter 5**.

The other side's settlement

7.14   As has already been said in **Chapter 1**, a fundamental part of any negotiation, and in particular mediation, is the mutual recognition of reality. Each side has to recognise its own reality and the other side's. Once that degree of common understanding has been achieved, finding common ground on which a settlement can be built becomes much easier.

So the third element of the pre-mediation analysis after analysing the client's risk-reward ratio, ie the benefits as well as the costs of settlement, is to do the same exercise for the other side. Of course this is not as easy to do. There is usually much less information available about what the other's goals are. However an intelligent estimate can be made. Some idea of how accurate the estimates are will be seen when proposals are framed and put forward at the mediation. The mediator may well be able to provide guidance during private discussions in either the exploration or exchange stages.

Carrying out this exercise will help clients work out what they can afford to do for the other side. This is not just in terms of how much money to pay.

Example 7.5

In an employment dispute, the employer may work out how much he thinks the employee will need until he finds another job. That is a money element. He may also work out that the employee needs help in finding a job, for example by receiving a positive reference or being able to continue to use his laptop and mobile phone number. These additional items cost the employer very little but can be of great value to the employee.

When devising proposals for settlement, always look to minimise the cost to the paying party and to maximise the benefit to the receiving party. The more clients have thought about how to do this in advance the easier it will be on the day.

A template in the form of a confidential checklist for working out a negotiation strategy for the mediation is at the end of this chapter.

Funding settlement

7.15   The paying party must consider how any settlement proposal is going to be funded. It is surprising how often parties attend mediation without having given any thought to the timing of payments, instalments, or any security that could be offered.

If the paying party needs time he must be able to show the receiving part that he cannot afford to pay the whole amount immediately, but he can afford to pay all the money over time and he has acceptable security available. In order to be able to show the receiving party this, the clients must have available at the mediation:

- (for individuals) an up-to-date statement of assets and liabilities, and bank statements, tax returns, valuations and redemption statements;

- (for businesses) three years of accounts, current management accounts and forecasts, bank statements tax returns and valuations; and

- tax advice on the timing and structuring of any payments.

It is astonishing how often halfway through the day there is frantic activity on telephones and e-mails to try and assemble this information.

It's not my problem

It is naive for a paying party to expect the receiving party to accept at face value what he says about his finances. After all they are actually in dispute at the mediation because trust has broken down.

The receiving party also has to consider how a settlement can be funded. It is naive for him to say that it is the other side's problem. All lawyers know that obtaining a judgment is the easy part of litigation. Actually collecting the money is the hard part. Recoverability is always something that needs to be considered.

If a client wants to receive money from the other side it is in his interests to help them pay it to him.

It is surprising how often the receiving party attends the mediation with no up-to-date information about the paying party's ability to pay. At the start of the litigation they may have carried out some searches on properties a party owns but by the time of the mediation they are almost always out of date. If up-to-date information is to hand it makes it easier to decide whether the paying party is bluffing when they say they cannot afford to pay.

Lawyers and their clients need to rebalance their preparation is discussed. They need to spend less time on the legal arguments supporting their case and more time on the practical ways of structuring a settlement.

Other stakeholders

7.16   In order to conclude a settlement the consent of people who are not parties to the dispute may be required. This point is often overlooked. Here are some examples of where authority or consent from others is often required:

- The property is jointly owned, eg by a man and his wife. The husband comes to the mediation as he is the actual party in the litigation. If he is going to agree as part of a settlement to a charge over the house to secure instalment payments, he will need the consent of his wife.

- If property is to be charged or sold as part of a settlement the consent of existing mortgagees or chargees may be required.

- If a party has borrowed money to fund the litigation and is going to borrow money to fund the settlement they will need the consent of their lenders.

- In corporate disputes, the person at the mediation representing the company needs to have the authority of the Board to negotiate and conclude a settlement on behalf of the company. Quite often the other side will want to be reassured on this point in order to avoid any danger of a settlement agreement being attacked by the company on the grounds that its representative did not have proper authority.

- The same point arises with partnerships or syndicates where one or two members are negotiating on behalf of the whole group. The other side will want to be reassured that they do have authority to bind all members of the group.

- If any of the parties have insurance to fund their legal expenses they will need to know how much the insurers want to receive as part of a settlement. Often legal expenses insurers do not attend mediations. It is not always possible to speak on the telephone or by email with the claims handling officer during the mediation. This can prevent settlements from being concluded. With other types of insurance, for example Professional Negligence insurance or Directors and Officers insurance, a representative usually attends the mediation. They do not always attend and the same problem about consent can arise.

Conclusion

7.17   To conclude:

- Always complete an PMA, preferably with your client.

- Do the maths.

- Remember to put values on the non-monetary factors.

- Work out your opening offer.

- Rebalance your preparation from polishing up your best legal points to working out settlement proposals.

- Consider how settlements can be structured and funded. Do this whether you are the paying party or the receiving party.

- Make sure that you have authority and consents from everyone, including insurers and funders.

Appendix 1

Confidential Checklist*

> In order for mediation to be successful you need to have discussed and considered with your client everything about the strengths and weaknesses of the case as well as the pos and cons of settling early. This can either be kept private or disclosed to the mediator if you think it would help the process. Key examples of information that should be considered are: cost implications, litigation risks, time restraints and mediation expectations

Confidential Checklist

Your case

List your evidence – Witnesses, documents, reports, statements etc.

1. _____

2. _____

3. _____

List damages:

1. _____

2. _____

3. _____

List your legal arguments concerning liability and damages:

Liability:

1. _____

2. _____

3. _____

---

*   Reprinted with the kind permission of the ADR Group.

Damages:

1. _____

2. _____

3. _____

List your strengths and weaknesses and any mitigating circumstances:

Strengths:

1. _____

2. _____

3. _____

Weaknesses:

1. _____

2. _____

3. _____

Confidential Checklist

Calculate your settlement range:

1. Would like to get
2. Would accept
3. Bottom line
4. Walkaway point

How did you value the case?

What elements are included e.g. special damages etc.

What is your best alternative to no agreement? (BATNA)

What is the worst outcome to no agreement? (WOTNA)

How much will it cost to go to trial?   £_____

How long will it take?   _____

What are your chances of winning in court?   _____%

What do the other side consider as their chance?   _____%

What questions / line of argument do you want the mediator to put to the other side?

Confidential Checklist

The other side's case

List their key issues:

1. _____

2. _____

3. _____

List their evidence:

1. _____

2. _____

3. _____

Guess their probable arguments regarding:

Liability:

1. _____

2. _____

3. _____

Damages:

1. _____

2. _____

3. _____

List their strengths and weaknesses:

Strengths:

1. _____

2. _____

3. _____

Weaknesses:

1. _____

2. _____

3. _____

Consider / guess the basis of their demands/offer:

How else may they have valued their demand / offer?

Chapter 8

When and Where to Hold a Mediation: Is It Important?

This chapter includes:

- How to decide when to hold a mediation
- Halsey and its descendants
- List of useful quotes
- What is the best day of the week for a mediation?
- Mediation venues
- Checklist for when choosing mediation venues
- Who to take to the mediation

When to mediate?

8.01   Complete freedom of choice in deciding when to mediate does not exist. Although mediation is sold as a voluntary process, in practice it is less voluntary than many people think. There are two main constraints on freedom of choice:

- contractual constraints; and
- Civil Procedure Rules.

Contractual constraints

8.02   More and more contracts contain clauses which oblige the parties to try and settle cases before going to litigation or arbitration. Often they stipulate a time limit by which certain steps must be taken. As soon as one party invokes these provisions the clock starts running. There used to be considerable doubt about whether the English courts would enforce such agreements, but the position is now different. The courts are increasingly willing to enforce mediation clauses.

The old position

Traditionally the English courts have been reluctant to enforce agreements to agree or agreements to negotiate. Some judges went so far as to say they were inconsistent with negotiation. In the case of *Walford v Miles* [1992] 2 AC 128, Ackner LJ said:

> 'However the concept of a duty to carry on negotiations in good faith is inherently repugnant to the adversarial position of the parties when involved in negotiations. Each party to the negotiations is entitled to pursue his (or her) own interest, so long as he avoids making misrepresentations.'

He went on to ask:

> 'To advance the interest he must be entitled, if he thinks it appropriate, to threaten to withdraw from further negotiations or to withdraw in fact, in the hope that the opposite party may seek to reopen the negotiations by offering him improved terms .... How is a vendor ever to know that he is entitled to withdraw from further negotiations? How is the court to police such an "agreement"?'

He concluded that:

> 'a duty to negotiate in good faith is as unworkable in practice as it is inherently inconsistent with the position of a negotiating party'.

The middle position

8.03   Ten years after Ackner LJ's comments, Colman J in the case of *Cable & Wireless plc v IBM United Kingdom Ltd* [2002] EWHC (Comm) 2059, held that where the parties have stipulated a mediation procedure that would be followed the clause was not void for uncertainty and could be enforced. He went on to say that, even where the agreement did not provide for an identifiable procedure, the court could still examine it to see whether or not it was expressed in unqualified and mandatory terms. This early identification of the need for precision in mediation clauses has been followed in subsequent cases.

A three-stage test has been developed in the Technology and Construction Court (TCC) and the Commercial Court. In 2007, the TCC said that the three stages were:

(1) the mediation clause must be sufficiently certain in that there should not be any need for agreement at any stage before matters can proceed;

(2) the administrative process for choosing the mediator and paying him must be defined; and

(3) the process or at least a model of the process for the mediation should be set out so that the detail of the process is sufficiently clear.

(See *Holloway & Holloway v Chancery Mead Ltd* [2007] EWHC 2495 (TCC).)

In 2012, the Commercial Court formulated the test as follows so that the parties must:

● make an unequivocal commitment to engage in mediation;

● define a model of mediation such as that provided by CEDR; and

- identify the mediator and the location of the mediation process in which the parties have to engage.

The present position

8.04 This approach was endorsed by the Court of Appeal in *Sulamerica CIA Nacional de Seguros SA & Ors v Enesa Engenharia SA & Ors* [2012] EWCA Civ 638. A helpful and clear recent formulation of the test was given by Hildyard LJ in *Wah v Grant Thornton International Ltd* at para 60:

'In the context the positive obligation to attempt to resolve a dispute or difference amicably before referring a matter to arbitration or bringing proceedings the test is whether the provision prescribes without the need for further and agreement,

(a) a sufficiently certain and unequivocal commitment to commence a process

(b) from which may be discerned what steps each party is required to take to put the process in place and which is

(c) sufficiently clearly defined to enable the Court to determine objectively

(i) what under that process is the minimum required of the parties to the dispute in terms of their participation in it

and

(ii) when or how the process will be exhausted or properly terminable without breach.'

(See Wah v Grant Thornton International Ltd [2012] EQHC 3198 (Ch).)

8.05 The courts have now gone further. In 2014 Mr Justice Teare held that he was:

'not bound by authority to hold that the dispute resolution clause in an existing and enforceable contract which requires the parties to seek to resolve the dispute by friendly discussions in good faith and within limited period of time before the dispute may be referred to arbitration is unenforceable'.

This was in the case of *Emirates Trading Agency LLC v Prime Mineral Exports Private Ltd* [2014] EWHC 2104 (Comm) where the clause in question provided:

11. Dispute Resolution and Arbitration

'11.1 In case of any dispute or claim arising out of or in connection with or under this LTC including an account of breaches/defaults mentioned in 9.2, 9.3, clauses 10.1(d) and/or 10.1(e) above, the Parties shall first seek to resolve the dispute or claim by friendly discussion. Any Party may notify the other Party of its desire to enter into a consultation to resolve a dispute or claim. If no solution can be arrived at in between the parties for a continuous period of 4 (four) weeks then the non-defaulting party can invoke the arbitration clause and refer the dispute to arbitration.'

He went on to give his reasons, which are almost the exact opposite of what Ackner LJ said in 1992:

> 'The agreement is not incomplete; no term is missing. Nor is it uncertain; an obligation to seek to resolve a dispute by friendly discussions in good faith has an identifiable standard, namely, fair, honest and genuine discussions aimed at resolving a dispute.'

He dealt with the problem of policing such clauses, which had troubled Ackner LJ, as follows in para 64:

> 'Difficulty of proving a breach in some cases should not be confused with the suggestion that the clause lacks certainty. In the context of a dispute resolution clause pursuant to which the parties have voluntarily accepted a restriction upon their freedom not to negotiate it is not appropriate to suggest that the obligation is inconsistent with the position of a negotiating party.'

He went on to say in para 64:

> 'Enforcement of such an agreement when found as part of the dispute resolution clause is in the public interest, first, because commercial men expect the court to enforce obligations which they have freely undertaken and second, because the object of the agreement is to avoid what might otherwise be an expensive and time consuming arbitration.'

In summary the present position is:

- the courts are in favour of enforcing mediation clauses;
- the clauses must still pass the three-stage test, ie be certain;
- if the clauses referred to a procedure such as CEDR or ADR group, those procedures must be a complete code of what is to happen when a reference to mediation is made.

Civil Procedure Rules

8.06 The effect of the CPR is that most parties in most disputes will eventually go to mediation unless:

- they settle without mediation, which they can always do if they wish; and
- they have an overwhelmingly good reason for not doing so, which is increasingly difficult to establish.

In practice mediation is now obligatory except in the strictest sense of the CPR. The question then arises whether it is better to go to mediation sooner or later.

The attitude of the courts

8.07 The place to start is with the Pre-Action Conduct Practice Direction and it is worth advocates being familiar with it.

It must be noted that this Practice Direction applies in all cases (para 2.3), even if a specific pre-action protocol also applies. It is not limited to mediation or ADR.

Para 4 deals with compliance.

'4.1 The CPR enables the court to take into account the extent of the parties' compliance with this Practice Direction or a relevant pre-action protocol (see paragraph 5.2) when giving directions for the management of claims (see CPR rule 3.1 (4)) and (5)) and were making orders about who should pay costs CPR rule 44.2 (5) (a)).

4.2 the court will expect the parties to have complied with this Practice Direction or any relevant pre-action protocol. The court may ask the parties to explain what steps were taken to comply prior to the start of the claim. Where there has been a failure of compliance by a party the court may ask that party to provide an explanation.

[...]

Examples of non-compliance

4.4 The court may decide that there has been a failure of compliance by a party because, for example, that party has –

(3) unreasonably refused to consider ADR (paragraph 8 in Part III of this Practice Direction in the pre-action protocol all contain similar provisions about ADR).'

Para 8 deals with Alternative Dispute Resolution.

'8.1 Starting proceedings should usually be a step of last resort, and proceeding should not normally be started when a settlement is still actively being explored. Although ADR is not compulsory, the parties should consider whether some form of ADR procedure might enable them to settle the matter without starting proceedings. The court may require evidence that the parties considered some form of ADR (see paragraph 4.4 (3))'.

It expressly suggests options such as negotiation and mediation.

'8.4 the party should continue to consider the possibility of reaching a settlement at all times. This still applies after proceedings have been started, up to and during any trial or final period.'

It also lists the specific Pre Action Protocols currently in force.

8.08   At para 2.2 (2) in Annex A it states that there is an expectation that the claimant should state the form of ADR that it considers most suitable and invite the defendant to agree. The defendant should say whether or not they accept the suggestion and if not why not and what alternative proposal they suggest. If ADR has not taken place during the pre-action correspondence and discussion the parties should review whether or not proceedings can be avoided before actually issuing proceedings. It must be borne in mind that this consideration of mediation takes place in a context of openness and cooperation in pre-action dealings between the parties and their representatives.

The point is that mediation is no longer:

- a fringe activity – it is a central part of litigation procedure in England and Wales;

- a sign of weakness – instead, suggesting mediation early on in a dispute gives a tactical advantage. Immediately the other side is on the back foot if it delays in responding to or ignores a request;

- a pseudo-day in court – the English tradition of adversarial litigation is now tempered by the expectations of cards on the table and co-operative litigation conduct as expressed in the Practice Directions and the problem-seeking approach of mediation.

How far can the courts help?

8.09   In the absence of a contractual obligation to go to mediation, the courts at present do not give much actual help to parties who want to go to mediation. The scope for making pre-action orders to facilitate mediation is limited. It has been known for courts to make an order which supports the mediation process by, for example, ordering pre-action disclosure of documents which one or both parties think are necessary for them to mediate.

Two potential disadvantages are often cited for going to mediation before proceedings are issued, even if a settlement is reached:

- A Settlement Agreement is legally binding but cannot be enforced by the court without issuing proceedings. There is an exception where the EU Mediation Directive applies.

- If a settlement is reached the court has no powers to make an order about costs. The Settlement Agreement has to deal with them. The exception is if the Settlement Agreement records agreement on all issues with costs to be assessed if not agreed. Proceedings can be issued for the assessment of costs (CPR 44.12(a), PD 46, paras 9.1–9.12).

By contrast, if proceedings are issued following a mediation, either to enforce the settlement reached at the mediation or because no settlement was reached, the court does have power to award pre-proceedings costs (CPR 44.2, Senior Courts Act 1981, s 51).

Mediation Settlement Enforcement Order (MSEO)

8.10   Mediation Settlement Enforcement Orders relate to cross-border disputes. The procedure for applying for one is set out in Pt 23 of the CPR where proceedings have commenced) or using the Pt 8 procedures (as amended by CPR 78.24 and PD 78). If the parties agree that one should be applied for, and this could be incorporated as a term of the Mediation Agreement or the Settlement Agreement the application is on paper. An MSEO can be enforced in the same way as any judgment or court order. If the parties cannot apply for an MSEO, the parties have to commence proceedings for breach of the settlement agreement, obtain their judgment and enforce in the usual way.

The court reinforces its avowed encouragement of mediation by its case management directions and in particular its cost sanctions. Advocates need to be familiar with the wide range of sanctions that the court can impose for not complying with pre-action protocols, court directions or unreasonably refusing to go to mediation. These can be found in CPR 44.2 and in particular CPR 44.2 (6). The most usual sanction is an adverse costs order.

Can I refuse to go to mediation?

8.11   The court has set out in a series of cases its attitude towards parties who unreasonably refuse to go to mediation. The starting point is a case from 2004, *Halsey v Milton Keynes General NHS Trust* [2004] EWCA Civ 576. In the line of cases that followed, the courts have wavered and sometimes contradicted themselves but the general message now is that they favour mediation. Even in the latest cases, see below, *Halsey* and the six factors are still referred to. Anybody contemplating whether to go to mediation has to bear in mind the *Halsey* factors.

The starting point is whether a party who is successful at trail but who refused to go to mediation be deprived of the usual costs order in its favour? The answer then and now is that it can, if the successful party unreasonably refused to go to mediation.

The six factors are the ones the court would take into account when deciding whether there had been an unreasonable refusal. If it did decide that there had been unreasonable refusal it was able to punish the defaulting party by:

● depriving it of its costs even if it had been successful at trial;

● imposing indemnity costs; and

● ordering a higher rate of interest to be paid on any damages.

The six *Halsey* factors are:

(1) the nature of the dispute;

(2) the merits of the case;

(3) how far other settlement methods have been tried;

(4) would mediation costs be disproportionately high;

(5) would mediation cause delay; and

(6) did mediation have a reasonable prospect of success.

These have been the subject of judicial consideration and findings and much comment from the mediation community. Advocates need to be familiar with the latest thinking.

The six Halsey factors

The nature of the dispute

8.12   Most cases are suitable for ADR. It is sometimes said that there are cases, which may not be suitable. The usual examples given are:

- the dispute is about pure construction of a document or point of law;
- there is a need for a binding precedent;
- there are allegations of fraud; and
- urgent interim relief is required, for example, injunction or freezing or search order

In practice these exceptions do not apply very frequently. If there is a need for urgent interim relief, that can be made in the usual way. This does not prevent there being mediation during the course of the proceedings. Applications for interim injunctions are often dealt with by undertakings anyway.

Regarding construction and binding precedent cases:

- Different interpretations of documents can be agreed.
- The need for a binding precedent or test case can arise but is comparatively rare. The small number of cases that the Supreme Court considers suitable for hearing each year (81 out of 229 applications between 1 April 2013 and 31 March 2014) shows the number of precedents that they think are required.
- At the Court of Appeal level there is the Court of Appeal mediation scheme (CAMS).

In a recent article in the *Law Society Gazette* ('Mediation: peace at any price?', 24 November 2014), Suzanne Rab, who has specialised in competition law both as a solicitor and a barrister, said:

'With mounting interest in Europe in private enforcement of competition disputes, it is timely to consider alternative forms resolution beyond a complaint to a competition authority, including mediation.'

She goes on to say:

'Competition cases can raise untested points of law and controversial economic theories. It can be in both parties' interests to avoid a precedent that is binding in future cases.'

It is often said that cases involving fraud cannot be mediated. The reasons why not have not been clearly articulated. It seems to be assumed that it is axiomatic that dishonest conduct cannot be countenanced by allowing it to go unpunished and coming to a settlement.

8.13   In practice many cases involving fraud are settled at mediation. This does not apply where criminal proceedings have been brought. They are not compromised by settlement at mediation.

In cases where there are allegations of civil fraud, both the claimant and the defendant can find a way of settling. Strong language is sometimes used at mediation both in written documents submitted to the mediator and in what is said on the day. Sometimes these allegations come close to being blackmail or defamatory but still the parties are able to find enough common ground to allow them to settle.

Advocates of mediation can, in an excess of zeal, frequently make allegations of questionable conduct that, if the case is not settled, might lead their clients to refer the matter to the authorities. This usually means the police or a regulator. They should be wary of doing this. Mediators might start to feel uncomfortable and terminate the mediation. On closer analysis their own clients may find themselves implicated. Common examples of questionable conduct are:

- forgery, often alleged in disputed wills cases and with good reason;

- mortgage fraud, often mentioned in disputes between property owners and investors;

- theft; for example in disputes over confidential information and proprietary information, maladministration of trust funds or abuse of powers of attorney;

- perjury; where the veracity of a witness who has given a sworn statement is challenged;

- harassment and intimidation by landlords and also in commercial disputes where there are said to have been physical threats against potential witnesses or parties/commercial dispute; and

- breaches of the Companies Act or Insolvency Act, which are in fact criminal offences, are often alleged in shareholder disputes or in claims brought by insolvency practitioners against bankrupts or directors of insolvent companies.

The merits of the case

8.14   A party who refuses to go to mediation because it thinks that it has a very strong case that will succeed at trial will not inevitably be acting unreasonably by refusing to go to mediation. However, as the court has pointed out on several occasions, many parties in a dispute believe that they have a strong case and will succeed at trial. Mediators are often faced with two sets of legal advisers, both advising their clients that they are going to win at trial. Even after making allowance for the inevitable bluffing and optimism bias sometimes this optimism is justified. Sometimes it is not.

The courts have not been as consistent and clear as practitioners would have liked on this point. The current position seems to that the party who refuses mediation simply because he thinks that he has a very strong case may still be acting unreasonably. There has to be some other factor.

But the courts are moving away from some of the earlier unhelpful remarks in for example in the case of *Swain Mason v Mills & Reeves* [2012] EWCA Civ 498, where Davis LJ seemed at para 74 to be creating a special category of reasons for refusal for defendants in professional negligence cases. Any advocates met with this sort of response by PI insurers to a request for mediation should refer to the list of quotations at **para 8.24** for useful, court-supplied ammunition.

Strike outs and summary judgments

8.15   The mediator is often told in the Mediation Statement that a party is contemplating making a strike out application. Sometimes the application is actually launched and the mediation takes place before the hearing. Both sides are negotiating knowing that their negotiating positions may be significantly changed for the better or worse after the hearing. It sharpens their appreciation of risk.

Sometimes it is said, either in the pleadings or in correspondence between solicitors, that the opponent's case is untenable and a strike out application will be made. Months pass and the mediation takes place. One of the first questions that the mediator asks the advocates is what happened to the strike out application? Nearly always the answer is nothing.

Advocates have to be able to answer the question whether it comes from the mediator or indeed their own client: if your case is so strong why not apply for summary judgement? Both defendants and claimants can apply. If it succeeds, a lot of costs are saved. If it fails, extra costs can be incurred. Clients often do not want to take the risk. They would rather settle.

It has to be acknowledged that the tests applied by the courts on interim or summary applications are different from the ones applied at trial. The burden of proof is not always the same.

In many strike out applications there is partial but not total success and there is still a rump of a case to be to be disposed of at trial. Is that risk better or worse than trying to negotiate a final settlement at mediation?

The acronym ADR can stand for many things. One is Agent of Devastating Reality. A party who is convinced that it has an overwhelming case but has not yet succeeded on a summary judgement application may still prefer to mediate. Sometimes the client on the other side has been advised by his lawyers that he does not have a strong case but is finding it difficult to accept that advice. All commercial mediators have anecdotes about lawyers in this position asking for their help in talking their clients round so that they can see sense.

8.16   Sometimes, but less often, it is the lawyers who are over-optimistic. Mediators can, by sharing their own experience of the uncertainties of litigation, even in very strong cases help a lawyer exit from the corner into which he has painted himself.

Experienced litigators acknowledge it is difficult to predict the outcome of trials. It was reported at the Chartered Institute of Arbitrators 2104 DAS conference that one of the biggest litigation funders had over a ten-year period achieved a 60 per cent success rate at trial. This is after the cases that they fund have been sifted by a panel of experienced lawyers, including retired High Court judges.

Another graphic example of this difficulty was recently provided in the case of *Excalibur Ventures LLC v Texas Keystone Inc* [2014] EWHC 3436 (Comm). In that case, Clarke LJ ordered indemnity costs against third party funders of the claimants who lost badly at trial. He concluded at para 110 that:

> 'in a case justice requires that, when the case fails so comprehensively, not merely on the facts but because it was wholly bad in law, the funder should, subject to the *Arkins* cap, bear the costs'.

He went on at para 112; 'to make an order for indemnity costs would not be to penalise but to recompense.' His summary of the claimant's case at para 58 described it as:

'based on no sound foundation in fact or law which met with a resounding indeed catastrophic defeat, speculative and opportunistic and grossly exaggerated in quantum.'

These comments were on a case which a firm described by the judge as top rank solicitors had provided a 17-page opinion saying that the claimants had a strong likelihood of success and the partner in charge told the lead funder that:

- the firm were so confident that they were on partial CFA, something that they had virtually never done;
- it had a 90 per cent chance of succeeding;
- it was the best claim he had ever seen;
- he had never lost a case in his entire legal career; and
- it was very unlikely that the case would go all the way to trial.

Extent to which other settlement methods have been tried

8.17   If the successful party at trial has rejected settlement offers before trial, this will be taken into account. If a successful party has made reasonable offers which were rejected by the unsuccessful party and it has declined to go to mediation, the court may find that the unsuccessful party was unreasonable in rejecting the offers and therefore there was no point in going to mediation. This happened in 2012 in the case of *ADS Aerospace Ltd v EMS Global Tracking Ltd* [2012] EWHC 2904 (TCC) – see paras 8 and 9(a)–(c) of the case.

The other settlement methods which are usually suggested are:

- negotiations;
- roundtable meeting; and
- Part 36 offers

Negotiations

The whole point about mediation is that it is a form of assisted negotiation. If the parties want to settle they can. They just have to get on with it. If a party believes that it has a strong case and wants to settle, it should make an offer. The more reasonable the offer, the more likely it will be accepted.

It is unhelpful for the court to find as it did in the *ADS Aerospace* case that it was not unreasonable for a successful party with a strong case to refuse to attend mediation when they had said they were prepared to engage in without prejudice discussions and there was no good reason why this approach should not be tried. If a unilateral attempt to initiate without prejudice discussions has failed but the other side are prepared to go to mediation how can a refusal to go to mediation be consistent with a good faith intention to try and settle?

An additional factor in that case was that negotiations would be quicker and substantially cheaper than mediation. The apparent speed and cost advantages of direct negotiations were considered in **Chapter 2.** There is no doubt that they can apply but they are usually exaggerated.

Roundtable meetings

Roundtable meetings are discussed in **Chapter 2**. They can and do work. For the reasons given there,, mediation is a more reliable alternative if the parties genuinely want to settle and achieve early finality.

Part 36 offers

8.18 Where a Part 36 offer has been made and not accepted, there is no settlement. Parties can discuss what improvements to the offer would have to be made in order for it to be accepted, or they can try and settle the case. The philosophies behind the making of Part 36 offers are nearly as varied as the parties making them:

- Make a very early offer and put the other side under pressure from the start

- Leave it to the last moment or to what they calculate as the psychological moment. This maximises the impact. Time is running out.

- Make an offer, which is more of an invitation to treat in order to open discussions rather than a final calculation of the offeror's exposure at trial.

- Make one offer and emphasise that it will never be increased.

- Make offers designed to cause anxiety where a party has the benefit of legal expenses insurance or funding.

It is surprising how often at mediations, even where the litigation is well advanced, that no Part 36 offers have been made. It is equally surprising how often Part 36 offers have been made by both sides and rejected and still a settlement is reached at mediation.

It is worth remembering that a successful party can still have an adverse costs order made against them for refusing mediation even if they made a Part 36 offer which was effective (*Dunnett v Railtrack* [2002] EWCA Civ 303 *and P4 Ltd v Unite Integrated Solutions plc* [2006] EWHC 2924 (TCC)).

This point was reiterated in the recent important Court of Appeal decision of *PGF II SA v OMFS Co 1 Ltd* [2013] EWCA Civ 1288. In this case the claimant accepted the defendant's Part 36 offer nearly 12 months after it had been made and one day before the trial was due to start. In that interval both parties had incurred a further £250,000 of costs. The court made no order for costs from 21 days after the Part 36 offer had been made. The defendant therefore failed to recover a considerable amount of its costs, which it could normally have expected to recover. This was because the defendant had ignored the claimant's offer to mediate. It had not refused; it had simply ignored the request.

Briggs LJ went on to comment about the weight to be attached to the fact that a Part 36 offer had been made. He did not accept that making a Part 36 offer and leaving the matter to go to trial because the offeror felt very confident about their case was reasonable. He explained in para 45:

'First, it is in my view simply wrong to regard a Part 36 Offer, without any supporting explanation for its basis, as a living demonstration of a party's belief in the strength of its case. As I have said, defendants' Part 36 offers are frequently made at a level below that which the defendant fears having to pay at trial, in the hope that the claimant's appetite for or ability to undertake, costs risk will encourage it to settle for less than its claim is worth.'

Whether the costs of mediation would be disproportionately high

8.19   There are cases where the costs of litigating or mediating can be disproportionate. This happens much more frequently with the former than the latter.

For low value cases, which fall within the small claims procedure, the court-administered mediation schemes offer an excellent opportunity to settle by means of telephone mediations at no cost. There are also schemes for fast-track cases for cheap, fixed-fee mediations to be administered through the Civil Mediation Online Directory.

The costs of the mediator are usually exaggerated. Quite often he is the cheapest professional in the mediation room. The lawyers' fees just for attending at the mediation almost always exceed his.

The mediator market is very competitive. If the mediator's fee is too high it is easy to obtain a reduction. How much a client wants to spend with his legal representatives in preparing and attending the mediation is a matter for him and them. The question of whether or not legal representation is necessary at mediations is discussed in detail in **Chapter 6**.

Delay caused by mediation

8.20   This is stated to be a factor and has featured in several cases, for example in *Palfrey v Wilson* [2007] EWCA Civ 94, *ADS Aerospace Ltd v EMS Global Tracking Ltd* [2012] EWHC 2904 (TCC), *Park Promotions Ltd (t/a Pontypool Rugby Football Club) v Welsh Rugby Union Ltd* [2012 EWHC 2406 (QB).

If the suggestion of mediation is made too close to the trial date a refusal may not be unreasonable. How long is too close depends on the circumstances. The following periods have been regarded as being too close: 2 months, 3 weeks, 13 days.

There are three problems with a late proposal of mediation:

• The peace premium has already been spent. Money, which could have funded a settlement has been spent funding litigation. In addition, another cognitive bias comes into play: the sunk cost bias. This is where people think that because they have already incurred a certain amount of expenditure they may as well carry on even though that might not be the best alternative.

• Costs have already been incurred. They can become an obstacle in themselves to settlement. Many mediations in fact turn out to be an argument over costs. This is even truer when mediations are taking place close to trial.

- Parties are on a war footing. Although they understand that mediation is about making peace not war they are ready for war. It can be more difficult for them to adjust their mindset.

In practice mediations do take place close to trial and sometimes even after the trial has started. Settlements are still achieved. As opponents of mediation point out, most cases settle rather than go to trial and many cases settle at the door of the court. If settlements can be done on the court steps by direct negotiation between the parties there is no reason why an assisted negotiation with the help of a mediator cannot also take place at this juncture.

Mediations can be arranged very quickly.

Example 8.1

In one case there had been two abortive mediations in a dispute arising out of the dissolution of a partnership of actuaries.

On the day of the trial the judge came in and said that unfortunately he had not been able to read all the papers because the case had been assigned to him at the last moment. He suggested that he spend the morning reading and reconvene at 2 pm and invited the parties to think about what they wanted to do.

He explained that his suggestion was based on his early reading of the skeleton arguments.

The parties adjourned. They started talking with the help of the mediator who had previously been involved. Initially this was by telephone but the mediator heroically made himself available.

The parties returned to court at 2 pm and asked the judge if he would mind standing the case over until 10 am the next day. He said that he would be delighted to do so.

The mediation carried on and resulted in a settlement just before midnight. Everyone including the judge was pleased.

Did mediation have a prospect of success?

8.21   This post-trial reconstruction of what was in the minds of the parties is difficult, but the court has to try and do it. Judges have been pragmatic. What has emerged is that:

- if at trial the losing party wants to apply for an adverse costs order against the winning party it must show that mediation would have had reasonable prospect of success; and

- this is not a heavy burden to discharge. As the court made clear in *Halsey* the losing party does not have to show that mediation would have succeeded but only that there was a reasonable prospect of success.

Given the various published success rates of mediation, which vary from 70 per cent to 85 per cent, one might have thought that the presumption was in favour of mediation being successful. In fact the courts have not adopted this approach. They have found various reasons to be acceptable as to why a winning party was entitled to refuse to go to mediation on the basis that there was no prospect of success. For example:

- One party believes that it has a strong case and the other had said they would never accept just a nuisance payment.

- Relations between the parties had deteriorated so much that there was no realistic prospect of success at mediation.

- In the immortal classic judicial formulation, there was 'insufficient room for manoeuvre to make mediation a venture which might have real prospects of success in achieving compromise'.

Such reasons suggest a worrying degree of unfamiliarity on the part of the judiciary with what actually happens in mediations. Commercial mediators have many anecdotes about how parties in the most unpromising circumstances were able to settle. After all, in about 40 per cent of commercial mediations there is a claim and a counterclaim. Both sides' lawyers advise their clients that they have a strong case. Both sides expect to be net receivers of money. In these circumstances it is not easy to see a way in which settlement can be achieved and yet most settle. There recently seems to have been an increasing reluctance by the courts to accept this reason.

8.22   The six *Halsey* factors are the most influential ones that the courts take into account but they are not the only ones:

- *Further information is required*

  This is often said and is usually exaggerated. If a party is going to allege that he cannot go to mediation until certain further information is available then it must be able to spell out how it could affect settlement.

  It is often said that the parties in a dispute cannot go to mediation without evidential certainty having been established. This approach is flawed. There is never evidential certainty even after the conclusion of the trial. Most of the claims that there needs to be full disclosure and full information are made by lawyers who are driven either by a legitimate concern to give full advice to their clients and to understandably protect their own backs or by a less than legitimate concern about earning some fees out of the case before it settles.

  It is dangerous to assume that a refusal to go to mediation because an expert report is not available will be sufficient. The most recent case on this point is *PGF* (see above).

- *The court made an ADR order which was ignored by the successful party*

  As was made clear in *Halsey* the more the court has encouraged a party to go to mediation and been ignored the easier it will be for the unsuccessful party to obtain an adverse costs order.

Halsey letters

8.23   Any advocate who wants to go to mediation and is meeting resistance from the other side should send a *Halsey* letter. This sets out why mediation is a good idea at this time and cross-refers to the specific *Halsey* factors. It might persuade the other side to drop their resistance. At the very least it provides a foundation for an application for an adverse costs order at trial.

Letters inviting mediation, whether *Halsey* letters or not, must not be ignored. The reply should acknowledge the *Halsey* factors and specify the ones that apply in this case and which make it reasonable to refuse mediation at this stage.

Precedents for *Halsey* letters, both pre- and post-action, are included at the end of this chapter.

The court supplies ammunition to advocates wanting to mediate

8.24   There are four recent cases that provide advocates with reinforcements that they can use in practice where the other side are resisting their invitation to mediate.

PGF II SA v OMFS Co 1 Ltd

In the *PGF II* case mentioned above, Briggs LJ said in clear words, which will be much quoted in correspondence about suggestions to go to mediation:

'In my judgment, the time has now come for this court firmly to endorse the advice given in chapter 11.56 of the ADR Handbook, that silence in the face of an invitation to participate in ADR is, as a general rule, of itself unreasonable, regardless of whether an outright refusal, or refuse to engage the type of ADR requested, or to do so at the time requested, might have been justified by the identification of reasonable grounds.' (para 34)

Garritt-Critchley v Ronnan and Solarpower PV Ltd

In *Garritt-Critchley v Ronnan and Solarpower PV Ltd* [2014] EWHC 1774 (Ch), the court ordered indemnity costs against the defendant who accepted the claimant's Part 36 offer after the trial had finished before judgment had been handed down. The claimants offered mediation, which was rejected in robust terms. The defendant's solcitors replied:

'Both we and our clients are well aware of the penalties the Court might seek to impose if we are unreasonably found to refuse mediation, but we are confident that in a matter in which our clients are extremely confident of their position and do not consider there is any realistic prospect your client will succeed, our rejection is entirely reasonable.' (para 4)

In this case this was a dispute over whether or not a binding contract had been made. The defendant's counsel described it as an all or nothing case.

His Honour Judge Waksman said at para 14:

'To consider that mediation is not worth it because the sides are opposed on a binary issue, I'm afraid seems to me to be misconceived.'

At para 22 he said:

'This gets back to the point about parties being too far apart. Parties don't know whether in truth they are too far apart unless they sit down and explore settlement. If they are irreconcilably too far apart, then the mediator will say this as much within the first hour of mediation. That happens very rarely in my experience.'

Northrop Grumman Mission Systems Europe Ltd v BAE Systems (Al Diriyah C41) Ltd

8.25   In *Northrop Grumman Mission Systems Europe Ltd v BAE Systems (Al Diriyah C41) Ltd* [2014] EWHC 3148 (TCC), the court concluded:

'where a party to the dispute, which there are reasonable prospects of success resolving by mediation, rejects mediation on grounds which are not strong enough to justify not mediating, then that conduct will generally be unreasonable. I consider this to be the position here.' (para 72)

Before arriving at this conclusion, Mr Justice Ramsay acknowledged that:

'As stated in Halsey, the fact that a party reasonably believes that it has a watertight case may well be sufficient justification for a refusal to mediate.'

He continued:

'The authors of the Jackson ADR Handbook properly, in my view, draw attention at paragraph 11.13 to the fact that this seems to ignore the positive effect that mediation can have in resolving disputes even the claims have no merit. As they state, a mediator can bring a new independent perspective to the parties if using evaluative techniques and not every mediation ends in payment to a claimant.' (para 59)

Saying it how it is, the current attitude of the courts and the reasons for it are best summed up in quotations from Briggs LJ's judgment in *PGF II*. In para 27 he said:

'the constraints which now affect the provision of state resources for the conduct of civil litigation (and which appear likely to do so for the foreseeable future) call for an ever-increasing focus upon means of ensuring that court time, both for trial and for case management, is proportionately directly towards those cases which really need it, with an ever-increasing responsibility thrown upon the parties to civil litigation to engage in ADR, wherever that offers a reasonable prospect of producing a just settlement at proportionate cost.'

In para 56 he concludes:

'The court's task in encouraging the more proportional conduct of civil litigation is so important in current economic circumstances that it is appropriate to emphasise that message by a sanction which, even if a little more vigorous than I would have preferred, nonetheless operates *pour encourages les autres*.'

Bradley v Heslin

8.26 *Bradley v Heslin* [2014] EWHC 3267 (Ch) is of particular help in boundary disputes. Mr Justice Norris says in this case about gates between two neighbours that:

> '23 Perhaps in times of scarce resources and limited (and in any event expensive) representation it is time to give those who know the worth of mediation in this context (both to the parties and to all Court users) some help. If in any boundary dispute or dispute over a right of way, where the dispute could not be disposed of by some more obvious form of ADR (such as negotiation or expert determination) and where the costs of the exercise would not be disproportionate having regard to the budgeted costs of the litigation, any District Judge (a) imposed a 2 month stay for mediation and directed that the parties must take all reasonable steps to conduct that mediation (whatever the parties might say about their willingness to engage in the process) (b) directed that the fees and costs of any successful mediation should be borne equally (c) directed that the fees and costs of any unsuccessful mediation should form part of the costs of the action (and gave that content by making an "Ungley Order") and (d) gave directions for the speedy further conduct of the case only from the expiration of that period, for my own part (recognising that certainly others may differ) I think that such a case management decision would be difficult to challenge on appeal.
>
> 24 I think it is no longer enough to leave the parties the opportunity to mediate and to warn of costs consequences if the opportunity is not taken. In boundary and neighbour disputes the opportunities are not being taken and the warnings are not being heeded, and those embroiled in them need saving from themselves. The Court cannot oblige truly unwilling parties to submit their disputes to mediation: but I do not see why, in the notorious case of boundary and neighbour disputes, directing the parties to take (over a short defined period) all reasonable steps to resolve the dispute by mediation before preparing for a trial should be regarded as an unacceptable obstruction on the right of access to justice.'

Is a neutral venue the best?

8.27 Many commentators emphasise the need for the mediation venue to be a neutral one. This, it is said, reduces any power imbalance between the disputing parties. It is perceived that there is a home advantage in holding a mediation on your own premises. Presumably it is thought that the host party can choose the best room for itself and more easily regulate the flow of food and drink to the other.

Apart from this sort of manipulation, there might be a fear of intimidation. Some lawyers' offices, which are a popular venue for mediations are very impressive. The architecture and provision is so lavish as to be intimidating. Presumably the message that their clients want to send to the other parties at the mediation when choosing their lawyers' offices is that we are powerful and rich.

Other things being equal it is probably better and safer to have a neutral venue. It reduces the scope for disagreements and resentments at the start of the day. Everybody is inconvenienced by going to premises other than their own, rather than just one party. In practice however other things are rarely equal. There are constraints.

Expense

Usually independent venues charge for their use. They also usually charge for refreshments including lunch and tea and coffee. There are often limitations on how long the mediation can continue because of staff needing to go home and the security of the premises to be ensured.

Availability

The better and more popular mediation venues can often be booked up weeks in advance. Start booking as soon as you have fixed the date for the mediation.

Suitability

8.28 There is a wide variation in the level of provision in various independent mediation venues. Some are purpose built or designed for arbitration and mediation meetings. Others are not specifically designed for arbitration and mediation meetings but for corporate presentations. They tend to have larger big rooms and fewer smaller rooms which are usually needed at mediations for private sessions. Hotels are a common choice but they do not always have a suite in the way that the purpose-built venues do. This means a lot of time can be spent walking around the corridors swiping cards to get to the other rooms.

A minimum of two rooms is needed. This is true even if most of the mediation (or indeed all of it is in is often the case in family mediation) is going to take place in a single room in joint sessions .The mediator may need to have some private time. Or one of the parties may wish to have time away from the others.

Ideally, for a two-party mediation there should be three rooms:

- one for each party, which is theirs for the day; and
- a larger one in which joint sessions can be held and in which the mediator can also spend time when he is not with either of the parties. It can also be used as a breakout room when there is a joint session later in the mediation, for example between lawyers or experts.

In most cases one of the parties offers to host the mediation. The venue is usually the office of their solicitors or the barrister's chambers. Many solicitors' firms and barristers' chambers now have mediation suites. Usually no charge is made for the hire of the rooms although sometimes it is, especially by central London firms.

If the mediator is also working as a lawyer in a set of chambers or in a firm of solicitors he may be able to provide the venue free of charge or at a modest cost. It will be neutral in the sense that although it is a lawyer's office it is a different lawyer's office from those of the parties' lawyers.

There is no point in arguing about venue or refusing to attend the mediation at the premises of the other side. The psychological advantage in fact lies not with the host but with the guest. It is much easier to walk out of someone else's office than your own.

Usually the parties share the cost of the room hire equally.

Often the mediation provider, if it is an administered rather than a self-administered mediation, makes the arrangements. Usually there is a charge at cost.

In London examples of good quality independent venues are the ICRC at 70 Fleet Street, the Chartered Institute of Arbitrators at 12 Bloomsbury Square and the Academy of Experts at 3 Gray's Inn Square. They all provide high-quality facilities with friendly and experienced staff.

In addition to the meeting rooms it is important to establish what else is provided:

- Are there staff to let people in and take messages?
- Will they make photocopies?
- Will there be printing facilities?
- Are there photocopy and printing facilities?
- Is there wi-fi?
- Will refreshments such as tea, coffee, or water be provided during the day?
- Will lunch be provided?

Checklist for mediation venue

8.29 Listed here are examples of the questions that should be asked when booking a mediation venue.

How many rooms are there?

Two is the minimum. Three is ideal for a two-party mediation. For each additional party you need at least one additional room.

When does the venue open and close?

What time does the venue open? What time does it close? If the staff need to leave, for example, at 7:30 pm, will the parties be able to stay on after this time and let themselves out?

Are the photocopying facilities?

Will there be a charge for photocopies? It is surprising how these can mount up if further documents are sent to the mediation and have to be circulated. If there are, who pays? Tired, stressed people can become very exercised by such questions.

Will there be printing facilities?

Will the printers work after the last secretary has left for the evening? Printing out the settlement agreement is always one of the trickier practical problems that arise late in the evening when everybody is tired and wants to go home.

Example 8.2

A mediation was held in the offices of the solicitors of one of the parties. The firm was a national firm and the mediation was actually held in one of their regional offices, which was not the usual office of the fee earner. The facilities were excellent. Time passed and settlement discussions dragged on. Eventually an agreement was reached. This host solicitor typed out the agreement on his laptop, which was connected to the firm's computer system. Sadly he could not access the printers. They were in a part of the building that had been locked up by the security guard for the night. Everyone was able to look at the settlement agreement on screen but not able to sign it.

The Mediation Agreement provided, as they nearly all do, that there was no legally binding settlement until all parties had signed a document recording the agreement. In the end the mediator went back to his hotel and arranged for the settlement agreement to be emailed to the hotel receptionist who printed out the agreement. It was all signed in the hotel bar.

Are all the rooms soundproof?

Quite often, especially in hotels rooms have removable dividers. Sound can travel. Quite often glass doors do not fit flush and sound can be heard. It does not matter how far apart the rooms are. It is the soundproofing that is vital not the propinquity.

Can people see into the room?

Many rooms in modern offices have glass doors and walls. Keep flipcharts covered up.

Are there CCTV cameras in the rooms?

Sometimes these are there for security purposes.

Example 8.3

A mediation was held in the offices of a City firm. One of the parties was put into a transaction room. This was a room in which information was made available to the legal team acting in a purchase of a company who came to inspect documents on site. The cameras were used to make sure that no information was removed. To start with, the firm declined to confirm that they would switch off the system but did so when the client put his coat over the camera which threatened to pull it off the wall.

Are refreshments provided and if so at what cost and who pays?

The bottom line

8.30   It is not worth fighting about the venue. There is no tactical or psychological advantage that cannot easily be neutralised by a skilled advocate with the help of a skilled mediator on the day. It is a truism of negotiation that power lies where the parties think that it lies. If both sides at mediation truly want to settle then the party who can walk out may have an edge.

Who to take to the mediation

8.31   As with the mediation file or bundle, the golden rule is less is more.

The fewer people who attend a mediation, the easier it is to settle. The minimum is a single person who has authority to sign a settlement that day.

Usually in corporate or commercial matters there will be present at least one person who was involved in the circumstances that led to the dispute and another person who has been brought in to clear it up. The latter is usually, but not always, more senior.

The advocate has to make sure that he understands:

● who has ultimate authority; and

● the dynamics between the team members, and in particular whether they will be playing the blame game amongst themselves.

The advocate also has to make sure that the senior person (the one with the authority to settle) has been fully briefed about the dispute. Often they are brought in late in the day and have received their briefing from the people who face criticism for having caused the dispute.

It is usually not advisable to take potential witnesses.

It can be useful for there to be one member of the team whose sole job is to make a note of what is said and done. This can be a more junior member of staff from either the representative's office or the client's.

Conclusion

8.32   To conclude:

● Mediation is not voluntary in any real sense.

● Do not resist going to mediation. That will only cause more expense, delay, stress and aggravation.

● Go to mediation sooner rather than later.

● Never ignore a request to consider mediation.

● Remember the results of the City of London 2014 Survey about what clients want: early settlement, cost containment, certainty (see **para 5.02** above).

● Do not argue about venues – it is a waste of time.

● It is easier to walk out of someone else's office than it is your own.

● Make sure that printing facilities will be available after 18.00.

● Keep your team as small as possible.

Appendix 1

Halsey letter inviting agreement to mediation (where proceedings have not yet started)

We write further to our letter of [DATE] in which we suggested that this matter should be mediated. We note that you have not yet accepted our invitation.

We are sure that you have discussed with your client the obligation of all parties to disputes, whether or not proceedings have started, are under an obligation to consider mediation. We refer you to the Pre-Action Conduct Practice Direction. In paragraph 8.1 it states that

> 'Starting proceedings should usually be a step of last resort, and proceedings should not normally be started when a settlement is still actively being explored. Although ADR is not compulsory, the parties should consider whether some form of ADR procedure might enable them to settle the matter without starting proceedings. The court may require evidence that the parties considered some form of ADR settlement'

You will be familiar with the requirement at paragraph 2.2 (2) in Annex A to which we referred in our previous letter.

You will be familiar with the 6 Halsey factors first set out by the Court of Appeal in 2004 in the case of *Halsey v The Milton Keynes General NHS Trust* [2004] EWCA Civ 576 and developed in a series of cases since then. The most recent and relevant is the Court of Appeal case of *PGF II SA v OMFS Company 1 Ltd* [2013] EWCA Civ 1288.

We refer to paragraph 34, in which Briggs LJ says:

> 'In my judgment, the time has now come for this court firmly to endorse the advice given in chapter 11. 56 of the ADR Handbook, that silence in the face of an invitation to participate in ADR is, as a general rule, of itself unreasonable, regardless whether an outright refusal or refuse to engage in the type of ADR requested, or to do so at the time requested might have been justified by the identification of reasonable grounds.'

For ease of reference we refer to paragraph 30 of the judgment, which summarises the advice given in paragraph 11.56. Briggs LJ says:

> 'The ADR Handbook, first published in 2013, after the period relevant to these proceedings, set out at length at paragraph 11. 56 steps which a party faced with a request to engage in ADR, but which believes that it had reasonable grounds refusing to participate at that stage, should consider in order to avoid a costs sanction. The advice includes:
>
> (a) not ignoring an offer to engage in ADR;
>
> (b) responding promptly in writing, giving clear and full reasons why ADR is not appropriate at the stage, based if possible on the Halsey guidelines;

153

(c) raising with the opposing party any shortage of information or evidence believed to be an obstacle to successful ADR, together with consideration of how that shortage might be overcome;

(d) not closing off ADR of any kind, and for all time, in case some other method than that proposed, or ADR at some later date, might prove to be worth pursuing.

It seems to us that you are disregarding this clear guidance are exposing your client to a costs sanction.

For the sake of completeness we refer to the 6 Halsey guidelines as they apply to this case:

1 Nature of the dispute

This case is not is not fall within any of the possible categories of cases not suitable for mediation referred to in Halsey, any of the succeeding cases or the AGR Handbook. It is a [give a brief description of the case, eg a partnership dispute or a contested probate case]. These are routinely dealt with at mediation.

2 Merits of the case

We accept that you have expressed a different view about the merits of the case. Parties to a dispute usually do. As Winston Churchill said: "Where you stand depends on where you sit." This does not mean that the case is not suitable for settlement.

3 Other settlement methods attempted

Apart from an inconclusive exchange of proposals in correspondence that has been no real attempt by the parties to whom engage in serious settlement negotiations. In our experience mediation produces better results because of the involvement of experienced neutral third party than other methods. If you disagree please specify why and say which method you propose.

4 Mediation costs are disproportionate

The costs for the mediator for a case like this are likely to be in the order of £2,500 plus VAT for a full day's mediation including preparation and travel. This is usually split equally between the parties.

It is for the parties to decide how much they want to spend on preparing and attending for the mediation. In the scheme of things they are not significant let alone disproportionate. In total the costs per party for preparation, attendance and sharing the mediator's fee are unlikely to exceed [£X ,000] plus VAT. This is considerably less than what each party will be spending in the early weeks of litigation if proceedings are started.

5 Delay

We have suggested mediation before proceedings have been started. Mediation at this early stage has 2 advantages:

● positions have not become too entrenched and the commercial realties have not been obscured by the legal thickets; and

● legal costs have not been incurred to such a level that they become an obstacle to settlement.

It is, in our experience, more productive for parties to spend their time ,money and effort on working out a settlement rather than in litigation

6   Reasonable prospects of success

As the court said in the case of *Philipp Garritt-Critchley v Andrew Ronnan and Solarpower PV Ltd* [2014] EWHC 1774 (Ch), at paragraph 22:

> 'This gets back to the point that port is being too far apart. Parties don't know whether in truth they are too far apart unless they sit down and explore settlement. If they are irreconcilably too far apart, then the mediator will say as much in the first hour of mediation. This happens very rarely in my experience.'

The Next Step

On the assumption that you now agree to mediation we propose that we invite the ADR Group to supply us with a list of proposed mediators. We will also ask them to administer the mediation.

We can host the mediation at our offices. We have 3 suitable rooms. There will be no charge for room hire or refreshments during the day. If you prefer another venue please let us know. If there are a venue charges we propose that they should be split equally between the parties.

We look forward to hearing from you by 10 AM on [14 days later]. In the meantime please can you confirm that you sent a copy of this letter to your client.

Yours faithfully

Appendix 2

Halsey letter inviting agreement to mediation (where proceedings have started)

We write further to our letter of [DATE], in which we suggested that this matter should be mediated. We note that you have not yet accepted our invitation.

You will know that this will be dealt with at the first CMC. The courts expect the parties to have worked out for themselves what they wish to do about mediation.

As the Court of Appeal said in the *PGF* case referred to below, 'there is a an ever increasing responsibility thrown upon the parties to civil litigation to engage in ADR,' and 'it a waste of its resources to have to manage the parties towards ADR by robust encouragement, where they could and should have engaged with each other in considering its suitability, without the need for the court's active intervention.' (para 27)

You will be familiar with the six Halsey factors first set out by the Court of Appeal in 2004 in the case *of Halsey v The Milton Keynes General NHS Trust* [2004] EWCA Civ 576 and developed in a series of cases since then. The most recent and relevant is the Court of Appeal case of *PGF II SA v OMFS Company 1* Ltd [2013] EWCA Civ 1288.

We refer to paragraph 34, in which Briggs L J says:

'In my judgment, the time has now come for this court firmly to endorse the advice given in chapter 11. 56 of the ADR Handbook, that silence in the face of an invitation to participate in ADR is, as a general rule, of itself unreasonable, regardless whether an outright refusal or refuse to engage in the type of ADR requested, or to do so at the time requested might have been justified by the identification of reasonable grounds.'

For ease of reference we refer to paragraph 30 of the judgment, which summarises the advice given in paragraph 11.56. Briggs LJ says:

'The ADR Handbook, first published in 2013, after the period relevant to these proceedings, set out at length at paragraph 11.56 steps which a party faced with a request to engage in ADR, but which believes that it had reasonable grounds refusing to participate at that stage, should consider in order to avoid a costs sanction. The advice includes:

(a) not ignoring an offer to engage in ADR;

(b) responding promptly in writing, giving clear and full reasons why ADR is not appropriate at the stage, based if possible on the Halsey guidelines;

(c) raising with the opposing party any shortage of information or evidence believed to be an obstacle to successful ADR, together with consideration of how that shortage might be overcome; and

(d) not closing off ADR of any kind, and for all time, in case some other method than that proposed, or ADR at some later date, might prove to be worth pursuing.'

It seems to us that you are disregarding this clear guidance and are exposing your client to a costs sanction.

For the sake of completeness we refer to the 6 Halsey guidelines as they apply to this case:

1   Nature of the dispute

This case does not fall, within any of the possible categories of cases not suitable for mediation referred to in *Halsey,* or in any of the succeeding cases or in the ADR Handbook. It is a [give a brief description of the case ega partnership dispute or a contested probate case]. These are routinely dealt with at mediation.

2   Merits of the case

We accept that you have expressed a different view about the merits of the case. Parties to a dispute usually do. As Winston Churchill said: "Where you stand depends on where you sit." This does not mean that the case is not suitable for settlement. As the ADR Handbook makes clear mediators can act as agents of reality.

3   Other settlement methods attempted

Apart from an inconclusive exchange of proposals in correspondence there has been no real attempt by the parties to engage in serious settlement negotiations. In our experience mediation produces better results because of the involvement of an experienced neutral third party than other methods. If you disagree please specify why and say which method you propose.

4   Mediation costs are disproportionate

The costs for the mediator for a case like this are likely to be in the order of £2,500 plus VAT for a full day's mediation including preparation and travel. These are normally split equally between the parties.

It is for the parties decide how much they want to spend on preparing and attending for the mediation. In the scheme of things and in particular having regard to the estimates of cost provided in the Precedent H they are not significant let alone disproportionate. In total the cost per party for preparation, attendance and sharing the mediator's fee is unlikely to exceed [£X,000] plus VAT.

5   Delay

We have suggested mediation at an early stage in proceedings with the Statement of Claim and the Defence now having been filed so that there is no danger of a stay for mediation delaying the litigation timetable. Carrying out mediation at this early stage also means that legal costs have not have been incurred to such a level that they become an obstacle to settlement.

6   Reasonable prospects of success

As the court said in the case of *Philipp Garritt-Critchley v Andrew Ronnan and Solarpower PV Ltd* [2014] EWHC 1774 (Ch). In paragraph 22 the court said:

'This gets back to the point that port is being too far apart. Parties don't know whether in truth they are too far apart unless they sit down and explore settlement. If they are irreconcilably too far apart, then the mediator will say as much in the first hour of mediation. This happens very rarely in my experience.'

The Next Step

On the assumption that you now agree to mediation we propose that we invite the ADR Group to supply us with a list of proposed mediators. We will also ask them to administer the mediation.

We can host the mediation at our offices. We have 3 suitable rooms. There will be no charge for room hire or refreshments during the day. If you prefer another venue please let us know. If there are a venue charges we propose that they should be split equally between the parties.

We look forward to hearing from you by 10am on [14 days later]. In the meantime please can you confirm that you sent a copy of this letter to your client.

Yours faithfully

Part B
The Mediation

Chapter 9

Mediation Process: Mediators' Tricks

This chapter discusses:

● What actually happens during the mediation process

● The techniques that mediators use

What do mediators do?

9.01   The three-stage process of exploration, exchange and formulation has been discussed in **Chapter 4.** The mediator's job is to try and take the parties through that process. But what does the mediator actually do? What does the advocate have to be prepared to cope with and to brief his client about?

Listed below is a selection of some of the techniques that mediators use. It is not a comprehensive list of every technique that a mediator might use. Although some suspicious advocates refer to 'mediators' tricks' these are not stratagems, feints, moves or ploys. They are things that mediators do. The well -prepared advocate is able to recognise them, explain to his client what is gong on and respond in the most appropriate way.

Small talk

9.02   A mediator will usually go to the parties' rooms before the mediation formally starts and introduce himself. These private chats are discussed in **Chapter 10**. He will engage the parties in small talk. Do not resist it or regard it as a waste of time. The mediator is trying to build rapport. During the day he will properly also take opportunities during lulls in proceedings to chat to the clients. Sometimes this happens in the absence of the advocate. There is nothing necessarily sinister about this. For example a mediator may have go to see a party and find that the advocate has gone to make a telephone call but his clients are there on their own. Some mediators will not come into the room until the advocate returns. Others will come into the room and start chatting about the case. Others will just chat about the client's business or the football results.

Warm smiles and cold eyes

9.03   It has been said that the best mediators, like the best spies, have warm smiles and cold eyes. Advocates should know that the mediator is doing a job. An essential part of it is to win the trust of both sides but be able to objectively assess and guide them both.

A well-known QC tells his clients that the mediator may be friendly towards them but he is not their friend. This is rather harsh. Most mediators think that they are friendly and indeed the friends of everybody at the mediation.

Workplace mediators are specifically instructed in the technique of omni-partiality. This means the mediator is encouraging all parties to think that he is on their side and are their best friend. The mediator is not biased against anybody. He is in favour of everybody.

Clients may be confused or misled by this. They really do think that:

● the mediator is on their side;

● he believes what they are saying;

● he is going to persuade the other side that they are wrong; and

● he has in fact become part of the team and is a mediation advocate.

They may feel let down when later in the day the mediator asks questions which they see as challenging. They can feel that has he deserted them. Skilled mediators will sense when this is happening and do their best to disabuse the client. It is something that advocates must also guard against. This is not to suggest that advocates should act as censors or insist, as some advocates do, that all communication and discussion goes through them. That is carrying control too far. This has already been identified as one of the common faults of advocates in **Chapter 6**. But they should remind their clients of what the mediator's role at mediation is.

Flipchart – pedagogy?

9.04   There is a school of mediators and mediator trainers who swear by the use of flipchart, whilst others deprecate it. Advocates should be aware that some mediators will, either during the Joint Opening Session or before the caucuses start, go to the flipchart and write up what they consider to be the key points and issues. Some of them can become quite pedagogic.

There is no point in resisting the mediator at this time if this is what he wants to do. It is worthwhile noting down what he writes on a flipchart in the way that it appears on the chart. It can be discussed with the client in private. The reason why it should be copied as it appears is that subconsciously or not mediators can present information on the flipchart in a way that reflects what they regard as important. Some of the more manipulative mediators may in fact be trying to prime the parties and their advisers by writing information on the chart in a particular order and phraseology.

Even mediators who do not use the flipchart in this way may later use the flipchart, which is usually placed in each caucus room. Be careful to cover up what is written on the chart. Many modern offices have glass walls. People from outside can see what is going on and read the chart. Mediators swap horror stories about confidential information being leaked inadvertently through the careless use of flipcharts.

Brainstorming

9.05   The mediator gathers everyone together with a flipchart and asks people to come up with ideas. Nothing is off-limits. The only rule is that no one comments on any idea or suggestion until the group has finished. Then the mediator sorts them out. The idea is to release the inner creativity in the group who will generate creative energy off each other. A variation on using the flipchart is writing all the ideas down on Post-It notes and sticking them on a whiteboard or even on the walls. They can be then moved around form clusters of suggestions or ideas.

In practice this technique although often taught to mediators is not much used in practice. It is a favourite of the Harvard Negotiation Project (HNP). It does not appear to take much account of research, which shows that group activity restricts rather than encourages creativity and that the best ideas comes from people sitting by themselves thinking. However, it is something that lawyers and their clients should be aware of and be prepared to participate in it if the mediator suggests it.

Be warned: 'brainstorming' as a term is sometimes replaced by 'thought shower' as it is considered less likely to cause offence to those suffering from a mental injury or disability.

The opening question

9.06   Mediators have different ways of opening the day's business after the Joint Opening Session. Whatever their usual approach is, what they actually say will be influenced by how the Joint Opening Session has gone. If it has been adversarial and confrontational some early remedial work may be required. The mediator may just be happy to let the advocates and the clients express their feelings of frustration and annoyance.

If there has been a standard Joint Opening Session, mediators tend to use one of the following opening gambits:

(1) What did you think of that?

(2) What did you think of what they said?

(3) How do you feel now?

(4) Well it seems to me that we have the following issues to deal with today.

(5) What do you want out of today?

Approaches 1 and 2

Approaches 1 and 2 are standard. Many trainers encourage mediators to use them. The intention is to open up the discussion and let the client in particular, but also his advocate, start to explain their side of the story even if it is only by commentary on the other side's version. However, there are difficulties with these approaches:

- They are open-ended and can invite a flood of talk.

- Approach 2 invites the client and the advocate to start arguing about the merits of the case even if only by way of refuting what the other side has set, unless of course they accept what the other side says, which would be a very positive but a very unusual thing to happen.

- Approach 1 carries the same danger. Both approaches are inviting the client and advocate to criticise the other side.

Approach 3

9.07   This is an indication that the mediator is going to take a holistic and healing approach to the day's work. It is inviting the client to, using a traditional mediators word, 'vent'. The pros and cons of venting are discussed later in this section.

Approach 4

This is more directive. The mediator wants to take control of the process by setting the agenda. This usually takes the form of making a list of legal issues. Many advocates also expect to spend the first two or three hours of any mediation discussing the issues before moving on to discussing settlement proposals. Advocates therefore have to be prepared to debate the case with the mediator if that is what he wants to do. The mediators who prefer this approach tend to be lawyers, and are usually senior barristers or former judges. An advocate who thinks that this may be what he has to do on the day will need to have his legal arguments carefully marshalled, with all the references to the books of authority and the cases ready as though he was making an application in court.

In fact, although some mediators might like to start doing this, they are often derailed by the clients expressing a desire to get on with settlement discussions. Many clients prefer to discuss settlement proposals sooner rather than later. And if an advocate does not want to spend his time debating the issues he can tell the mediator that right at the start. There is no requirement or obligation to get bogged down in legal detail. As has been made clear in this book there is a positive advantage in not doing so.

Example 9.1

An example of this happened in a mediation about a pension release scheme. It was a significant but not huge amount of money in the order of £500,000–£800,000.

The mediator explained that he had identified five issues which he thought need addressing first. He told the parties this at the Joint Opening Session. He repeated it in the first caucus with the claimant, but it became clear that in fact, having heard what both parties had said in the Joint Opening Session, there appeared to be a way to structure a settlement.

The mediator went into the other room. He returned quite soon. There was an air of disappointment and surprise about him. He explained that indeed there did appear to be way of settling this case and perhaps it would be better to concentrate on structuring settlement than discussing his five issues.

The two sets of financial advisers, not legal advisers, met and emerged with the framework for a settlement. The details had to be worked out. When it came to discussing how much money was going to be paid by whom and when, legal issues of liability and risks of adverse costs orders at trial were of course mentioned as negotiating tactics.

The concept of fairness was mentioned many times by both sides. Each side defined fairness by reference to legal rights and possible grounds of liability, but in the end what prevailed was:

● the commercial reality that a settlement could be achieved;

● the willingness and ability of the parties through their own financial advisers to engage on the day in working out most of the detail; and

● the legal issues really only coming in to play when agreeing a final figure and of course legal costs.

The case settled. The mediator is entitled to take credit for that. It settled because his agenda for the day was not followed and party autonomy was asserted. However, he did manage the process even if it had not been his first choice and shepherded the parties to signature.

Approach 5

9.08   This indicates that the mediator is going to engage in a very important task: expectation management. Of course, advocates do this with their clients as well. Sometimes the clients listen to what their advocates say. If certain cognitive biases such as selective perception, confirmation bias and optimism bias come into play, they will not fully absorb what was in fact said.

Sometimes the advocates as well as the clients have expectations that they will be fortunate or even unlikely to realise at either mediation or trial. This is where self-auditing becomes so useful: see **Chapters 7** and **18**.

If a Pre-Mediation Analysis (PMA) has been carried out as explained in **Chapter 7**, neither the advocate nor the client will have difficulty in dealing with this enquiry from the mediator. If it has not been done, there may be some false starts and dithering while the client and the advocate work out what it is that they do want from the day.

In a nutshell there are two basic types of mediators' opening enquiry:

● those that invite the parties to look at the past; and

- those that invite the parties to look to the future.

Advocates should be equally prepared to deal with both.

Venting

9.09   The invitation to vent has the disadvantage of:

- being open-ended; and

- encouraging not just a flood of talk but also a torrent of emotion.

As discussed in **Chapter 5** the role of emotions and how they influence a party's decision making is important. In practice advocates should be careful about encouraging their clients to give free expression to their emotions. Usually the emotions are negative ones such as anger, frustration, ill-will or revenge. Sometimes they are not directed at the other side but they are still negative, for example a sense of loss, which induce feelings of sadness and a dwelling on the past.

There is a view, which in some circles has become an article of faith, that expressing emotions – even strong ones – in a forceful or passionate way is a good thing. If it does not happen settlement will be impeded. As Brown and Marriott say, 'unexpressed emotions sabotage settlements.' This view is not universally held. Research has shown that In fact expressions of anger or temper do not make people feel better. They can even make them feel worse.

The work of Professor Brad J Bushman and others has cast doubt on the cathartic theory, which uses the hydraulic model of emotions. Based on Freud's theory that expressing anger was much better than bottling it up, the hydraulic model posits that frustration leads to anger. Anger builds up inside an individual in a similar way to the way hydraulic pressure builds up in a closed environment until it is released. People who bottle up their anger and do not let it out will eventually explode in aggressive rage. Bushman tested the theory that venting by letting people get their anger out of their system should make them feel less, not more, angry. The results of his research were that it did the opposite. People who vented their anger became angrier.

Distraction works better, hence the clear advice in this book to encourage clients not to ruminate on their frustrations and resentments but to imagine and build the future. You cannot control the past. It can control you. You can control the future. You do that by creating it.

Expressing negative emotions, particularly anger in public aggravates the situation. Even if the speaker feels better, the act of expressing anger tends to generate stress chemicals such as cortisol that affect the prefrontal cortex.

In a nutshell, stress makes it more difficult for people to think about settlement. Their nervous systems react to the threat. The prefrontal cortex, which is the part of the brain that deals with rational thought and goal setting, shuts down. The older part of the brain, which deals with instinct and response, fires up. This means that the listener stops being receptive to what is being said to him and stops being capable of thinking about settlement.

There is a difference between people feeling emotion, acknowledging emotion and expressing it. There are also different ways of expressing the same emotion. Anger does not have to be expressed through loud voices, obscenity, obstructive behaviour, confrontation and table banging. A calm modulated statement by a client, that when they think about what has happened to them they feel angry, will do, and it helps secure the moral high ground. That is always a useful location to occupy when beginning peace talks.

Despite what Brown and Marriott say about suppressed emotions, expressed emotions can also sabotage settlement.

Open questions

9.10   Mediators use these all the time. These and other interrogative techniques and responses are discussed in **Chapter 6**. Advocates and their clients must be prepared to deal with them. Clients must be warned that these questions will be asked and they should not see them as intrusive or hostile. The more that they have thought about what questions might arise and their responses the easier it will be on the day.

Some mediators can even when gently asking open questions appear to be cross-examining. Some clients find any question challenging. The advocate should always be ready to explain that the mediator is acting as devil's advocate. If the mediator is not acting as devil's advocate he should be asked what he thinks that he is doing (see also 'reality testing' below) – be prepared to provide lots of explanation.

Reframing

9.11   It is an important part of the advocate's role to identify how his client is feeling and to agree with him the best way of communicating and managing feelings and emotions. One technique which mediators are taught to use for dealing with emotion is reframing. This can take two forms:

- paraphrasing what the speaker has just said in less confrontational or toxic language; and

- echoing what the speaker has just said so that they can hear how their own words sound when they are not spoken by them but to them.

Properly used by skilled mediators, reframing is a useful technique. Advocates can use it themselves with their clients or when talking to the mediator. But they should be prepared to experience it being used by less skilful mediators. When this happens, clients can feel patronised.

Example 9.2

A well-known lady mediator came into the room of one of the parties in a significant dispute about a national franchise. The client was a high-powered 'type A female' businesswoman. She had been successful in creating a business. The mediator asked in soothing tones: 'Well, how do you feel after that?' There was a caressing emphasis on 'feel'. The client nearly exploded. 'I have not come here for therapy,' she declared.

The mediation settled when the discussion was able to move away from concerns about feelings and empathy to discussing delivery dates, discounts and marketing support.

Guiding and steering

9.12 This is not when the mediator tells you what he thinks you should do. It is where, by the tone of voice, the phrasing of questions, the facial expressions and general demeanour, he is indicating what he thinks.

So indications that the client may be prepared to make an improved offer will be met with smiles and encouraging nods of the head. Or, when the offer is made, there may be a marked lack of smiles and nods but a spreading of the hands and a brief monotone 'OK, if that is what you want to do' as an acknowledgment.

Questions such as: 'Where do you think the sympathy of the court is going to lie?' or 'How do you think that point/ argument will play with the judge?' are clearly inviting the parties and their advisers to re-consider their forceful expressions of confidence in the outcome at trial.

Mediators do give cues and clues by what they say, whether they intend to or not. Experienced and skilled mediators know this. They usually take care, unless they are very tired, to self-censor. It is safe for advocates to assume that, if they pick up a cue or clue from what an experienced and skilled mediator says, they were intended to.

The wise advocate will be on the look out for them and when he spots them be ready to explore them with his client and the mediator. Do not be shy in engaging with the mediator. There is nothing wrong with asking the mediator questions such as: 'Am I right in thinking that.......?' or 'I am getting the impression that …. Is that correct? ' Clients are paying for the mediator's services. Make the most of what he has to offer. Work with him not against him

Reality testing

9.13 This has been described by a very experienced City commercial solicitor as 'the most powerful tool of the trade employed by the mediator.' He goes on to describe it as 'whereby the mediator forces the parties to consider and assess the risks that they face in continuing with the litigation.'

If a mediator engages in reality testing it is not just the legal merits of the case which are discussed, but also:

- calculation of damages;
- costs;

- the likelihood of recovering any award of damages or favourable costs order; and

- the number and quality of witnesses.

Sometimes the reality testing can appear hostile. Advocates are usually prepared to cope with it without becoming overly defensive. They must warn their clients to expect this and advise them that:

- they may have to participate in these challenging conversations, especially when questions of evidence and credibility are being discussed;

- when the mediator is applying reality therapy he is not necessarily expressing his own view – he is acting as devil's advocate and putting another point of view; and

- the client should not feel as though they are being victimised – the mediator will be doing the same thing in the other room.

In practice mediators who engage in intrusive and energetic reality therapy are usually inclined to let their views be known on the merits of the parties' cases as well.

Many mediators think that reality testing is what their job really is about and they do not do much else at mediations. Some even take it to the extent of scaring the clients about the torment they will suffer at trial. This is known as trashing and bashing – one of the 25 models of mediation practice. This can unnerve some clients. Wise advocates will have already explained to their clients exactly what happens at trial.

This overconcentration on trial and litigation overlooks the desire that clients have for certainty and finality and the benefits of settlement generally. They are, despite what some advocates and mediators think, more than saving legal costs and a possible adverse judgment. This is discussed in more detail in **Chapter 5**.

In Chapter 7 it was explained why advocates and clients need to rebalance their preparation for mediation. Some mediators need to do it as well. A sensible advocate will make sure that the mediator is concentrating on settlement and not on legal and forensic evisceration of the case.

Feeding the habit: settlement junkies

9.14   Craig Pollock, writing for the Chartered Institute of Arbitrators, an organisation which has recently decided to embrace, or at least come to an accommodation with, mediation, puts forward the bracing view that:

> 'Mediation advocates are well advised to view mediators as "settlement junkies" who are prepared to feed their habit (settlement) by almost any means. [...] The mediator's sole ambition in the mediation is settlement (hence the term "settlement junkie").'

It has to be acknowledged there are some mediators who are fixated on settlement. They tend to be relatively newly accredited and inexperienced mediators, anxious to try out their new professional skills and of course to build up a back catalogue of success. They can press parties too hard, usually doing this by a combination of:

* guillotining the parties' explanations or discussions;

* over-emphasising the risks of litigation and the dire consequences of losing;

* telling horror stories of ironclad cases that ended up wrecked and rusting;

* emphasising how costs can escalate;

* pushing a settlement too hard; and

* expressly or at least impliedly criticising the parties and their advisers for not seeing the obvious benefits of settlement.

Creating a wedge

9.15   Some mediators worry that lawyers can be the main obstacle to settlement. They can let this show in two ways:

* suggesting that the lawyers do not understand the case and the legal points (lawyer mediators, especially senior lawyers are prone to this); and

* non-lawyers tend to appeal directly to the clients and suggest that lawyers are only feathering their own nest.

Usually mediators use these tactics out of an excess of zeal, not because they are being cynical, divisive or obstructive. It has to be recognised, however, that there are some mediators who are highly manipulative and who seem to think that they can dictate to the parties and their advisers exactly what should happen both as to the process and the outcome.

There are mediators who have been known to tell clients in front of their lawyers that the main obstacle to settlement is their lawyers. It might be true. Even if it is, this is not the best way of making the point. There is no advantage to the clients in having a public row with the mediator. Advocates have to be robust and resilient. Advocates should continually reflect on what they are doing during the day to check if they are becoming part of problem, rather than the solution. It can and does happen.

There is no point in the advocate engaging in hand-to-hand combat with the mediator. If it is thought that the mediator is pressing the client too hard too quickly, prime the client to tell the mediator: 'I need more time. I am beginning to feel a little railroaded.'

Having a private word with the mediator to express concerns is much the best way of dealing with settlement junkies. Having a row in front of clients is not.

Separating clients from lawyers

9.16   Mediators often suggest that there be a meeting of lawyers only. There is no reason not to attend such a meeting. Sometimes these are actually:

- attempts to find out what clients really want and they really think about the merits of the case and the settlement zones;

- opportunities for an explanation of a particular point that is proving to be an obstacle, usually of a legal nature;

- a chance to actually have a haggling session away from the clients and the need to showboat; or

- a chance for the mediator to seek guidance on how they would like to move the process forward.

More rarely, but still frequently, the mediator suggests a meeting without lawyers and with just the clients, and in particular the decision-makers. Most mediators make the suggestion when the process is stalling. Some clients can be unsure but most are ready to do it. Some advocates are uneasy. They will defer to their clients, but they insist on an intensive pre-meeting briefing. In practice there is no reason for advocates to advise against it, provided that the mediator is going to be present during the meeting. This will:

- neutralise any imbalance of power;

- prevent anyone feeling bullied or harassed; and

- ensure that an accurate report of what was said is received by both rooms.

Champagne, chardonnay and cappuccino

9.17   Mediators want to discuss settlement with each party. Some do it sooner rather than later. They are anxious to find out what settlement range the clients have in mind and need to have a feel of how far apart the parties really are. They adopt different approaches:

- One very successful and experienced commercial mediator has on more than one occasion gone into one room, after only a hour into the mediation and asked: 'If after two days of mediation I can only bring you a figure of [£XX] what would you say?'

- Others come in and say: 'Well this looks like a £200,000 settlement doesn't it?'

- Others try and adopt a lighter and less direct approach and ask the clients for three figures:

  — the figure that if you settled on tonight you would be delighted – so delighted that you would buy your lawyers a bottle of champagne;

  — the figure which is not a bottle of champagne, but lets you buy them a bottle of chardonnay or merlot; and

  — the final figure, which is not that, but at least the job is done and you buy them a cup of coffee while waiting for the train.

  These figures, the mediator assures the parties, are for his consumption only. He will not disclose them to the other side.

Many clients and their advocates are reluctant to disclose figures to the mediator. This can be because:

- they have not worked them out;

- they do not want to acknowledge, even to themselves, that they are bluffing and are prepared to move radically from the position stated in their mediation statements and correspondence; and

- they are suspicious. There are some solicitors, particularly commercial litigators in large City firms, who regard as risible the idea that the mediator will not make use of or disclose in some way this confidential information. They just do not think he will be able to resist the temptation in order to feed his settlement habit.

Exchange offers

9.18 The subject of offers, and in particular how to frame them and when to make them is discussed in **Chapter 10**. This is just a reminder that some mediators prefer sequential exchange offers and some simultaneous. Be prepared do either.

Attention has already been drawn to the paradox of anchoring (see **Chapter 18**). The important thing is to stay flexible and to have discussed in advance with the client that simultaneous exchange of offers may be requested.

Guessing offers

9.19 The mediator comes into the room with an offer from the other side. Before delivering he asks those around the table to guess what it is. Do not be quick to dismiss this as a silly game. Think about it. The reason the mediator doing this is not just to provide some light relief or entertainment – it is to gauge how well each side is reading the other.

The ability to read the other side and to see the pictures in their heads is a key skill to be acquired and practised by mediation advocates. It is deeply unimpressive when experienced and highly paid lawyers say: 'I do not know' or 'I have no idea'. Advocates who respond in this way tend to be inexperienced or underprepared or not really convinced that mediation is a better way of dealing with their client's case than litigation.

Sealed offers

9.20 Mediators use several different techniques to try to close the gap when the parties are in the deal zone but cannot quite reach final agreement. One technique which often works is sealed offers:

- The mediator asks each party for their last, best and final offer.

- This is disclosed to the mediator on a confidential basis. Neither side sees each other's offer.

- The mediator looks at them both and reports to the parties how far apart they are. He does not tell them in figures how far apart they are – he simply indicates whether they are very close or still a distance apart.

- Usually the parties want to know how far apart they are. If both parties consent to disclosure the mediator tells them.

- Nearly always, but not inevitably, the parties review how near they are and decide to take the extra step to conclude the deal.

- This does not always happen and the mediation can come to an end without a settlement. What happens on many occasions is the opposite of settler's remorse. It is the sense of a missed opportunity. Where the parties are really not very far apart having disclosed final offers they usually make another attempt in the next 48 hours and they usually succeed.

A question that always gets asked is what happens if the sealed offers overlap. There are two choices:

- The mediator can give that offers back to the parties and ask them to think again as they have overlapped..

- The mediator can split the difference between the two offers so that settlement is made at that point.

Split the difference

9.21   This again is a traditional way of bridging gaps. In the final stage usually one party or the other suggests splitting the difference. More often than not, if people have genuinely tried to settle they will split the difference. If relations have deteriorated during the negotiations it will probably be rejected. This is why it is important for mediation advocates to try and preserve good spirits and good humour as discussed in **Chapter 6**.

Some clients and advocates deride the concept. It is too hackneyed and unworthy. Mediation is a nobler calling than horse trading or gambling.

There is a danger of being sucked into splitting the split. This occurs where one side says that they will split the difference and the other side says that it will not. The rejecting side now knows where the other side will move to – they then offer to split the difference between their previous figure and the half-way point. The ways to avoid this are for the parties to give their response to the mediator on a private and confidential basis (he does not disclose what either side said) or to use the auto-settler.

The auto-settler

9.22   A variation of simply splitting the difference that has been developed is the auto-settler. This guarantees a settlement without relying just on luck.

The two parties have that their positions and make their final offers. In one final attempt to settle each is asked to make a final offer. Whoever makes the biggest movement wins.

Example 9.3

● The claimant will settle at £200,000. The defendant has offered £150,000. The difference is £50,000. If they split the difference the settlement would be at £175,000.

● The claimant offers to settle at £190,000. The defendant offers to settle at £165,000. The defendant has moved by £15,000 and the claimant by £10,000. The defendant wins. The settlement figure is £165,000.

● Movement is calculated in absolute figures. It is not calculated by percentage movements.

● If each party moves by the same amount, the settlement figure is is the midpoint, ie splitting the difference. In this example, if they have both moved by £10,000 the settlement point would have been £175,000.

The skill is trying to guess how far you have to go without going to the midpoint. How well are you reading the other side?

Mediator's proposal

9.23   Some mediators think that it is useful for them to formulate a suggested proposal for settlement. They may do this simply by commenting on other proposals. Or they may make a stand-alone proposal, which originates from their previous hints and comments. Or they just work one out and introduce it to both rooms.

Other mediators are very reluctant to do this. The reason is not that they lack imagination, but that they do not want to be seen as selling a particular proposal. The debate and discussion can become about them and their proposal rather than about the parties their solutions.

The mediator devising a proposal is not the same as a mediator suggesting possible modification to proposals to try make them more acceptable to all parties. A proposal does not become more acceptable simply because the mediator makes it. Advocates must be prepared to say why a proposal put forward by mediator is unacceptable. They should be not be reluctant to do that provided they do it courteously and constructively.

Mediators recommendation: during or post mediation

9.24   Some mediators make recommendations. This is similar to, but not the same as, developing or suggesting a proposal. Usually the recommendations are made after the mediation has finished without a settlement. They form a view of the best way solution for all parties. Some mediators write to the parties telling them this as a matter of course. They regard it as part of their after sales service. Others only do if requested. Some may invite the request. Others, even when invited to make a recommendation, decline to do so. They think that it is moving too far towards the adjudicative model. An advocate who does not want the mediator to make suggestions or recommendations should say so early on or at the first hint that the mediator might be thinking this is an appropriate thing to do.

'I'll try and persuade them': a mediator's endorsement

9.26   Some mediators, in an attempt to promote settlement, will ask a client if he can accept a proposal. They add the rider that if he can they will back it. Some go further and say they will recommend it to the other side and try and persuade them to accept it. Mediators who do this are investing their own personal and professional capital in the proposal. Personally endorsing a proposal in this way can make it difficult for the client to resist. Advocates have to weigh up whether the mediator is just feeding his habit or providing food for thought.

Tossing a coin

9.27   This has been a traditional way of making decisions for centuries. If the mediator suggests tossing a coin as a way of closing the final gap, think hard before rejecting it. It is intended as a face-saving way of achieving settlement. Very often in mediations the parties are down to the last £500 or £5,000 and become stuck. The money in the scheme of things does not make a lot of difference. It is more a question of:

* 'I have already gone further than I had intended.'
* 'There is an end to this process of me giving way.'
* 'This is the proverbial last straw.'
* 'I can be obstructive and sit here saying that I am not going to pay you another £500 because I can and you are going to squirm and eventually concede. That will make me feel better.'

Or it is more calculated and is refined bluffing of the sort that poker players indulge in. Or it's not even that and is simply a power-play.

If tossing a coin is suggested and accepted settlement follows. The outcome is usually accepted with good grace both by the winner and the loser. It was just a matter of luck.

If the suggestion is not accepted it can at least free up thinking.

Secret weapon

9.28   The mediator is in a unique position. Only he knows what is being said in both rooms. He can only disclose what the parties authorise him to. This knowledge has been called the mediator's secret weapon.

Sensible advocates know this and explain it to their clients, which is why it always an excellent idea to listen to what the mediator is saying and what he is not saying.

The mediator has the inside track. The parties are paying for him. They might as well make the best use of him.

Conclusion

9.29   To conclude:

- Remember Core Principle 1: the purpose of mediation is to make peace not war.

- Mediators want to achieve this, but can only do so with the help and consent of the parties and their representatives.

- The tricks described in this chapter are used to achieve the common aim: settlement.

- Being familiar with them will prevent inappropriate use and feelings of being manipulated.

Chapter 10

The Stages of the Mediation Days

This chapter shows in outline format what happens at various types of mediation – civil and commercial, family, workplace and community. It assumes:

For the CIVCOM

- A full day's mediation lasting eight hours
- A dispute between two parties
- A neutral venue with a start time of 10am
- A mediator using the facilitative model with caucuses and simultaneous not sequential exchange of offers
- A working lunch

For the FAMILY

- a Mediation intake assessment meeting (MIAM)/intake meeting
- Three sessions of two hours
- No attendance of lawyers at the sessions but consultation by clients during the process
- Preparation of a Memoradum of Understanding

For the WORKPLACE

- A dispute between two employees
- An intention that if possible they both remain employees
- A memorandum of agreement
- A follow-up session

For the COMMUNITY

- A dispute between two neighbours – one male and one female – who do not live next door to each other
- A co-mediation carried out by two mediators – one man and one woman

- No legal proceedings have been issued but police have been involved and have warned the parties to try and sort it out otherwise they may be facing a caution or a summons for breach of the peace
- Each party has a close member of their family living next by
- Follow up session

Civil and commercial mediation

Mediation Clock

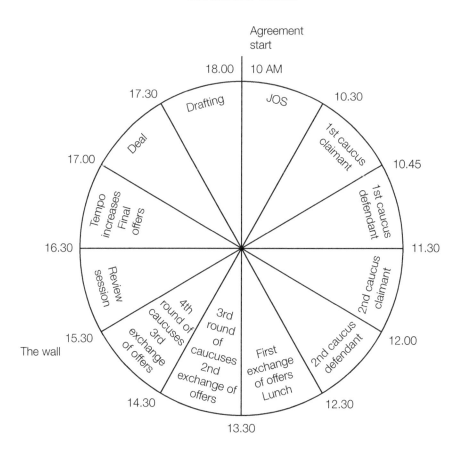

Variations

10.01 Please note that this timetable is only for purposes of illustration. It is not prescriptive in any way. There will always be variations. One of the hallmarks of mediation is that it is a flexible process. For example:

- Variables such as the nature of the dispute, the size of the teams on each side and the individual style of the mediator will influence the format and timing.

180

- There is no joint session. The mediator goes straight into private sessions with the parties.

- There is an extended joint session. Some mediators like to keep the parties together for as long as possible. They only move into private sessions when the joint session has run out of steam.

- The mediator initiates a sequential rather than a simultaneous exchange of offers.

- The mediator does not invite offers until after lunch. The traditional hour for putting forward proposals amongst some civil and commercial mediators is 15.00. Apparently this is to avoid the dangers of premature offers. Clients, if not their advocates, often start to show signs of impatience. They want to know if the other side are serious about trying to settle or if everyone wasting their time. These points are discussed below in more detail.

The pace of mediations varies. Sometimes momentum is generated early on and maintained. At other times it takes a while for any momentum at all to be generated. It is not always easy to keep going. Quite often momentum can be lost and has to be restarted.

The time splits are only indicative. But they are based on several hundred mediations.

Stage 1: Arriving at the venue

10.02   The parties arrive at the mediation. More often than not the mediation takes place in the offices or chambers one of the party's lawyers. Sometimes it is in a neutral venue such as a hotel or conference centre. The choice of venues is discussed in **Chapter 8**. There are five fundamentals.

Be on time

Lawyers know that they have to be punctual for court hearings. They should be just as punctual for mediations. If the clients are late that is bad enough. If the lawyer is late it can be disastrous. Clients become stressed, worrying about whether their lawyer is going to turn up. Just when they need reassurance, the person who can give it is not there. Clients can start to lose confidence in themselves, the process and the advocate. The other side, who have arrived on time, will start to develop a negative interpretation of events. They wonder whether or not the late arrival is being deliberately obstructive and disrespectful or just incompetent. Being late never sets the right mood for mediation.

- Always aim to arrive at least 30 minutes before the mediation is due to start. This extra time is never wasted. You can talk to the mediator or the lawyers on the other side, set up your laptop or run through your opening statement.

- It has to be admitted that barristers usually arrive later than the rest of the team, but not always.

- Clients do find it reassuring if all their legal team is already there when they arrive.

- Catch the train before the obvious choice. Build in spare time. Do not assume that there will always be taxis available at the station. Check and pre-book.

Where is the venue?

10.03   It is essential to make sure that the advocate and the clients know where the venue is. This sounds obvious but some modern office developments are not in city centres and are called imaginative names that are unknown to Satnavs and taxi drivers. The Inns of Court can be a nightmare to navigate for the first timers. Locals usually underestimate the time it takes to walk from the station with a trolley full of papers.

Embarrassment in the waiting area

The parties find themselves all together in the reception area. This can be awkward. What is the etiquette? Should they acknowledge each other? Should they go and say hello? Should they pointedly ignore each other or display a false bonhomie? There is usually a lot of embarrassed shuffling and glancing.

Sometimes the parties start to interact. If done in a positive and friendly way, it is helpful. Usually it is not and at best is guarded and rather stiffly polite. There is always a danger that people who are in dispute with each other and under stress will start arguing and create the wrong mood for peace talks.

If the advocate has arrived early he can meet his clients and manage the situation. He can show them to their room, defuse any negative tensions and rally them before they meet the mediator and the day gets under way.

Often the parties are asked to stagger their arrivals to avoid these sorts of difficulties. Try and keep to the suggested timetable.

Meeting the mediator

Sometimes the mediator is also waiting in the reception area with some of the parties. What should the parties do? Most clients will have looked up the mediator on the internet and know what he looks like.

Lawyers and their clients must be scrupulous to avoid giving any appearance of influence with the mediator. Parties under stress can be oversensitive to suggestions that a mediator might be biased in favour of the other party. It is much better for advocates not to initiate contact with the mediator even when they know each other. Wait until he approaches you. He may not. Most mediators will politely keep themselves to themselves. He is not being standoffish. He is being mindful of the appearance of bias. In any conversations with the mediator in front of the other side, avoid referring to any previous dealings or common acquaintances.

Dressing less formally than your client

10.04   The importance of dress is discussed in **Chapter 16,** but the safe rule is to dress up, not down. As the day progresses, men can loosen their ties as everyone loosens up. Jackets can be taken off as a sign of serious intent to really be involved. You cannot dress up in the same way.

Mediations are not court proceedings, but a degree of formality, at least in the early stages, in conduct and dress is normal. Like it or not, people receive messages from what those around them are wearing. Think about what messages and signals you want to send. Advocates are best advised to avoid wearing clothes that can be interpreted as making a personal statement.

Stage 2: Chats with the mediator in your room

Signing the mediation agreement

10.05   Before the mediation formally starts the mediator goes to each party's room to introduce himself. Each team has a separate room, which is theirs for the whole day. Joint sessions usually take place in a third larger room, which the mediator also uses when he is not with either of the parties. This preliminary chat is an opportunity for:

- the mediator to ask the parties to sign the mediation agreement if it has not already been signed. Usually he asks everybody who is present at the mediation to sign the agreement. This is to make sure that they are individually bound by the confidentiality provisions. This is explained in more detail in **Chapter 12**.

- the lawyers and their clients to discuss any issues with the mediator before the mediation formally starts, eg there have been new developments or some concern about the procedure for the day.

- the mediator to confirm with the parties that they would like to have a joint session. This is discussed in more detail in **para 10.07**. Some mediators can be very insistent that there is one. Others are happy to go with what the parties want.

- the mediator to ask the clients if have any concerns or worries about the process so that they can discuss them privately with him before the mediation formally begins. For example, clients can be concerned that the other side will be aggressive or lose their temper.

- clients to express an almost universal concern – that the other side are not really attending the mediation in good faith to settle or that there is no one present in the other room who has authority to settle. The mediator can explain how he intends to deal with that.

The mediator will want to make sure that:

- he knows who everybody is and why they are present at the mediation;

- everybody understands what the Mediation Agreement says; and

- everybody understands the intended procedure for the day.

Mediation agreement

10.06   The mediation agreement is the key document. This is discussed in detail in **Chapter 13**. It sets out the obligations and rights of the parties and the mediator towards each other as a matter of contract. Many clients come to mediation without having read the mediation agreement beforehand.

This is a bad idea. Advocates must go through the mediation agreement with their clients and explain it to them before the mediation. Some solicitors do not even send it to clients in advance. The advocate usually just tells his client that it is standard and he has read it.

It is undesirable to say the least if the first time that the client sees the mediation agreement is on the day when he asked to sign it. Clients, especially if they not sophisticated users of legal services, will find it difficult to absorb what is being said to them by the mediator about the mediation agreement on the day. Their minds are already on other things and avoidable stress is induced.

A checklist of the terms in a mediation agreement is at **Chapter 13.**

Not ready to start?

Sometimes parties are not ready to start on time. This can be because people are late, new issues have arisen or they simply need to talk to their lawyers. If more time is needed before the mediation formally starts, just ask for it. Most mediators are helpful and can assist in resolving any outstanding issues before the mediation formally gets under way.

If one side needs a lot more time, the mediator may say that he wants to start talking with the other party if they are ready. There is no point in objecting to this. It makes good use of time and sets a cooperative mood.

Lawyers only meetings

Sometimes the mediator may ask lawyers to meet him alone without their clients. This is quite common, where there is a strict timetable for the mediation. The mediator will want make sure that the lawyers understand the time pressures and the milestones for reaching certain stages in the mediation if a settlement is going to be achieved within the time limits.

Stage 3: Joint Opening Session

10.07   The traditional model for mediation assumes that there will be a Joint Opening Session (also known as a plenary session). This is where all the parties and their lawyers sit in the same room with the mediator. The purpose of a Joint Opening Session is to:

- allow the mediator to introduce himself to everybody and to make sure that everyone knows who each other is and why they are at the mediation;

- explain the purpose of mediation and the ground rules for the day, eg that mediation is voluntary, confidential and without prejudice;

- set the mood for settlement discussions; and

- give each party the opportunity to say what they want to the other for the purpose of the mediation – the mediator makes his opening statement and then invites the parties to make theirs.

Mediator's statement

10.08 Each mediator has his own style and way of saying things. Most opening statements include the following topics.

The mediator:

- introduces himself: some mediators go through their CV to establish status and authority, whilst others simply say 'Good morning' and who they are;
- asks everyone to switch off their mobiles;
- goes round the table asking people to introduce themselves. Clients should be told about this so they do not become confused. All they have to do is give their name and position, for example: 'I am X Y and I am the contracts manager,' or 'I am W Z wife of A B';
- makes sure that the mediation agreement has been signed – if this has not been done the mediator may circulate the agreement for signature; and
- gives key explanations.

The mediator usually reminds everyone of the following:

- The purpose of being at the mediation is to try and reach a settlement.
- His role is to help the parties do that. He is not there as a judge or arbitrator but as a facilitator. He may ask some reality testing questions to help him gain a better understanding.
- Mediation is a voluntary process in the sense that the parties cannot be forced to settle. They can be forced to attend but not to settle if they do not want to.
- The parties can leave at any time but, if they want to leave, to give him 10 minutes notice before walking out.
- All communications on the day, whether in private session or in a joint session, are confidential and without prejudice.
- Until all parties have signed a document recording the settlement there is no legally binding agreement.
- Parties must have authority to settle. He may ask the parties and their representatives to confirm that they do. Do not allow clients to misrepresent their authority. If it will be necessary to seek authority, eg from insurers or a director before a settlement can be agreed, say so at the outset. If the fact that authority is limited is only disclosed later it causes the other side to feel misled. Trust is lost and the momentum and goodwill that has developed can quickly evaporate.

10.09 The mediator explains the procedure he intends to follow:

- he will invite each party to say what they want to; and
- either he will keep the Joint Opening Session going for as long as he thinks it useful or he will break up into caucuses and then shuttle between the rooms.

Some mediators emphasise that the procedure is flexible and that they will do what the parties want and tell them that this is their day. Others emphasise that while the dispute and the solution belong to the parties, the process belongs to the mediator.

The mediator may also confirm:

- He is independent. Any potential conflicts of interest should in practice have been resolved before he was appointed.

- He will destroy notes and papers after the mediation. This in practice is becoming more difficult to do because many mediators are now required to have professional indemnity insurance. Their insurers expect them to retain sufficient documents to enable any claim that might be made against them to be investigated and defended.

The mediator usually concludes by:

- asking the parties if they would like to say anything – most do;

- reminding them of the purpose of mediation, which is to make peace not war; and

- asking the listening party not to interrupt the speaker.

The parties' opening statements

Who goes first?

10.10   It is customary for the claimant to go first but there is no absolute rule about this. In practice if not in theory there is no particular advantage in going either first or last. There is no burden of proof to discharge. Mediation is not a trial. It is entirely a matter for the parties and their lawyers whether or not they want to say anything. Some mediators actively encourage clients to say something. Whatever the choice it is essential that:

- the decision has been made in advance; and

- the speaker has made notes and rehearsed what he wants to say.

Should the client speak or should he leave it to his advocate?

There are a number of advantages to the client saying something:

- He has the chance to speak directly to the other side and their lawyers. This is something that he would not be able to do at trial. He may feel that this is sufficient acknowledgement. The importance of allowing clients to be heard and acknowledged was discussed in **Chapter 5**. Clients who do not feel that they have been acknowledged may find it difficult to get into a settlement mindset.

- He has the chance of impressing the other side and show that he will be a credible and sympathetic witness.

- He can show that the other side that he is a human being. Quite often the decision maker on the other side will not have seen him before. The tendency for disputants to demonise each other is frequently an obstacle to settlement. Those who were not involved in the circumstances giving rise to the dispute can easily form a negative impression of the other side based on what they have been told by their own side.

- He can make an impact statement to explain the effect that the dispute has had on him, his family or business. If a client comes across as genuine and likeable he has a much better chance of receiving a favourable settlement than if he comes across as dishonest, unreasonable and vengeful.

There are, however, disadvantages:

- The client becomes too emotional and gets confused, stressed or angry. The other side may interpret this as a sign of weakness.

- He is not adequately prepared and tries to make it up as he goes along. He starts to ramble and can easily lose his audience.

- He may make an ill-advised remark, which makes the other party angry or disclose information that his lawyer was keeping secret until later.

- He may contradict what has previously been said by him or on his behalf in correspondence or witness statements.

- The other side may provoke him. Although mediators ask everybody not to interrupt the speaker, in practice lawyers and clients do interject with corrections, questions and adverse comments.

If the client wants to make a statement should his advocate make one as well?

10.11 It is always worthwhile the advocate making a statement. If the client wants to make a long statement in which he explains the whole factual background of the dispute, his views about what has happened in the past, who is to blame and what should happen in the future, the advocate need only make a short statement. If the client wants to limit himself to an impact statement the advocate can make the usual fuller statement, which is discussed below.

If both the client and the advocate are going to make statements who should go first?

If the client is only going to make an impact statement, he should speak after his advocate. The emotional power of what he has said will be the last thing the other side hear. If the client is going to make a much fuller statement he should speak first. This will give the advocate an opportunity of correcting anything that his client may have got wrong or to reinterpret what he has said in case there has been a misunderstanding.

Generally it is better if the advocate makes the opening statement. But there are many mediators who think the opposite and actively encourage the clients to speak to them and the other side in the Joint Opening Session. Some can be insistent. If the client or the advocate is uneasy about the client speaking publicly, be firm with the mediator.

There is a significant difference between the client speaking to the mediator in private, which the advocates should allow and speaking to the other side in public. On balance the risks outweigh the benefits. Unless the client is be able to stick to a script that he has agreed and rehearsed with his adviser he is not going to do himself or his case any good. In practice, in a stressful situation sticking to a script is not always easy for clients to do.

An exception: apologies

10.12   Often what the aggrieved parties at mediation really want is an apology. They will never be able to obtain that in court. No judge can order another party to apologise. If an apology is to be given then it is better that:

- it is given early rather than later, as this creates the right mood for settlement and may remove one of the biggest obstacles to settlement; and

- it is given by the client, as will have much more impact if a genuine and personal apology is given. Apologies given by lawyers on behalf of clients although they may be genuine never have the same force.

What to say in the opening statement?

When preparing what to say be absolutely clear on two questions:

- What is the message I want to convey?

- Who am I delivering the message to?

The message is:

- Settlement is a good idea for both sides.

- You and your client realise that.

- You want to be sure is that the other side realises it as well. Set out in a neutral and conversational way the reasons why it is a good idea for both sides to settle rather than fight.

Deliver your message to the decision maker on the other side. That will not be the lawyer. In a calm, courteous and conversational way address the decision maker. In corporate disputes the decision maker will often not have been involved in the original dispute. He will have been brought in either to clear up the mess or to sanction a settlement. Until now he may only have heard his own team's version of events. This is the opportunity to explain your client's side of the story. Often decision makers hear things for the first time at mediation.

How long should the statement be?

The statement should not last more than 10 minutes and must never go beyond 20 minutes. After 20 minutes people stop paying attention. As with all presentations it is much better not to read from a script but to speak from notes. Rehearse so that the message is expressed clearly in a confident and fluent manner. There is no point in repeating what has been set in court papers or mediation statements. Refer to them but not repeat them. It just wastes time and energy.

Is this advocacy?

10.13   When making a statement, the advocate is really acting as an interpreter explaining his client's perspective, not selling his client's case. The fundamental differences between speaking on behalf of a client at mediation and speaking on his behalf at court are:

- in court the advocate is analysing the legal and evidential issues and trying to persuade the judge that his arguments are correct on the other side is wrong;

- at mediation there is no judge to persuade – it is unrealistic to expect lawyers and their clients to publicly change their minds about their case;

- in court, because it is warfare, advocates attack the other side, whereas at mediation it is peacemaking – advocates needs to build bridges with the other side;

- in court advocates deal with legal issues, whereas in mediation they deal with personal and commercial issues; and

- in court judges can be persuaded by legal argument, whereas in mediation the decision makers amongst both sets of clients are not persuaded by legal argument, but by commercial and personal considerations.

Advocacy at mediation is not the same as advocacy in court. It is more a matter of interpretation and explanation than aggression and demolition. Advocates will make much more progress with the other side if they can identify obstacle to settlement and outline possible solutions.

As explained in **Chapter 5**, legal points cannot be ignored completely. They should be at least acknowledged. In all cases both sides have strengths and weaknesses. Nobody will believe a lawyer who says that he has told his client that he has 100 per cent chance of winning a trial. It is much better while asserting that that the client has a strong case, which he has been advised he will win at trial, to acknowledge that there is always a degree of uncertainty. It is that uncertainty which is one of the main drivers for a settlement.

10.14   Some commentators advise representatives when speaking to be passionate. For the reasons given in **para 9.09** above, this can be bad advice In civil and commercial mediations. Being passionate is often interpreted as meaning that the speaker should express himself forcefully, even if it means becoming angry and demonstrating that that he is angry by shouting or table banging. This is said to convince the other side of the strength of conviction in the case and the authenticity of the speaker's point of view. In most mediations this is a unwise tactic.

Aggressive presentations, which involve attacking the lawyers or their clients on the other side, are counter-productive. When people feel under attack they become stressed and, as explained at **para 9.09**, stop being receptive to what is being said to and cannot think about settlement.

Expressing anger is also counter-productive. It is true that expressing anger can make someone feel better. The problem is:

- this feeling is short lived;

- expressions of anger can be because of the release of dopamine in the brain, leading to further expressions of anger, so that a further dose of dopamine is released. People become trapped in a cycle of anger;

- people who are angry are also stressed. As explained in **para 9.07**, people who are stressed find it difficult to engage in a way of thinking that is conducive to settlement. This again is largely due to the interruption to the activity of the prefrontal cortex; and

- the other side seeing this expression of anger may perceive it as a weakness. They may interpret it as evidence of lack of self-control, which they might be able to exploit at a trial before the judge.

Concluding the opening statement

10.15   By all means be assertive in presenting an assessment of the problem to the other side. There is a difference between being assertive, aggressive and offensive. Of course no advocate will ever publicly admit in an opening statement that he does not have confidence his client's case. Nobody expects this to happen. Finish the opening statement by reiterating that you and your client are ready to engage in constructive settlement discussions. Do not end with a rousing battle cry.

Visual aids

In practice these are not usually of any value in the Opening Session. The disadvantages are:

- they interrupt the flow of the verbal presentation;

- the technology does not usually work smoothly; and

- the technology can be difficult to set up especially for the visiting side.

If the visual aid is a chart or summary to explain a point, make a copy and hand it round so that the other side can take it back to their room with them. If the visual aid is potential evidence for use at court, such as a surveillance video or a tape recording, it is better to play it first to the mediator so that he can assess the impact on the other side and then to the other side in a session devoted just to that. If it is introduced as part of the opening statement the impact will be diluted.

Plans and photographs are useful. Refer to them and provide copies for the other side to take away. Handing them out while the advocate is talking will distract the listeners and the impact of what is being said will be lost. Make sure that you have enough copies for everyone and some spares.

What to do when the other side is talking

10.16   You may find what the other side is saying is insulting, boring, irrelevant, and just wrong. Do not do what many lawyers and their clients do in the circumstances:

- stare out the window and clearly demonstrate that you are not paying any attention at all;

- laugh, shake your head and indicate disagreement; or

- whisper to other members of your team.

Instead, remind yourself that the purpose of being at mediation is to try and achieve a settlement:

- Do not do anything that makes this more difficult. Pay attention while the other side is speaking.

- Note what is being said and what is not being said.

- Ask yourself why they are expressing themselves in a particular way.

- Look at the speaker's body language.

- Consider whether what he is saying conflicts with what he is doing. Is there evidence of cognitive dissonance?

- Look at what other members of the team and in particular the decision maker are doing.

Even when being attacked and insulted there is always something to learn. Staying calm and receptive under attack is not easy but skilled advocates can do it.

Advocates and clients on both sides must bear in mind that each side is looking at the other and trying to read them. Be careful what messages are being transmitted by body language.

Should you agree to a Joint Opening Session?

10.17 The answer is 'yes' if either the other side or the mediator suggests it. Holding a Joint Opening Session used to be axiomatic. They seem to be falling out of fashion, but they do have benefits:

- They allow the mediator to set the mood and explain the ground rules.

- They give the parties the opportunity of speaking directly to and observing the other side's decision maker and influencing him.

- they give clients the opportunity of making sure that they have been heard and acknowledged and of impressing the other side as a genuine human being and a strong witness.

There are sometimes good reasons for not agreeing to a Joint Opening Session:

- There has been a history of intimidation or extreme confrontation and your client is feeling stressed by it. Sometimes clients are under medical care as a result of other side's conduct

- Relations are so bad between the parties that they will not be able to restrain themselves from engaging in public and angry arguments.

- The subject matter of the dispute is sensitive and people still feel awkward or embarrassed, for example in a sexual harassment case.

- There is no need for a Joint Opening Session because there have already been extensive settlement negotiations, which have failed. Both parties are confident that they know all the relevant facts and also each other's positions very well. There is nothing more to learn. They just want to start the negotiation. In fact there is always something to learn. In practice some sort of joint session usually takes place later in the day.

Stage 4: Private meetings with the mediator

10.18 Private meetings with the mediator are also called caucuses. They are an important part of most mediations. Even where the mediator prefers to have an extended Joint Opening Session and to try and keep the parties together for as long as possible there will be some private meetings. There is no fixed order in which they take place. After the Joint Opening Session has concluded some mediators go and see the claimant first. Others see the defendant first. The order can be influenced by what has been said in the Joint Opening Session. The mediator may wish to clarify some preliminary points early on in the process with one party.

There is no set length of time for a caucus. Mediators are aware of the problems of time management. There is always the danger that a party may feel ignored if the mediator spends a long time with the other party. Sometimes it is necessary for a mediator to spend more time in one room than the other. There may be simply more issues with one party that have to be discussed.

As a general rule the first round of caucuses last about 30–45 minutes. The second round is often longer. As the day progresses caucuses gradually become shorter as the momentum towards settlement increases. This process of the mediator going from one room to another having private sessions in each row it is sometimes called 'shuttle diplomacy'.

If at any time during the day an advocate or his client feel that they are being neglected or that the mediator is spending too much time with the other side they should tell him and ask him why. He may, subject to the rules of confidentiality, not be able to give a full explanation. He may only be able to say that it is necessary at the moment. Mediators will not take offence at being asked these questions. It is easy to lose track of time at mediation.

Stage 5: First exchange of offers

10.19 There is no uniform approach to first exchange of offers. Some mediators ask parties what their proposal for settlement is in the first caucus. This is quite rare but the mediator wants to find out how far the parties have prepared for this mediation by thinking about settlement. Other mediators like to prolong the exploration stage so that both they and the parties feel that all the issues have been fully discussed. They believe that this enables the parties to make a better-informed decision on what proposal to put forward. They delay proposals until five or six hours into the mediation. There are other mediators who believe that the dangers of a premature offer are less than the dangers of offers being delayed for too long. They believe that settlements are achieved not by exchanging legal points and arguing about evidence but by discussing proposals. The sooner you have proposals to discuss, the better.

Experienced mediators will quite frequently tell the parties at the beginning of the mediation day of the milestones that will have to be met if progress is going to be made. For example they may say that unless the parties have made an agreement in principle by 16.00 (assuming the mediation is due finish at 18.00), they will not have enough time to prepare the written settlement agreement. Working back from this means that the first proposals must be made by 1400 at the latest. That leaves two hours for further negotiation.

In practice many mediators encourage the parties to exchange proposals before lunch. This is not always possible but at least it provides the parties with a timeframe.

Stage 6: Lunch

10.20   There are three schools of thought regarding lunch:

- Have lunch brought in for the parties to eat in their own rooms and keep on working. This maintains the momentum.

- Have lunch brought in and all the parties eat together. The theory is that this will encourage parties to interact and will help lower the barriers to settlement. Momentum is maintained in a different way. Many deals are concluded over a meal. In practice bringing disputing parties together on the day they are thinking about their disagreements and arguments and expecting them to interact in a sociable way is unrealistic. It is a sad fact that at mediation the parties do not usually want to be together in the same room.

- The parties make their own arrangements and go out and have something to eat. This can disrupt momentum. But they go out at different times. The mediator can still be working with one party while the other is out having lunch. When they return he can work with them while the others go out for lunch. The advantage of going out is that it gives people a break. Mediation can for many clients be stressful, claustrophobic and pressured. Fresh air and a walk can help them absorb the new information that they have received, clear their minds and re-energise them for the afternoon session.

In practice during the day some clients will need to make contact with their office or respond to telephone calls. Their life is not put on hold just because they are in a mediation. Some of course will need to go out for a cigarette or re-park the car.

Stage 7: Second exchange of offers

10.21   The parties having had a chance to digest their lunch and the first offers are invited by the mediator to put forward revised proposals.

Stage 8: Private sessions continue

10.22   There is no fixed process or limit to the number of exchanges of offers that can take place. Some mediators advertise the fact that their cases settle after two exchanges. After the second exchange a significant change often takes place in both rooms. They either decide that they want to try and settle today or that they do not. By now they will have been at the mediation for about five hours. Usually they decide they want to continue to try and settle. The mediator will give guidance if asked on what he think needs to be done in both rooms to close any gap and resolve any outstanding issues.

In civil and commercial mediations it is common for there to be a claim and a counterclaim. At the start of the mediation day both sides say that they expect to be net receivers of money. This in most cases makes it difficult to settle a dispute. However it is still the case that most disputes where there is a claim and counterclaim settle on the day. The turning point comes when one party decides that it will not insist on being a net receiver. That usually takes place at the third exchange of offers.

Stage 9: The wall

10.23   Assuming that the mediation started at 10.00, the low point in every mediation is usually about 15.30. Parties hit the wall. No settlement has been reached. Both sides are feeling frustrated and think that the other side is being unreasonable. They start telling the mediator and each other that is all a waste of time and they might as well go straight to court.

Experienced mediators do not become discouraged. They have seen this happen many times before. They explain this to the parties and encourage them and their advocates not to give up and to persevere with the process. On most occasions it pays off.

It is usually the clients who express frustration. The advocates have been through the process before. They know that the frustration will pass and a settlement can be achieved even though it does not look likely at this precise moment. Sometimes it is the advocates who say that it has all been a waste of time and that there is no prospect of settlement. Advocates who are tempted to do this should remember why everyone one is at the mediation: to reach a settlement. No one reaches a settlement on the day by walking away. In any case the clients have paid for eight hours so they might as well make full use of them. Experienced mediators will be able to assess the situation and suggest ways of moving forward. One of them is a review session

Stage 10: Review session

10.24   There is no prescribed pattern for a review session. Sometimes the mediator, as part of general discussion with a party, starts reviewing where the parties have got to so far, what they have done to get there, why there appears to be a blockage, and asks for suggestions for moving forward. He may rather more formally tell the parties that he has identified the obstacles to settlement having been listening to both sides for five or six hours. He will tell them what they are. He may do this in a joint session. Or he will tell them separately in private. In both cases he does the same thing:

- summarise without breaching confidentiality where he thinks both parties are;

- identify what is impeding progress; and

- explain what appears to be needed to speed up progress.

The mediator might just ask everyone to come into a joint session and simply ask them where they think they are and what they would like to do to make progress. He may be hoping for a creative brainstorming session. In practice it can easily turn into a blame shifting session with tempers becoming frayed and positions becoming even more entrenched.

Sometimes clients and their advocates can regard this identifying of obstacles to settlement as a criticism of them. Sometimes it is, but this is where the effective advocate is more resilient and robust. He listens very carefully to what the mediator says and how he says it. Having decoded what the mediator is saying he will ask the mediator for guidance. Good mediators give it.

This is where the effective advocate is really important. If he has been sensible during the mediation so far he will have:

- avoided extreme demands or statements of position;

- avoided backing himself and his client into a corner;

- made it clear that if new information was received he and his client have an open mind and would re-evaluate their position;

- carried out an analysis of the various options and scenarios with his client before the mediation and will have continued the process during the mediation especially during the times when the mediator was with the other party; and

- reassured his client that it is not a sign of weakness to change your mind. As the great economist J M Keynes said: 'When circumstances change I change my mind. What do you do?'

Stage 11: The caucuses continue

10.25   The parties reflect on what the mediator said during the review session. Often it is at this stage that the mediator suggests face-to-face meetings between either the lawyers without clients or the clients without lawyers.

If the mediator suggests them always accept his suggestion. He knows what is happening in both rooms. Nobody else does. He would not be suggesting these meetings without a reason. It is sensible to insist that the mediator is present. This avoids face-to-face meetings turning into unpleasant rows with threats and accusations of blackmail or intimidation being made.

When such meetings take place they nearly always add a fresh impetus to the momentum settlement, which may have stalled. In particular when the decision makers from each side meet they often have the necessary authority to take that vital decision that unlocks settlement.

Stage 12: Settlement

10.26 At last, an offer is made by one party that the other can accept. The parties are in agreement. There is no legally binding agreement yet. It has to be reduced to writing.

Stages 13 and 14: Drafting agreement, signature and copy documents

10.27 Many people think that this is the easiest part of the day. The hard work has already been done. Settlement has been reached. In fact this is one of the most dangerous periods of the day. This is discussed in detail in **Chapter 14**.

Eventually the settlement is reduced to writing and agreed. It has to be signed. Some mediators like to have a signing ceremony where everybody gets together to do it. There is always a danger that one party is feeling that they have given away too much. Frustration with each other may still be high. There might be displays of bad temper or sarcasm, which can upset everything. It is more efficient for each party to double-check the agreement in its own room and sign it.

Stage15: Farewells

10.28 Some mediators like to have a moment of theatre and gather everyone into the same room and give a speech of congratulation. Sometimes this is appropriate. In practice most of the time the parties just want to go home. Usually they will say goodbye to each other and shake hands. But often one side refuses and just wants to leave without even seeing the other party. The lawyers at least usually observe the professional courtesies and say good-bye to each other and shake hands.

Mission accomplished.

Family mediation

10.29 This model assumes that a husband and wife wish to divorce. They have three children. Neither is eligible for legal aid. Each has consulted solicitors. Divorce proceedings have been drafted but not yet served. The husband works full-time and has adequate pension arrangements. His wife works part-time and has more limited pension arrangements.

Relations between them are bad. The husband has moved out of the matrimonial home. There are no allegations of domestic violence. The three children are all upset by the break up and it is affecting their behaviour and performance at school.

MIAMs

10.30 MIAM stands for mediation information and assessment meeting. Under the family procedure rules it is compulsory for all parties who wish to issue court proceedings for a remedy about finances or in relation to children to refer the matter to family mediation. There are exceptions, for example if there is a risk or evidence of domestic violence. In practice most divorcing couples must now attend at least one session family mediation.

The MIAM or the intake meeting is the first step. The normal procedure is for the party's solicitors to make a referral to a family mediator. The mediator will contact each of the parties and arrange a MIAM. This can be a joint session or each of the parties can attend separately. The mediator takes information from the client's and asked them what they would like to discuss. He will explain about mediation and other ways of resolving outstanding issues without going to court. If the mediator considers that mediation is suitable he will tell the parties and ask if they would like to try mediation. This is their decision. It is not compulsory to go through the mediation process. It is compulsory to consider going through the mediation process. If the parties want to go to mediation process the mediator will draw up a negation agreement and asked the parties to sign it.

Mediation sessions

The mediator will agree with the parties how many sessions to schedule. Where there are issues about finances and children normally three to five sessions are scheduled over a period of weeks. In complicated matters, then there are many more sessions. Much depends upon the degree of cooperation between the parties.

First session

10.31 Most sessions are held jointly with the parties together in the same room with the mediator throughout. A session usually lasts between 90 minutes and 2 hours. It is possible to have private sessions.

The mediator helps the parties structure their discussions by identifying issues, which have to be addressed. An important part of this is highlighting what information is required. At this stage neither the husband nor the wife will have completed a Form E. There is therefore a lot of information gathering to be carried out.

Subsequent sessions

At the end of each session the mediator agrees with each party what information they are going to gather and provide at the next session. For example details about pensions.

In structuring the discussions, the mediator usually compiles a list of issues that have to be worked through. He tries to achieve incremental agreement. At the end of each session he confirms what has been agreed so far and what the agenda is for the next session. He is trying to develop the habit of cooperation and build up a sense of convergence.

In the intervals between sessions the parties can consult their lawyers. It is rare for lawyers or any other advocates to attend any of the sessions. Sometimes a mediator may suggest that they do bring lawyers along, for example if each party attends a session and tells the other that their lawyer has got it all wrong. The mediator may wish to find out whether there is a conflict of legal advice or whether the parties are, as they often do, simply hearing what they want to hear.

Mediators cannot give legal advice. A significant number of family mediators have no legal training. Mediators can explain but they cannot advise. Usually mediators advise the parties to take legal advice on what their legal rights are, what might happen at court if the parties do not reach their own settlement and on the meaning of any agreement that could be drawn up.

If the parties reach an agreement the mediator prepares a Memorandum of Understanding. It is not legally binding. It can be made legally binding if it is turned into a court order. The mediator usually advises the clients to have this done for them by their own solicitors.

Some mediators prepare a draft Memorandum of Understanding and send it to the parties that so that they can consult with their solicitors before confirming that it is what they have agreed. The Memorandum of Understanding is then issued to both sets of referring solicitors who can then incorporate it into a court order.

Workplace mediation

10.32   This model assumes that the mediation will take place in a single day, between two employees who are in dispute and lasts for eight hours and is not part of an in-house mediation procedure.

Most workplace mediations are commissioned by the HR Department. They have a dispute between employees and have not so far been able to resolve it. They want to avoid it becoming a formal grievance and/or disciplinary matter. The objective is to enable both employees to remain in employment and to have resolved the cause of the friction between them.

It is a confidential process. Mediators do not report to HR what was said to them by the employees privately or what was discussed in any joint sessions.

Arrival

The mediation is usually held at the employer's premises preferably at a location that is not the employees' usual place of work. The mediator is shown to his room. That is where most of the discussions will take place during the whole day.

The mediator asks each of the employees to come and see him in the room separately. Some mediators keep this first meeting brief and confine it to introductions and possibly signing the Mediation Agreement.

The first private session

10.33   The mediator tries to identify who is the principal claimant and sees them first. If one employee is more junior they are usually seen first. Each employee is invited to tell the mediator how he or she sees the situation and to give their explanation of how the problem has arisen. Even in this first session the mediator will be trying to find out if the employee is ready willing and able to have a joint session with the mediator and the other employee. Quite often they are not. They have probably not been talking for some time and indeed have been trying to avoid each other.

The first session usually lasts about an hour.

The second private session

The mediator has now heard from each employee. They are not yet ready for a joint session. So the mediator holds a second round of private sessions. In this round the mediator tries to shift the focus from how the employee feels about what has happened in the past to thinking about how the other employee might see things and what could be done to improve relations. The mediator will, within the bounds of confidentiality, be able to exchange information and comments from each employee to the other. He can start to see whether the respective lists of grievances, explanations and goals overlap at all. Ideally by the end of this round each employee will have started to come up with some suggestions for the future or at least expressed a willingness to try and come up with some.

Lunch

The mediator eats his sandwiches and the employees make their own arrangements.

Joint session

10.34   If the employees have agreed, a joint session is held which takes up most of the afternoon. By now the mediator will have been able to develop a shopping list of what appears to be live issues that have to be tackled. This afternoon session can be an intense and draining experience for the employees. Good mediators will make sure that there are breaks every 45 minutes or so. The objective is that the employees will during the afternoon be able to speak to each other, give explanations and offer apologies for the past. For the future they will be able to suggest changes or improvements and offer assurances.

This is not intended to be a legally binding agreement. It is rare for whatever agreement is reached by the employees to be written down in a memorandum of understanding or agreed protocol.

Sometimes the employees are not ready to have a joint session. The mediator having completed their rounds of private sessions (and they can hold more than two if they think that it will help) brings the day to an end and tells the employees that they will be in touch with to arrange a follow-up session.

The mediator speaks to each of the employees on the telephone to see if they want to try a joint session. If they do it is arranged and usually takes place a week or so later.

Conclusion

The mediator reports to the HR Department either that the employees have sorted out their disagreement or that they have not and the dispute remains unresolved.

Community mediation

10.35   The procedure is more like the model of workplace mediation described above than the civil and commercial model.

In this model we assume that two neighbours, who are both council tenants are complaining about each other's behaviour. One is complaining about excessive noise from their sound system and the other is complaining about the other being too nosey and interfering.

The mediation will be a co-mediation and last four hours.

Arrival

Nearly all community mediations are held in the parties' houses. Ideally the two co-mediators will have met up and travel to the parties' homes together.

The mediators tell each neighbour that they have arrived, introduce themselves and confirm which neighbour they will be seeing first.

First private session

10.36   The mediators visit the home of the first neighbour. It is rare for any representative to be present. Sometimes there is another family member or friend. After introductions and reminders about the purpose of mediation they invite the neighbour to tell their side of the story.

The Mediation Agreement will not usually have been signed in advance. The mediators explain what the agreement says and asks the neighbour to sign it. Ideally this should be done before the mediation session starts. Some mediators prefer to encourage the parties to start talking before asking them to sign the agreement. There are obvious potential dangers about confidentiality being broken if discussions start and the neighbour never signs the Mediation Agreement.

The first session usually lasts about 30-45 min. After the first session with the first neighbour the co-mediators have a debrief usually outside. They go and see the second neighbour. They go through the same procedure.

In both sessions by a combination of open questions and active listening the mediators will be trying to draw out what the underlying grievances and motivations are. They will also be planting the seeds of the idea of a joint session. Ideally this should take place on the same day after the first round of private sessions.

In practice relations between the neighbours are usually so bad that this does not happen. Nearly always one neighbour says that they feel intimidated by the other.

Second private sessions

10.37 If there is time the co-mediators will hold a second round of private sessions. This will follow the same format as the first round. But the mediators will now have each neighbour's point of view of the other. This is this is the exchange stage discussed in **Chapter 4.**

Joint session

If a joint session can be arranged it does not usually take place on that day. This is mainly because of time constraints and the desire of the parties to meet in a neutral venue. Warring neighbours usually do not want to have their opponents in their house.

After the second round of private sessions the mediators will say goodbye to each neighbour and explain that they will be in touch by telephone to follow up and hopefully to arrange a joint session. The joint session normally takes place about two weeks later at a neutral venue. The mediators will by this time have been able to prepare a list of issues that have to be resolved. They can see how much common ground there is.

Emotions can still be running high with both parties being suspicious and wary of each other. This session takes skilful management. The objective is to reach an agreed way forward. If this is possible the mediators summarise what has been agreed. The agreement is not usually recorded in writing by way of a memorandum of understanding.

Conclusion

The mediators report to the referring body such as the Housing Department or Social Services Department that an agreement is reached. They do not disclose any details about what has been said to them or what they have said to the parties.

Follow-up

Sometimes, if resources permit and the circumstances suggest that it would be a good idea, there is a follow-up. This is usually by telephone. Sometimes there can be a follow-up face-to-face session.

Conclusion

10.38 To conclude:

- Mediation is a flexible process and the stages described in this chapter will not always be followed in the same way.
- Making yourself familiar with the likely pattern of events and walking clients through them will reduce stress levels for everyone.
- Reducing stress in any way that you can improves the chances of settlement.

Chapter 11

Physical Preparation

This chapter discusses the physical preparation for a mediation. It concentrates on two topics:

- The position paper or mediation statement
- The file of documents (mediation bundle) for use at the mediation

Why do mediations fail?

11.01 The two most common reasons why mediations do not produce a settlement on the day are:

- lack of preparation in advance; and
- lack of engagement in the process on the day.

Preparation for mediation

11.02 Is preparing for mediation the same as preparing for a trial in court? Most lawyers and clients do prepare for mediation in the same way that they prepare for trial. In other words they prepare for a fight. As discussed in **Chapter 1**, this is not what mediation is for. Why do they do it?

The main reasons seem to be:

- the clients want to explain themselves;
- the clients want to justify themselves;
- they want to make the other side feel guilty;
- they want to unnerve the other side with a show of legal and commercial strength;
- the lawyers want to win the argument and show that the other side is wrong;
- the lawyers want to exercise their professional skills, mainly legal analysis and advocacy; and
- it is easier for lawyers to prepare for court – that is what they are trained to do and they are practiced in it.

Nearly all of the paperwork that is sent to the mediator and the other side is about the strength of the legal case. Rarely is there any analysis of settlement.

For the reasons discussed in **Chapter 5**, legal rights cannot and should not be ignored. Briefly this is because:

● clients use them as a yardstick for fairness;

● they represent the default position for what happens if settlement is not achieved;

● they are one of the risk factors; and

● clients are paying for legal advice and it does have some influence on them.

The trouble is that parties, and especially their lawyers, over-concentrate on the legal analysis at the expense of the commercial and personal analysis. What is wrong with this?

● *The PMA is relegated in the list of priorities or is not done at all before the mediation*

  If the PMA is not properly completed, the client will not be in a position to take an informed decision. He will not appreciate his range of options. He will not understand either the risks and associated costs of not settling or the benefits of settling. He will be more prone to flawed decision-making as the cognitive biases discussed in **Chapter 18** come into play.

● *The client's goals are not articulated*

  As explained in **Chapter 16**, going to a mediation without clear goals will make a successful outcome less likely and make the whole process more difficult for the client

● *The nuts and bolts of settlements are not identified and so the engine of settlement is not built*

  As explained in **Chapter 10**, doing this on the day makes the whole experience more stressful for the clients. People under stress find it more difficult to concentrate on settlement. It is much easier for them just to argue.

● *They will not have thought about the other side*

  The importance of seeing the pictures in the other side's head and understanding their reality has been discussed in **Chapter 16**.

11.03   At the mediation, the mediator will be encouraging both sides to look at the situation from each other's point of view. Homework does pay off.

Clients attending mediation and their advisers need to rebalance their preparation. It should be:

● for peace talks;

● proportionate; and

● prompt.

What this means in practice is:

● *Co-operating with the other side in the preparations for the mediation*

There is nothing to be gained by arguing about the choice of mediator, what documents to include in the mediation file and dates for exchanging mediation statements. There is much to be lost. Raising the level of antagonism sets the wrong mood for the mediation.

Parties at mediation will need to try and establish a good enough working relationship to be able to discuss proposals and negotiate with each other. They will not be helped if their lawyers have been arguing before they get there.

● *Not wasting time, money and effort*

Much of the advice given to advocates and their clients about preparing for mediation assumes that they have unlimited time and money to spend on preparation. In practice this is not true and there are limits. Think twice before:

— preparing huge mediation files which look like trial bundles (this is discussed in more detail at **para 11.28**);

— spending time arguing with the other side about the index or the contents of the mediation file;

— drafting 10-page mediation statements that read like case summaries or skeleton arguments for court, or worse, preparing instructions to counsel to do it – that will produce a document that is well structured and expressed but late, long and forensic; and

— delegating it all to the most junior and least experienced member of staff.

Common faults in preparation

11.04   Many mediators complain about the poor standard of preparation. The main complaints are about:

● out of date information – often, up-to-date information about valuations management figures or schedules of loss are not available;

● documents that parties want to rely upon are not brought to the mediation and have to be emailed or even couriered over during the course of the day;

● mediation documents being delivered late to the mediator – it is difficult for a mediator to be well prepared at the mediation if he only receives the documents the day before. . As a general rule, you should deliver the documents that you want the mediator to absorb at least a week before the mediation. It is also much more efficient if the mediation statement and the file of documents can be delivered at the same time.

Cutting corners

11.05   Preparing for mediation in a proportionate way is not the same as cutting corners. Try and avoid:

● just copying the last hearing bundle (see **para 11.27**);

● not updating information – carrying out a PMA will help prevent this (see **Chapter 7**);

- not having a review meeting with the client (and if counsel is being instructed, with counsel as well) until the day before or even on the day of the mediation.

- relying on the fact that mediations are not as formal as court hearings:

  — the mediator, unlike a judge, cannot punish a party if, for example, there are missing documents:

  — there are no formal rules of evidence and burdens of proof. However, as explained in **Chapter 1**, at mediations, information gaps are often obstacles to settlement. If the parties have different information they are more likely to have different views of the dispute. The more shared information there is, the greater the chance of a shared view. With a shared view it is easier to identify the common ground. The more common ground there is the greater the chance of settlement; and

  — the parties who do not settle on the day can try again, but this does cost the client money.

Guidance notes

11.06   Most appointing bodies issue guidance notes on mediation preparation. These can be helpful; however, they can cause stress and uncertainty. Mediators may issue their own guidance either in the form of notes on their website, in their Mediation Agreement or more usually in their email confirming the booking. Some of the guidance can be very prescriptive. Attention is drawn in **Chapter 13** on the Mediation Agreement to some examples of draconian requirements. Some mediators issue directions or stipulate (as the Jackson ADR Handbook puts it). Others are more relaxed.

Advocates should read them as soon as they become available and consider whether or not they are going to be able to comply. If there is any doubt telephone the mediator and discuss the problem. Most mediators will be very accommodating. They do want to do the mediation after all.

Pre-mediation conversations were discussed in **Chapter 3**. They are worth having. Advocates should not wait for the mediator to telephone them but should take the initiative. Most mediators will telephone after they have received the mediation statement and the mediation file. There is no need to wait for this stage.

What to talk about

11.07   The advocate should make sure that the mediator agrees that the conversation is private and confidential. Make it clear what he can disclose to the other side and what he cannot. The following topics may be discussed:

- background information about your client;

- who will be there and what role they will play;

- any personality issues;

- any sensitive issues;

- what the obstacles to settlement are;

- what issues are will have to be dealt with at the mediation;

- previous negotiations and offers and why they failed; and

- previous mediation experience of both and the clients and the advocates. Advocates who have never attended a mediation should tell the mediator. Everyone has to do it for the first time at some time. Most mediators will be happy to explain the process and answer any questions.

- The advocate should also ask the mediator to raise any concerns about the other side with the other side, eg who will have authority to settle, or should there be a joint opening session. Within the bounds of confidentiality most mediators will do this.

Pre-mediation meetings

11.08 Pre-mediation meetings are rare in England and Wales but more common in Scotland. Some mediators encourage the parties' lawyers to meet them before the day of the mediation. These meetings are often similar to the pre-hearing procedural hearings in arbitrations. For most mediations they are of limited value. If the dispute is complicated and there are a large number of parties a case management discussion can be useful, but most of it can be done by email or conference call.

Sometimes a meeting with the mediator is useful for the client. This is especially true if the client has no experience of mediation or is reluctant or suspicious about the whole process, but make sure that:

- all discussions are private and confidential;

- that it is clear whether the mediator will make an additional charge for such a meeting, or whether it is included in the standard fee, and tell the client; and

- the mediator knows what the meeting is for and what issues are likely to be raised.

Mediation statements and files

11.09 Ideally mediation statements and mediation files (aka bundles) should be prepared at the same time. In practice, the mediation file is usually sent to the mediator before the mediation statement. This is the wrong way round.

Advocates should prepare their mediation statements first. Doing this has the following advantages:

- it sets out the framework for preparation;

- it will isolate and identify the main issues and any gaps have to be plugged before the mediation. In a building dispute for example it may be clear that the schedule of remedial works, which has been prepared for the Particulars of Claim is now out of date;

- it will simplify the selection of documents to be included in the mediation file;

- it will make it easier for the mediator to understand the documents if he has a roadmap to read before he starts; and

- it helps focus the minds on settlement rather than legal argument.

Both sides organise and highlight the legal arguments that are in their favour. They gloss over the weak points in their case. They usually ignore any discussion about settlement apart from saying:

- they are attending mediation with a view to settlement;

- any settlement must reflect the relative legal strengths of the clients' cases, and their own client's case is of course always the strongest;

- the other side should be under no illusion that if the case does not settle their client will fight the case vigorously all the way to trial and they are confident of success;

- they may refer to previous offers or negotiations but often they do not; and

- they usually do not explain what issues have now been dealt with or fallen away. They sometimes, but not always, identify new issues that have developed since the proceedings were commenced. Sometimes these new developments are reserved for the mediation itself so that everybody is taken by surprise.

Why are the documents prepared before the statement?

11.10   There seem to be four reasons:

- The preparation of the document file can be delegated to a junior member of staff. There may already be a document file in existence that has been produced for a court hearing. Sometimes that is simply copied in full and sent as the mediation file.

- It takes more thought and concentration to prepare a mediation statement than it does a mediation file. Lawyers and their clients are usually under time pressure. The inevitable tendency is to leave this task until the last moment.

- Clients, either because of time pressure or because they simply do not want to think about the problem, may be late in giving instructions to their lawyers. Often the lawyer will prepare a draft mediation statement and send it to his client for approval. He then has to wait before sending it to the mediator. To avoid delay when sending the draft to the client for approval, stipulate a deadline for replying or otherwise it will be sent it to the mediator as drafted.

- Clients may not have paid their lawyers for doing this work. Clients need to understand that, although mediation is much cheaper than litigation, it is not free.

Must I prepare a mediation statement?

11.11   The answer is 'No'. Many mediations take place without the parties having produced mediation statements and successfully end with a settlement. However, it is a good idea to prepare one.

The disadvantages of not producing mediation statements

11.12   There are some disadvantages of not producing mediation statements:

- It takes longer for the parties and the advocates to move from the advocacy phases to the problem-solving phase.

- There is more opportunity for parties to say to each other that they do not understand each other's case. This may not in fact be true but they say it anyway. They invite each other to explain it. This usually means that there is a great deal of going back over the history of the dispute and the litigation. This delays the time when the parties start to think about solutions for the future rather than problems of the past.

- The lawyers and clients have probably not taken the trouble to ask themselves: 'What do we want to achieve out of this mediation?' Therefore, they tend to be more reactive and less proactive for the first three or four hours.

What is the purpose of a mediation statement?

11.13   The purpose of a mediation statement is not what the Jackson ADR Handbook says it is. In section 14.67, advice is given on the Content of the Position Statement:

'Outline of the parties' case on the issues

… the statement needs to clearly set out the party's position in relation to each of the issues. The statement may make brief reference to statements case defences, key documents or evidence and matters of law that support the party's position. *It is important that this document persuades the other side of the merits of the case, and therefore the strength of the parties negotiating position in relation to the disputed issues of fact or law.'* [emphasis added]

Changing people's minds

Advocates are often told that their job is to persuade the other side. If this means to change their minds it is misguided. Mediations are often not a case of one side being right versus the other side being wrong, but of both sides being right. It is a question of how to manage two set of legitimate interests (the interests are at least legitimate in the eyes of the disputants.)

It is unrealistic to think that a lawyer is going to publicly change his mind in front of his client. Or that the client will suddenly say he has been wrong all along. The only exception is if there has been some crucial new piece of information, which completely changes their worldview. That does not happen in practice.

If a bombshell is delivered at the mediation the other side will retreat to their bunker. They will terminate the mediation and go back to their office to absorb the new information and reassess their position. If they have been told about the bombshell in advance they have the chance to do this before the mediation and acknowledge that there is reason for a fundamental shift. It sometimes, but rarely, happens. After all, as has been said many times, news is never as good or as bad as it first seems.

Much of the advice about how to persuade people at mediation stems from the continuing confusion between a dispute and a case (see **para 1.17**). The distinction is habitually ignored. For example, the Jackson ADR Handbook (2013) says:

> 'The mediator may ask each party to provide him or her with a statement setting out their *case***.'**

It goes on to say:

> 'The position statement is not intended to be a formal document like a statement of case used in litigation. The document is primarily intended to ensure that the mediator is fully briefed on *each side's case*. Where statements are disclosed by the parties, they form an important tactical function of giving the opposing party an insight into the strength of the other side's *case*.'

11.14   However, in a nod towards principled negotiation it concludes: 'However, it should be written in a non-confrontational style.' In other words the content can be confrontational but the style should not be.

This continues a tradition expressed for the last 20 years.

In *Making Mediation Work For You* (LAG, 2012) the authors say:

> 'In civil proceedings the parties are usually only able to mediate once they have sufficient information about the other party's *case* and *evidential certainty.*'

In *Mediation: A Psychological Insight into Conflict Resolution* (Bloomsbury Continuum, 2004) Strasser and Randolph say:

> 'Each party and/or their legal advisor, makes a short opening statement … setting out the main points of their *case*'.

In *Mediation Advocacy* (Nova Law and Finance Ltd, 2010), Goodman says that it is an essential feature of mediation preparation that each representative sends to the other:

> '[a] *statement* of their client's *case* and *submissions* that they wish to make … Like any effective written advocacy it should aim to overwhelm the opposing party and deflate expectations.'

There has not been much development since the denizens of the CEDR Training Faculty Messrs Mackie, Mills and Marsh were saying in *Commercial Dispute Resolution: an ADR Practice Guide* (Butterworths) in 1995:

> 'The opening statement should be concise yet *forcefully demonstrate* the strength of the *case*.'

The bottom line

Given this approach, which causes confusion for representatives and clients, is it really surprising that the take up for mediation has remained so low? What is needed is a rebalancing in preparation and representation There needs to be far less emphasis on preparing the legal case and more on working out the commercial settlement. Advocates needs to concentrate on making commercial deals not legal points.

Who is the mediation statement for?

11.15   All draftsmen need to be clear in their own mind about two things:

● who their audience is; and

● what is their message.

Mediation statements have various audiences: the client, the lawyer on the other side, the mediator, the other side's client. They all have different perspectives.

The lawyer on the other side

The lawyer on the other side will know the case. He will have read the documents and the pleadings and will already have formed his opinion about the case and advised his client accordingly. Unless there is some radical new argument or revelatory piece of information he is unlikely to be persuaded by what is written in a mediation statement. He is more likely to be influenced by indications of the way forward and possible settlement proposals.

Mediator

If the mediator is a lawyer he can understand legal documents. When he has read them he will still not have the in-depth knowledge of the issues and evidence that the parties and their lawyers have. It is useful to highlight the key points for him in the mediation statement.

Client on the other side

It is the decision maker on the other side that should be the primary audience. He may be a lawyer, but usually will not be. He seems to be ignored in most mediation statements. Be clear what message you want to send to him. Think carefully about the best language to use – it will not be the language of lawyers.

Own client

Some mediation statements appear to be written for the draftsman's own client rather than the other side's. There is a forceful repetition of all the other side's weak points and mistakes and all the client's strong one. Clients may find it reassuring.

The draftsman must ask himself if a partisan and exaggerated presentation of his client's case is likely to influence the decision maker on the other side. If the answer is no then why do it?

Is your message clear?

11.16 The draftsman must be certain in his own mind what message he and his client want to convey. If that is not clear to him then it will be clear to the other side. Whatever the message is, it must be set out clearly in the mediation statement so that there is no confusion. Often the message is buried in a mass of detail or left until the end. Most mediation statements are too long and contain too much detail. The decision maker reading it loses concentration. He needs to be told in clear non-legal terms early on in the document what the key message is.

The mediation statement is not a restatement of case

11.17 Despite what the Jackson ADR Handbook advises, the mediation statement is not a restatement of case. Advocates who simply restate their client's case are wasting time and an opportunity to start engaging with the other side for the purpose of negotiation and settlement.

Setting the scene for peace talks

The main purpose of the mediation statement should be to set the scene for peace talks. Each side should be persuaded to think that it is in their interests to settle the case. This is not achieved by telling each other how indefensible their position is. It is more usually achieved by emphasising the benefits of settlement. If there is any doubt about this, clients and advocates should ask themselves how they react when they receive a mediation statement telling them their case is rubbish, their witnesses are liars, their legal analysis is flawed and that they are inevitably going to lose at trial.

Although many believe that attack is the best form of defence it is not the best form of encouraging someone to give you what you want. A mediation statement, which is a reasoned and reasonable assessment of the current situation between the parties, will make a better impression on the other side's decision maker than a partisan and adversarial presentation. Explain the client's point of view about his own case and the other side's. Show, do not just assert. Do not attack and criticise the other side. They will retreat into defence mode.

Chapter 5 emphasised the importance of the client feeling that they have had an opportunity to state their side of the case and to be heard and acknowledged. Some clients want the lawyers to do this for them in the mediation statement. If they want this to be done in an aggressive and tendentious way, warn them of the risks. In fact clients will feel more satisfied that they have been heard and acknowledged if they do it in person at the mediation. They will be able to do this either publicly in the Joint Opening Session or in a private session with the mediator or the other side.

Setting the agenda

The mediation statement allows an advocate to set the agenda by highlighting those issues, which the mediator will have to address during the day if settlement is going to be achieved. Of course different clients have different agendas, but is it is surprising how much agreement there is, even between the receiving party and paying party, on what the key issues are that have to be addressed.

If that's their attitude I'm not coming!

All mediators tell stories about being telephoned by the lawyer for one of the parties who says that his client has decided not to go ahead with the mediation after he has read the other side's mediation statement. This is either because he has been so insulted by what has been said or so discouraged by the extreme expression of position that he thinks that there is no point in carrying on with the mediation. A lot of time and effort can be spent in trying to persuade the outraged client to change his mind and attend the mediation.

What to put in the position paper

Head it 'Confidential'

11.18   The question of confidentiality at mediation is complex. It is discussed in detail in **Chapter 12**. Avoid any arguments in the future over mediation papers and information by clearly including at the head of the document words such as:

> 'For the purposes of mediation only. Without Prejudice and confidential to the parties at mediation'

That is sufficient. Some advocates go further. Here are some examples:

- 'Without Prejudice Subject to Mediation Privilege.'

  As discussed in **Chapter 12**, the court has decided that there is no such thing as mediation privilege (see *Brown v Rice* [2007] EWHC 625 (Ch)). What the draftsman is probably trying to do is import the provisions of the mediation agreement about confidentiality, not calling witnesses or making collateral use of the information and documents produced at the mediation.

- The following example illustrate a different approach:

  'This Position Statement is provided for use only in the mediation on XXX and it is served on a without prejudice basis. Nothing in this statement restricts the claimant raising further arguments in relation to any matter or issue during the mediation or at a later stage should matters remain unresolved and all such rights are hereby wholly and expressly reserved.'

- Another example provided: *'without prejudice save as to costs.'* This was in lower case italics.

- A further example was:

  'WITHOUT PREJUDICE SAVE AS TO COSTS. PREPARED SOLELY FOR THE PURPOSE OF THE MEDIATION ON XX. STRICTLY PRIVATE AND CONFIDENTIAL.'

  This was in bold capital letters.

Confidential information for the mediator

11.19   There may be information which a party does not wish to disclose to the other side but wants the mediator to know. For example it might be information about the client's health or an important witness. This can be sent in a separate confidential note to the mediator. There is no requirement to inform the other side that you have sent the mediator a confidential note.

The vocabulary blacklist

The following is a list of quotations from phrases used in mediation statements and opening statements over the last 12 months. They serve no useful purpose. In fact they usually have a negative impact especially on the decision-makers.

- 'Your client is a liar.'

- 'You do not understand the law.'

- 'Even on your own case you will inevitably lose at trial.'

- 'I know more about this case than you do' – said by counsel to his own client and to the other side!

- 'We have come here today to give you an opportunity to explain to us your case which we do not understand.'

- 'In the light of the defendant's views as to the merits of its case you should be under no illusion that if a satisfactory settlement cannot be reached the defendant will continue to strenuously defend the proceedings.'

- 'We are here to settle but not at any price. If we cannot achieve settlement today then we will pursue the case vigorously to trial.'

- 'We are supremely confident of our case.'

- 'The claimant approaches mediation in a genuine attempt to bring these proceedings to an end. However that sentiment must be measured against the reality of the defendant's position in circumstances where the available evidence makes it plain that its position is a highly unattractive one.'

- 'The defendant is aware of the costs and risks associated with any claim. However the defendant is confident in its counterclaim and if there is to be any settlement at mediation (or at all), that counterclaim is going to have to be taken into account.'

How long should it be?

11.20   Most guidance issued by mediators or mediation providers say that the mediation statement should be no more than four pages long. More realistically six pages is a sensible working maximum. Multi-party and very complex disputes will take longer to explain, but very few need more than 10 pages. Most mediation statements are too long rather than too short.

Exchange mediation statements or not?

11.21   The usual practice is to exchange mediation statements. This is normally done two or three days before the mediation. They have probably already been sent to the mediator.

Reasons to exchange

- It is the usual practice so why depart from it?

- Both sides know what each other is telling the mediator.

- There is less chance of an unpleasant surprise or ambush at mediation, which helps to build trust between the parties and set a co-operative mood for the mediation.

- Some lawyers and clients prefer not to disclose all relevant information in advance but to keep something in reserve as a surprise to use at the mediation. They usually hope that it will have a shock impact on the other side, which will cause them to radically change their position. Sometimes it does. Usually it has the opposite effect. It slows down momentum because the other side needs to absorb and evaluate the new information. This takes time. Quite often a big surprise leads to a premature termination of the mediation.

Reasons not to exchange

11.22   Some lawyers prefer not to exchange. They send the mediation statement to the mediator but do not want the other side to know what they are saying to the mediator. The usual reasons are:

- They are providing information that they think is helpful to the mediator but which they want to keep confidential from the other side. An example would be information about their client's health or a change in his financial circumstances.

- They are being frank in indicating their client's real position as opposed to public position regarding settlement.

- Their client feels very strongly about some issues and they want to avoid the risk of alienating the other side by a forceful expression of these views.

- They are not convinced about the other side's bone fides. They suspect that they may not be attending the mediation in good faith to try and settle, but rather for tactical reasons to find out information which they can use in the litigation.

Exchange is better

No one expects a party in a dispute to reveal all the weak points in their case and their bottom line for settlement. However it is useful for the mediator to be told by each party how they are approaching the mediation and what they consider are the real issues that require consideration. If the statements have been exchanged it removes reasons for suspicion. Any concerns about confidential information can be dealt with by sending a supplementary confidential note to the mediator.

Examples of opening and closing paragraphs in mediation statements

11.23 You must decide whether the following examples are good or bad role models.

Opening paragraphs

'The defendant comes to this mediation with a genuine desire to settle the claim and, within certain parameters, an open mind as to how assessment might be achieved. Is in both parties' interests for settlement to be reached as soon as possible. Combined costs are fast approaching £200,000. If the matter proceeds to full trial, there is a real risk that they will exceed the value of the property, which is the principal asset in the estate and the focus of the dispute.

A settlement is, however, unlikely to be reached unless a realistic view is taken of the merits of the claim. The defendant considers that the claim is weak.'

Closing paragraphs

'Accordingly as matters stand, the defendant finds it difficult to imagine that he might agree to any terms of settlement that would involve him making a contribution towards the claimant's costs. To be clear, under no circumstances will the defendant consider making any contribution towards any success fees for which the claimant might be liable under the terms of the CFA either with your solicitors and counsel. This must be regarded as a red line, which will not be crossed'

'*Mediation*

The claimant approaches this mediation in a genuine attempt to bring these proceedings to an end.

However that sentiment must be measured against the reality of the defendant's position in circumstances where the available evidence makes it claim that its position is a highly unattractive one.

Settlement will require the claimant to take a pragmatic and realistic view of its position and the risk to it of a substantial adverse costs order'

'*Settlement*

The way in which this whole matter has been handled by the claimant has left a bitter taste (in particular the events of [DATE])). The defendant is aware of the costs and risks associated with any claim as such. The defendant recognises that there are benefits to settling both the claim and counterclaim.

However the defender is confident in its counterclaim and if there is to be any settlement at mediation (or at all), that counterclaim will have to be taken account of.'

'The defendant denies the existence of both loans and is prepared, unless inexorable settlement can be agreed, to pursue the matter through trial.

That said, the defendant is aware of the cost of litigation. Whilst it strongly believes that it will be successful defence of its claim, it is aware of the recoverable costs of litigation stop it therefore enters mediation every hope and which that the matter can be resolved on a mutually acceptable basis.'

A checklist for a mediation statement may be found at the end of this chapter.

Do you need a mediation file?

11.24   The answer to this question is 'not always'. However, in nearly all civil and commercial mediations, a mediation file of documents is produced. It has two purposes:

- to help the mediator understand the background to the dispute and to see the documentary evidence which supports either side's assertions; and
- for the parties to use as reference material at mediation.

Does the document file need to be agreed?

11.25   The answer to this question is 'no'. Keep in mind these practical points about document files or bundles:

- It is a good idea if, at the mediation the mediator, the parties and their lawyers all have the same documents in front of them in the same order. A paginated indexed file is desirable but not essential.
- There is no need to spend a lot of time agreeing the index or the contents of the mediation file. Each party is entitled to send the mediator what they would like the mediator to read. Advocates who try and exclude documents have not really understood the nature, purpose and process of mediation.
- In practice, at most mediations the document file is hardly referred to.
- Schedules of figures, photographs and plans are consulted. Copies of court orders and pages of correspondence between the litigation lawyers are not.
- The usual law of documents applies to mediation as it does at court – the one document that everyone wants to see is the one that has not been brought.

What to include in the mediation file

11.26   The golden rule is less is more. Include:

- pleadings;
- key documents referred to in the pleadings;
- correspondence about settlement;
- plans and photographs;
- schedules of loss, damages, etc; and
- costs details for both sides, eg Precedent H.

Keep out:

- court orders;
- interim applications;
- a complete set of witness statements. It is rarely worth including all the witness statements, so be selective. Some may contain a coherent and helpful account of the factual background to the dispute, but usually there is a lot of repetition of information contained in other documents;
- summaries of witness statements. If there are particular paragraphs or sections that you want the mediator to read tell him what they are.

In practice the mediation file is often a copy of a file that has already been produced in connection with the litigation. There has been no attempt to review it for relevance for the mediation. This is understandable. It takes time and money to review and create a bespoke mediation file. It can be cheaper and quicker just to make an extra copy of something that has already been produced. The disadvantage of this is that:

- irrelevant material may be included; and
- it can cost the client more money in mediator's fees. It is imperative when appointing the mediator and considering the mediation agreement that it is established exactly what preparation time is included in the fee.

Preparation time

11.27 Most mediators include a reasonable amount of preparation time. This is usually between two and four hours. Others include all preparation time in their standard fee. Some mediators appear to be very slow readers and the parties can receive an unpleasant shock when they receive a significant additional invoice for reading time.

A checklist for the mediation file is to be found at the end of this chapter.

What to take to the mediation

11.28 There is an important distinction between documents that are produced especially for the mediation and documents that have been produced for the litigation.

Documents produced for the mediation

These are not usually evidence as such, but presentations of figures, illustrations or summaries, for example an up-to-date schedule of loss or some plans showing alternative rights of way or boundaries. Take note of the following points to remember:

- They should always be prominently marked: 'FOR THE PURPOSE OF MEDIATION ONLY – WITHOUT PREJUDICE'.

- Always make sure that you take with you enough copies for all attendees plus some spares.

- Print out copies. Do not rely on them being emailed to attendees or only being available on someone's iPad. Figures in a schedule on a screen never have the same impact and authority as those on a printed page. Also it can be very inconvenient if several people have to cluster round one screen.

Documents produced for the litigation

The key documents will have been included in the mediation file. The eternal question for lawyers is: How many of my litigation files do I take with me to the mediation? Does one take it all or make a selection? Of course the answer depends to a large extent on how many there are. The golden rule is that if you are not going to take everything make sure that you have someone back in the office who will be available to email or scan documents that you have not brought with you and are now needed.

It is essential to tell your client to do the same thing, ie bring what they think they will need and have someone available who can email or scan material that they have left behind. It is amazing how often clients will say, for example: 'I have an up-to-date bank statement but I have not brought it with me'.

It is safer to take everything. All lawyers are familiar with what happens when a document is not available. Everybody assumes that it has much greater significance thanin fact it has.

Draft settlement agreement

11.29 When preparing for mediation, the concentration is on the mediation statement (position statement) and on the mediation file (bundle). But it will save time and stress later if at this stage advocates could do two things:

- draft the settlement agreement at the same time as the mediation statement is drafted;

- draft a template and the boilerplate clauses and bring a selection of alternative clauses.

Doing this will stimulate thought about what a settlement could look like and what is capable of being achieved and how, and what further steps are to be taken as part of a settlement. Sometimes these can be technical, for example serving notice in order to trigger a release clause in a contract. Thinking about this in advance reduces the risk of overlooking something. This will also make life easier for everyone at the mediation. It can be difficult after a hard day's negotiation to start drafting a settlement agreement from scratch. People are tired and want to go home. It is much easier if there is an outline document, at least, to work from.

Settlement Agreements are discussed in more detail in **Chapter 14**.

Conclusion

11.30 To conclude:

- Prepare for peace not war.

- Be crystal clear what message you want to send in all communications and contacts with the other side.

- Remember that the decision makers will probably not be lawyers.

- At most mediations the documents in the mediation file are rarely consulted.

- Most mediation statements are too long and contain too much about the law and not enough about ways in which settlement could be approached.

Appendix 1

Checklist of Items and Documents to Take to Mediation

- Laptop and memory stick
- Calculator: one is always needed. The calculators apps on the laptops never work as well and cannot be handed round so easily for people to double-check calculations
- Draft settlement agreement or Tomlin order
- Draft special clauses that might be needed as alternatives, for example:
  — confidentiality
  — non-compete
  — non-derogatory remarks
- Draft ancillary documents such as:
  — a reference in unemployment case
  — a public announcement or press release
  — form of charge
  — statement of assets and liabilities
- Up-to-date office copy entries and company searches
- Up-to-date valuations
- Up-to-date costs information in printed form
- Security documents: if any security could be offered
- Up-to-date bank statements
- Mortgage redemption statements
- Draft accounts, management accounts
- Up-to-date valuations
- Consents from mortgagees and co-owners
- Headed notepaper or a template on the laptop for any undertakings or side letters that might need to be drafted at short notice
- Telephone numbers, especially mobile numbers, and email addresses of anybody that might need to be consulted for example:
  — Counsel

- — Accountants

- — Co-directors

- — Insurers and funders

- — Partners for authority

- — Specialist colleagues to help when a knotty company or conveyancing problem arises during the drafting of the settlement agreement

- Copies of any funding agreements such as conditional fee agreement (CFA), damage based agreements (DBA) before the event (B) or after the event (NTE) insurance policies or third-party funding agreements

- Notes of any tax advice

  It is essential that clients understand the tax implications of making or receiving payments. Often they have not taken any advice and try and do so during the course of the mediation. Or they have received some informal advice on the telephone. Rarely has the actual Calculation of the tax consequences being worked out

- Copies of any written opinions or reports from counsel or expert witnesses. You may not disclose them to the other side but you may show them to the mediator

  Having them ready to show to the mediator if need be indicates a high level of preparation and a willingness to explain to the mediator and threw him to the other side why your client is taking the position that he is

- Stationery. For example notebooks, post-it notes, highlighters, stapler, hole punch, of course some of these items will be available in well resourced mediation venues such as Counsel's Chambers or solicitors offices or the IDRC or the Chartered Institute of Arbitrators but not all of them will have everything to hand and not all venues are well resourced

- Tissues and mints to hand round as needed

- Favourite snacks for when the hospitality runs out. It is essential that everybody feels well fed and watered

- Change of shirt/blouse: if you expect it to be long mediation a change of essential clothing and topping up of personal hygiene can not only refresh you mentally and give you a 2nd burst of energy it can also make the atmosphere more pleasant

- Money and change for parking and late-night taxis home. This is particularly relevant for the senior staff so that they can make sure that the junior staff are looked after

Digital storage

Many documents are now stored digitally. As was said above, if you think that a document might need to be shown to the mediator or the other side, print it out in advance and take it with you. Even in high-tech offices, printing from iPads and laptops is not always a straightforward operation and attachments can often not be read. Handing round an iPad to a group of people for them to scroll through a document is never as effective as handing out printed copies for them

Checklist for Mediation Statement

Warning

In bold capitals at the top of the front page include words such as:

'**FOR THE PURPOSE OF MEDIATION ONLY, WITHOUT PREJUDICE AND CONFIDENTIAL.**'

If it is for the mediator's eyes only and not for disclosure, say that in **BOLD CAPITALS**

The nut graph

This is the paragraph in any column in which the essence of the story is told. Keep it to 140 words, for example:

'This is a claim under the 1975 Inheritance Act. The parties are brother and sister. The brother has issued proceedings claiming that his mother's will did not make reasonable provision for him. The will divided the estate equally. It consists of the mother's house in which the brother lived during his parents' lifetimes and in which he still lives and the whole estate is worth approximately £750,000.

The claim form is at pages 1–2, supporting witness statement at pages 3–20 and a copy of the will is at exhibit 2 at page 29. Respondent's witness statement is at pages 40–51.'

The parties

Say who they are, what they do and who is representing them.

The litigation

If proceedings have been issued, summarise in two or three lines what stage has been reached and what the next step is.

Key documents

Identify any particular documents that you want the mediator to have studied beforehand.

The current position

This is not a restatement of your case and all the best points. These can be found in the pleadings and witness statements (if any). It is a non-contentious summary of your client's assessment of the current position, in particular identifying what live issues appear to be preventing settlement.

What has changed?

Help the mediator to come up to speed quickly with what he's going to have to deal with at the mediation. Identify:

- issues which have been agreed or dropped; and

- changes in issues, for example new medical evidence or an upcoming application for security for costs, etc.

Aids to understanding

In a complex case it can be useful to prepare:

- a cast list;

- a chronology; and

- an organigram of companies and parties.

In boundary disputes or damage to property claims, photographs and plans can be useful if not already included in the pleadings.

Settlement negotiations

Include copies of any offers and explain why they were not accepted.

Figures

Make sure that you have up-to-date figures for the amount that is being claimed or disputed. If they are still being produced, tell the mediator this and explain that they will be available on the day.

Costs

Include copies of your Precedent H if not already in the bundle; even if it is state what your costs to date are excluding VAT, and what new money will be spent taking this matter to trial. Identify any funding arrangements outside.

Attendees

State the names and positions/roles of any attendees.

Sub-edit

Cross out as many adjectives and adverbs as you can. Ask yourself:

- Who am I trying to influence with this document?
- What is my message?
- How would I feel if I received this document?

Send to the client for comment but do not allow the client to write the document. If there is something that he particularly wants to be said it can be said in the opening statement on the day. Remind yourself and the client that mediation is to make peace not war.

Appendix 3

Checklist for Mediation File (Mediation Bundle)

Index

It is well worth preparing the index:

- It helps the mediator navigate.
- You can send a copy to the other side for agreement.
- It makes you think about what to include and identifies what is missing.

Why have a bundle?

Remind yourself of the purpose of the bundle:

- for the mediator to know what the background to the dispute is; and
- for the parties and the mediator to use as reference at the mediation.

Remind yourself at all times that in most mediations the bundle is hardly referred to and in many cases never even opened.

Documents

- Include documents that are referred to in:
  - the pleadings;
  - the position paper (mediation statement);
  - offers and rejections; and
  - key correspondence. This is correspondence not contained elsewhere. Exclude all the ephemeral tit-for-tat litigation emails and letters.
- Pleadings – include the latest version and exclude all that have been superseded.
- Expert reports – identify the key sections that the mediator should read
- Witness statements – these are rarely useful unless they contain information that is not included elsewhere or unless other documents are referred to. Do not bother with witness summaries.

Chapter 12

Legal Issues

In this chapter the following legal issues are discussed:

- Confidentiality: can the courts find out what happened at the mediation?

- Enforceability of settlement agreements made at mediation: can a party get out of the settlement?

- Liability of mediators: if the mediator did not do a very good job, can he be sued?

The discussion does not dwell on the theoretical framework or on the historical progress of these concepts but emphasises the practical up-to-date position.

Confidentiality

12.01 Mediation is sold on the basis that it is a confidential process. How confidential is mediation in practice? Why does it matter? Does it add anything to the protection from disclosure bestowed by the concept of without prejudice privilege?

There is a basic distinction when discussing confidentiality at mediations between without prejudice privilege and mediation confidentiality. Some of the discussions appear to confuse them.

In the UK, mediators are trained to treat the confidentiality of a mediation process as sacrosanct. In their assessment at the end of their training they will fail if they do not make sure that they and the parties observed the strictest confidentiality. The one exception to this is family mediation,where disclosure of financial matters is not treated as confidential.

Why is confidentiality important?

Confidentiality goes to the essence of the mediation process. The job of the mediator is to encourage the parties to a dispute to reveal to the mediator what their true interests and needs are and to share their evaluation of alternatives to litigation.

Mediation is sold as an opportunity for clients to devise their own solutions to their dispute. These solutions can be much more creative than ones that the court could grant. They need to know that if they discuss in confidence matters that are not apparent in the pleadings, correspondence or the witness statements, they will not be disadvantaged.

Most settlement negotiations are without prejudice. They are, to that degree, confidential. However, that usually applies where the parties negotiate directly with each other not through a third-party neutral or other intermediary. That is a bilateral negotiation. With the mediator there is a third party involved and therefore the negotiations to a degree are trilateral. This introduces an extra element of complexity. A party can say to itself in bilateral negotiations: 'I can decide right now what I tell the other side and whether I trust them to keep what I tell them confidential to the process and not to try and make improper use of it later'.

In mediation a party has to decide:

● whether or not he wants to discuss confidential matters with the mediators;

● whether he can rely upon the mediator to keep the information confidential to himself; and

● if he permits its disclosure to the other side, whether he can rely upon the other side to keep the information confidential.

The decision on whether or not to disclose has to be taken in circumstances of stress and uncertainty and sometimes under time pressure. There may also be pressure from the other side and from the mediator. It may also have to be taken in circumstances of distrust and against a backdrop of miscommunication and suspicion. If the mediator is going to do his job he needs to encourage people to open up. Most mediators and most parties at an action find this easier to do this if they trust each other and are reassured that the process is confidential.

Without prejudice

12.02 The basic points regarding without prejudice are as follows:

● This applies in English law to all genuine settlement discussions, whether oral or written.

● The courts have decided that as a matter of public policy it is sensible to encourage settlement discussions and support the without prejudice rule. This means that unless one of the established exceptions applies, settlement discussions cannot be referred to later except in without prejudice discussions.

● It is not necessary for the label without prejudice to be used but it is sensible if it is.

● Using the label of without prejudice on a letter will not make that letter privileged from disclosure if in fact it is not part of genuine settlement discussions.

● The without prejudice privilege is well-established but it is not absolute.

The exceptions

12.03 There are nine exceptions to the without prejudice rule, the eight *Unilever* exceptions and the one *Oceanbulk* exception.

The eight *Unilever* exceptions are well known and were established in the case of *Unilever plc v Proctor and Gamble Co* [2000] 1 WLR 2436.

The court may order disclosure of without prejudice statements to provide evidence:

(1) that without prejudice communication has resulted in a concluded compromise – in other words was a deal reached or not?

(2) of an estoppel, ie where a clear statement is made on which the other party is intended to act and does in fact act;

(3) that the concluded agreement should be set aside on the ground of misrepresentation, fraud or undue influence;

(4) of what the other party said or wrote in without prejudice negotiations if the exclusion of the evidence would act as a cloak for perjury, blackmail or other unambiguous impropriety;

(5) of negotiations in order to explain the delay or apparent acquiescence, for instance, on an application to strike out proceedings;

(6) as to whether the claimant acted reasonably as to his loss in his conduct;

(7) of an offer expressly made 'without prejudice except as to costs'; and

(8) in the case of matrimonial communications, which are based on the public interest in the stability of marriage, where the person making the statement is likely in the future to cause serious harm to the well-being of a child.

The *Oceanbulk* exception was created in the case of *Oceanbulk Shipping & Trading SA v TMT Asia Ltd* [2011] 1 AC 662, where the Supreme Court took their cue from the House of Lords in *Ofulue v Bossert* [2009] UKHL 16 when they indicated that the list of exceptions was not closed at (8). The ninth exception comprises:

(9) admissions which aid the court in the interpretation of concluded agreements.

Mediation confidentiality and privilege: does it exist?

12.04 Mediation confidentiality does exist. It is in addition to without prejudice privilege. The High Court held in *Farm Assist Ltd (FAL) (in Liquidation) v Secretary of State for the Environment, Food and Rural Affairs (DEFRA)* [2009] EWHC 1102 (TCC) that there are two sources:

● Express confidentiality, which is a creation of contract. It arises solely out the mediation agreement signed by the parties and the mediator. The different types of confidentiality clauses, which appear in mediation agreements are discussed in **Chapter 13**.

● Implied confidentiality between the parties and between the parties and the mediator, which is analogous to what exists in arbitration.

Mediation privilege as a special privilege does not exist. The court was invited to find that there was a special category of privilege called mediation privilege in the case of *Brown v Rice* [2207] EHWC 625 (Ch). It declined to do so. The courts have commented on the concept of mediation privilege in later cases such as *Cattley v Pollard* [2007] EWHC 16 (Ch) but have declined to find that it exists. Although

Briggs LJ has argued in favour of mediation privilege, and he is the current champion for mediation in the Court of Appeal, there does not seem to be much enthusiasm for it either among the judges or the legislators to create what would be analogous to an extension of legal privilege.

What is mediation confidentiality?

12.05   In simple terms, mediation confidentiality covers three things:

- the contents of discussions between the parties whether in the presence of the mediator or not;
- the contents of discussions between a mediator and a party; and
- any documents produced for the purpose of the mediation for example a mediation statement or position paper.

These restrictions on disclosure apply whether or not a settlement is reached at the mediation. Usually it also covers the admissibility of evidence if a settlement is not reached, so that:

- a mediator cannot be called as a witness; and
- documents produced for the purpose of the mediation and statements made during mediation cannot be used in evidence in the subsequent trial.

As with without prejudice privilege, mediation confidentiality is not absolute, and there are the following exceptions:

- if the court thinks that it is in the interest of justice to hear what happened at mediation either from the parties or the mediator;
- by waiver – the consent of all the parties and the mediator is required;
- by express exception in the mediation agreement – these usually provide that disclosure be made to prevent the commission of crime; and
- if the EU Mediation Directive (2008) applies. (see below)

12.06   The obligation of confidentiality does not belong just to the parties as without prejudice privilege does. It also belongs to the mediator. This is so whether there is an express duty of confidentiality arising out of the mediation agreement or an implied one. The parties may agree to waive confidentiality as they did in the *Farm Assist* case but the mediator is entitled to apply to the court to restrain disclosure or to resist a witness summons.

The EU Directive applies to cross-border disputes. Under Art 7, each State is required to ensure that mediators are not compelled to give evidence of information arising out of or in connection with the mediation in subsequent arbitration or litigation unless either the parties agree or it is necessary for overriding considerations of public policy. There are specific exceptions to:

- protect children:
- prevent harm (physical or psychological) to a person: and
- 'implement or enforce the mediation agreement'.

The Cross Border Mediation (EU Directive) Regulations 2011 (SI 2011/1133) gave effect to this Directive in the UK. Regulation 9 provides that, subject to reg 10, mediators and the administrators of mediation have the 'right to withhold mediation evidence' in court or arbitration proceedings. Regulation 10 provides that a court may order mediators of administrators to 'give or disclose evidence' where:

- all the parties agree;

- it is necessary for the overriding considerations of public policy in accordance with Art 7(1)(a) of the Mediation Directive; and

- it is 'necessary to implement or enforce the mediation agreement'.

How do these rules of without prejudice privilege and express and implied confidentiality apply in practice?

12.07 Some commentators are worried about the encroachment on the confidentiality of the mediation process by the courts. They point out, for example:

- The *Oceanbulk* exception could be extended beyond just explaining the factual matrix or surrounding circumstances to assist the court in its responsibility to construe contracts. The court could extend its enquiries into the surrounding circumstances to investigate not just what happened in terms of chronological facts but also the basis on which the parties negotiated and what their approach and conduct was like.

- There must be a temptation for this sort of judicial intervention and enquiry if there is to be greater compulsion for parties to go to mediation. Courts will hesitate to order parties to go to mediation unless they have confidence in the competence and ethical standards of mediators and the general efficacy of the process. After all, as the senior judiciary constantly reminds everyone, mediation takes place in the shadow of the law.

In practice there are few problems. It is worth remembering as Mr Justice Edwards-Stuart recently reiterated in the TCC (in *AB v CD Ltd* [2013] EWHC 1376 (TCC)) that:

> 'I shall just interpolate at this point that all parties agree that in the light of the authorities it is open to the court when determining whether or not a binding compromise has been reached in relation to the dispute to examine without prejudice correspondence for that purpose. The object of the without prejudice rule is to prevent communications between the parties being put before the court in relation to questions of liability and in relation to the underlying dispute'.

In that case the Court heard evidence from the mediator.

12.08 In **Chapter 14**, there is a discussion about drawing up settlement agreements and what happens if no final agreement can be signed on the day but heads of agreement are prepared or offers are left open to acceptance after the mediation has finished. The courts can look behind the without prejudice privilege to see whether or not a compromise was in fact agreed and made.

In practice problems of confidentiality rarely occur. There are several precautions that mediators and advocates and their clients should take and usually do, which is why problems are rare, but sometimes they overlook them:

- Make sure that everyone understands the Mediation Agreement.

- Does it say that the confidentiality provisions cover all conversations with the mediator both before and after the mediation?

- Make sure that all conversations with the mediator before the mediation agreement is actually signed are expressed to be confidential. This is the usual rule.

- Some mediators take an eccentric view that they are not entitled to have confidential discussions with one party before the mediation agreement is signed and the mediation formally commenced. This is apparently to avoid the appearance of bias.

- Does it expressly say that everything that is disclosed by a party to the mediator remains confidential to the mediator until he is given permission to disclose it to the other side?

- If it does not, consider stipulating that the mediator may not disclose anything to the other side without express consent. Relying upon the mediator to self-censor could be dangerous, especially with evaluative and settlement fixated mediators.

- If it does, make sure during each mediation session with the mediator and particularly at the end of each session what can be disclosed.

- There may be some information which the mediator might wish to disclose at his discretion if he thinks that it will help the other side develop their thinking about settlement proposals. If the mediator is given permission to disclose at his discretion check when he returns what he disclosed and how it was received.

Be clear what and why questions are being asked

12.09   Often in mediation each side asks questions of the other. They may require factual answers, which will come out in the dispute, especially the litigation proceedings, in any event. Advocates need to be realistic and acknowledge that it is increasingly difficult under CPR for parties to conceal relevant facts and information. The courts believe in the 'cards on the table' approach and the cards have to be face up.

Sometimes the questions are designed to elicit information, which is not disclosable in the normal way, for example:

- *Questions about a party's financial position*

   This may be relevant to the other side's risk/reward calculation. The question of recoverability always has to be factored into a party's risk assessment.

- *Questions about how a proposal is made up*

   When an offer is made, the receiving party may ask how it was calculated. If it has been calculated using discounts for litigation risk, a detailed explanation may give the other side an insight into how confident the offeror is about the case. For this reason some parties prefer to give global figures including all claims, interest and costs and with no breakdown.

Receiving parties usually find an offer more compelling if accompanied by an explanation of how it has been put together. Mediators often ask for a breakdown. They want to see why the parties are apart. Being able to compare the relative calculations of risk and of the value of benefits helps them do that.

A practical solution is to provide the mediator with the breakdown but not give him permission to disclose to the other side. He can then tell the other side that he knows how it has been calculated but is not at liberty to reveal the details. The other side may be reassured that that there is apparent science behind the proposal and it is not just a figure plucked out of the air.

When asking a question through the mediator, be prepared to explain why the question and the information sought is relevant. In the end advocates have to realise that refusing to disclose information can erode any sense of trust. A modicum of trust is needed to achieve any sort of settlement in any sort of negotiation.

Beware of eavesdropping

12.10 Although much useful progress can be made by discussions or conversations on the way or in the washrooms, everyone has to be careful that they cannot be overheard. The same applies when stepping outside for some fresh air and standing near a doorway or window. Some chambers in Lincolns' Inn are notorious for being susceptible to eavesdropping, both deliberate and inadvertent.

Take care when speaking with the other side not to fall within the exception without prejudice privilege, which permits disclosure evidence of perjury, blackmail or other unambiguous impropriety. Threats or hints of duress must be avoided. Clients must be advised according, especially if there is a chance that they will be able to discuss settlement with the other side directly without lawyers being present.

Need to be consulted

Those attending the mediation need to have the necessary authority to settle. In practice, others who are not present may need to be consulted even if their authority is not strictly required. For example:

- Third-party funders and insurers may be entitled to be informed about what is taking place at the mediation even if their consent to settlement is not actually required. In practice their consent is often required.

- Parties may well feel the need to tell their spouses or partners what is happening.

- Others may want to seek advice from their accountant. Disclosure to any of these will have to be authorised by the mediator and the other party.

Binding provisions

12.11 Advocates will also want to be sure that the confidentiality provisions in the mediation agreement bind the recipients of the information. Confirmatory emails or texts are usually exchanged. Particular care needs to be taken in three situations:

(1) *Duties to third parties*

Some of those attending the mediation make it clear that they are under legal or statutory duties, for example liquidators, trustees in bankruptcy, accountants, or HMRC investigators. They usually bring this to the attention of everybody at the start or before the mediation. The standard confidentiality three provisions are amended to allow them to comply with any legal or statutory duties that they may have.

(2) *Tactical mediation*

This is where there is a suspicion that the other side is attending the mediation for tactical reasons. Although many mediation agreements provide that the parties confirm that they are attending in a genuine good-faith attempt to try and settle, there are clients and lawyers who attend mediation for other reasons. These include:

- They want to find out information.

- They may want to test what the lawyers are like or how the potential witnesses are likely to perform at trial.

- They may be testing the likely reaction to a Part 36 offer that they are thinking of making.

- They may simply want to undermine the other side's confidence in their own case or try and drive a wedge between the client and his legal representatives.

- Where the other party is being represented by lawyers on a CFA or a DBA or where there are insurers involved, they may want to put pressure on the funders or lawyers by making offers which might cause them to think twice about continuing to act or provide funding or cover. As explained in **Chapter 7**, any sensible representative will have discussed these zones of uncertainty with clients before the mediation.

(3) *Hard bargains*

The natural inclination for all negotiators is to try and get the best deal for themselves. Sometimes a negotiator finds himself in a much stronger position than the other side and wants to exploit it to his maximum advantage. This can happen where there is an imbalance of power between the parties, for example, where there is a large well-funded corporation on one side and a financially destitute individual on the other.

There are two considerations to bear in mind:

- The European Code of Conduct for Mediators specifically requires mediators to address imbalances of power. A powerful party should be careful about what it says to the mediator and the other side about how much more powerful it is.

- Agreements, which have been obtained in circumstances of duress or other unconscionable conduct, maybe set aside. This is discussed in more detail in **Chapter 15**.

Parties to mediation must be aware they cannot say whatever they like at mediation and be absolutely certain that their words will not come back and cause them problems.

Can mediators be witnesses?

12.12   The answer is yes. But advocates and parties must remember:

- In most Mediation Agreements, the parties agree not to call the mediator as a witness. Some agreements go further and say that if a party does call the mediator as a witness they must indemnify him as to his costs, including paying a professional rate for his time. This at the least recognises that there is no absolute bar under English law to a mediator being called as a witness.

- The circumstances in which mediators could be called are not certain but seem to be the same as those giving rise to the exceptions to the without prejudice rule or mediation confidentiality.

- Many mediators have adopted the practice of destroying their notes and other documents provided to them for the purpose of the mediation. They see this as a defensive mechanism because it will mean that their evidence will be less reliable and therefore less relevant to the trial.

- It should be noted that the 'I cannot remember anything' defence to a witness summons does not work. As the court held in *Farm Assist:*

  'Whilst the Mediator has said clearly that she has no recollection of the mediation, I accept that this does not prevent her form giving evidence. Frequently memories are jogged and recollections come to mind when documents are shown to witnesses and they have the opportunity to focus.'

- Mediators should be aware that they are often required to retain their notes for professional indemnity insurance purposes. If a claim is made against a mediator, his insurers will not be happy if he has no recollection of what occurred. Many professional negligence actions, brought several months or years after the events complained of, become a battle of the attendance notes.

The question of mediator liability is discussed at **para 12.17** of this chapter.

Can settlement agreement made at mediation be enforced?

12.13   There are two different scenarios:

- where the mediation takes place after proceedings have been started; and

- where the mediation takes place before proceedings have started.

Where proceedings have started

The usual procedure is for there to be a Tomlin Order. The fact that this is not a judgment making it more acceptable to the paying party. Its advantage is that if the paying party does not comply with the terms of settlement, the innocent party can immediately apply for judgment and enforce the order. It is not necessary to commence fresh proceedings to enforce the agreement.

Part 40.6.2 of the CPR as set out in the White Book (2013) sets out the three orders that the court can make in conjunction with a Tomlin Order:

'(i) that the proceedings be stated to enable the agreed terms be put into effect

(ii) that, if the agreed terms require it, then payment out monies paid into court and provision for accrued interest thereon

(iii) for costs be assessed, whether between the parties or out of public funds'.

There is further discussion about settlement agreements and Tomlin Orders is in **Chapter 14**.

Where there are no proceedings

12.14　The parties sign the settlement agreement. This is a contract and all the usual rules for drawing up effective contracts apply. If one of the parties does not perform, the innocent party has to issue proceedings to enforce the settlement agreement.

In practice now, most mediation agreements provide that, in order to be legally binding, any settlement has to be recorded in writing and signed by the parties. This was discussed in **Chapter 13**.

In mediations where the parties are legally represented there are mercifully few problems. Where parties represent themselves more difficulties arise. This is particularly true where the mediator is not legally qualified or declines to be involved in drawing up of the settlement agreement.

The agreement is not signed on the day

12.15　Problems can still arise when a mediation produces a settlement but the agreement is not signed by all the parties on the day. If there is still an appetite for settlement, the problem can arise, as has been seen in *Brown v Rice,* if there are subsequent discussions. The question is: what rules are governing the formation of a contract that is a settlement agreement? Does the settlement agreement have to be in writing in accordance with the stipulations in the mediation agreement? Or do the ordinary rules of without prejudice discussions leading to a concluded settlement apply? In other words, can a legally binding settlement agreement be concluded either by exchange of e-mails or by telephone calls?

In the case of *Brown v Rice,* the court held that the subsequent telephone calls, purportedly setting out offers left on the table at the previous day's mediation, did not form a concluded agreement. This was for two reasons:

- There was not sufficient certainty about how, if the offer had led to a concluded agreement, the proceedings were to be disposed of. Was it by Tomlin order or by judgment?

- The mediation agreement stipulated that any agreement, in order to be legally binding, had to be in writing and signed by the parties.

The mediator was not called to give evidence. By contrast, in the more recent case of *AB v CD Ltd,* the court directed that the mediator attend the trial to give evidence on what was said in telephone conversations that took place after the mediation day. The court considered whether or not these telephone conversations took place as part of the mediation and on the terms of the mediation agreement.

The relevant clauses in the mediation agreement provided that:

'Clause 1

The parties with, unless and until one of the parties withdraws from the mediation or it is otherwise determined, use their best endeavours to resolve their dispute by mediation and will take all such steps as may be necessary to participate fully in the mediation process ("the mediation") including the taking of all preparatory steps for the mediation hearing ("the hearing"). The provisions of the code of procedure set out in the appendix hereto, as supplemented or varied by this agreement, shall apply to the mediation and are incorporated in and form part of this agreement.

Clause 2

The parties appoint a person named in the mediation particulars as the mediator.

Clause 3

The hearing shall take place at the date, time and play set out in the mediation particulars. If the dispute has not been resolved at the end of the time allotted for the hearing, then, with the agreement of all the parties and the mediator, this hearing may be continued or may resume at such time and place as the parties and the mediators may agree.'

Clause 8, which the judge identified as being important provided that:

'Clause 8

The hearing shall continue during the time allotted and shall determine upon the happening of any of the following events:

8.1 The mediator, in his absolute discretion, determines that no useful purpose will by served by continuing the hearing.

8.2 The mediator, in his absolute discretion, determines any reason that the mediation ought to be terminated or adjourned, and a mediator shall not be required to give its reasons for so determining

8.3 One of the parties withdraws from the mediation.

8.4 The parties reach agreement.'

Clause 9 ,which the judge also identified as being important, provided that:

'Clause 9

If agreement is reached between the parties, the same shall not be legally enforceable unless incorporated into a written settlement signed by them or their representatives who shall be deemed to have full authority to enter into such settlement agreement on their behalf.'

12.16   The judge found:

- The agreement by the claimants to leave their offer open, made during the hearing, after the conclusion of the hearing and the defendant's agreement to consider it did amount to an agreement by the parties to continue the mediation until the defendant either accepted or rejected the offer or it was withdrawn. However, he concluded that there was no evidence before the court that the parties agreed to extend the mediation process beyond this.

● The sensible decision to continue to use the helpful services of the mediator was made to facilitate settlement but was made on an ad hoc basis, not on the terms of the mediation agreement.

● A binding agreement was reached when the claimant's solicitor telephoned the mediator to communicate the claimant's acceptance of the offer of the defendant's figure for damages, together with the claimant's costs to be assessed on the standard basis if not agreed, and the mediator then communicated that acceptance to the defendant's solicitors. It was by the second conversation that the agreement was concluded. It was a term of the agreement that the action would be disposed of by way of a Tomlin Order.

Can mediators be sued?

12.17   The answer is an unequivocal 'yes'. In the UK, there is no mediator immunity as there is in some jurisdictions such as the United States and Australia where there are some forms of immunity.The barriers to successfully suing a mediator are:

● *The limitation and exclusion of liability contained in most mediation agreements*

These are standard form documents. There is considerable doubt in the mediation community as to whether or not these limitation clauses will in fact be upheld. Some mediators do not even include them. They presumably rely upon not being in breach of contract or being negligent, their professional indemnity insurance, and the difficulty any claimant will have in establishing breach, causation and loss.

● *Establishing breach*

There is no reported case in the UK on what constitutes a breach of the standard of care that a mediator should display when carrying out the mediation. Some examples are obvious such as inadvertently or deliberately disclosing confidential information without permission, leaving his notebook in one room open at a page showing confidential information that he has been given in the other room, for example an explanation of their BATNA.

Evaluative mediators, who give advice and offer opinions on the merits, put themselves in the same position as anybody else who volunteers advice. If the mediator advises negligently and the recipient can show reliance, then on the face of it there is a claim against the mediator.

A mediator who fails to communicate accurately what one party has asked him to tell the other side is negligent and also in breach of contract. If he is instructed to pass on information including a proposed settlement and does not want to do so, he must tell the parties asking him that is not going to do it. He cannot just not do it without informing the party who has asked him to.

12.18   A mediator can always refuse to accept instruction if he wants to. What effect such refusal may have on the mediation is another matter. The reason for not accepting the instruction will have to be a very good one and not just because the mediator thinks it is ill advised or might upset the recipient and set back progress towards a settlement.

If he fails to communicate an acceptance of an offer when instructed to it would be negligent and in breach of contract. Anecdotally there is evidence of mediators failing to communicate an acceptance and the mediation has failed. In subsequent telephone calls between the solicitors it was discovered by the offering solicitor that no acceptance had been communicated. In the end a deal was done on the same terms that had been proposed at the mediation. There was little direct loss apart from a small amount of additional legal costs. But there was a complaint against the mediator to his appointing body, which led to a refund of fees.

If a mediator mis-communicates what he has been told to pass on, either inadvertently or deliberately, he is negligent. It might disentitle him to claim his full fee because he not provided the service that he contracted to provide. However, it might be difficult to show that the breach has caused any loss at all let alone a quantifiable one.

Clearly the parties are entitled to expect that the mediator will not misrepresent their position to the other side or the other side's position to them. As has been explained in **Chapter 9**, some mediators encourage a party by telling them that if he can accept this proposal they will go and do their best to persuade the other side to accept. Mediators who do this put themselves in a difficult position. They become advocates for the other side's proposal. In their enthusiasm they may say that the proposal they are putting is the other side's final proposal and is not negotiable. The mediator may not have been told is that it is. He may be misinterpreting the message that the other side is giving them. This is why it is always good practice, if negotiations appear to be stalling and perhaps reaching final deadlock, to speak directly to the other side's lawyers or to encourage clients to speak directly to each other. Any miscommunications whether deliberate or not will be revealed and can be corrected.

Even if a settlement could have been made at the mediation but because of a mistake by the mediator it was not, this does not mean that there is an actionable breach. It is always open to the parties to speak after a failed mediation to find out what each other's present thinking is. There is always room for further negotiation direct between the parties. The chain of causation can easily be broken.

There is a distinction between negligence and poor service. Mediators who do not read the papers properly beforehand or who arrive at the mediation late and tired because they have been working late the previous day may not give their best.

The level of service could be so bad as to amount to breach of contract rather than just a failure to meet reasonable expectations. The first thing to do is to write a polite measured detailed letter of complaint to the appointing body or, if is a self-administered scheme, to the mediator.

12.19   It is a sadly the case that many mediators, even experienced practitioners and lawyers, react in a very defensive way to any sort of criticism. Sometimes this is because the mediators are so busy and famous that they think that they are beyond reproach. Other times it is because they do not have enough work and want to hang on their fees. The CMC may need to be enlisted. Details of their complaints procedure can be found on their website.

The difficulties in suing mediators is recognised by the professional indemnity insurance market. Insurers regard mediators as a low risk. This explains why mediators are charged very low premiums compared with what solicitors. barristers and other professionals who engage in mediation related activities have to pay.

Mediation, which is intended to reduce litigation, is spawning litigation. The courts are not showing any disinclination to take in these cases and make mediation law. Sooner or later there will be more cases against advocates and mediators.

Conclusion

12.20   To conclude:

- Make sure that clients understand that the mediation process is without prejudice and is confidential, ie they cannot discuss it with anyone else who is not bound by the confidentiality provisions in the mediation agreement.

- Make sure that clients understand that the courts can, in certain circumstances, enquire into what happened at the mediation.

- Settlements made at mediations are legally binding.

- Ensure that someone with sufficient authority to settle is present.

Chapter 13

The Mediation Agreement

This chapter covers:

- The standard terms in a mediation agreement for civil and commercial mediations
- A checklist of points for a mediation agreement

General

13.01 Judging by the number of parties at mediations who do not read the mediation agreement before they sign it, the importance of the mediation agreement is not understood. Most mediations are creatures of contract. The rights and duties of the parties towards each other are set out in the agreement. This includes the rights and duties of the mediator.

There is a difference between self-administered and administered mediations. In that in administered mediations the mediation provider will usually send out their standard mediation agreement it to be signed and returned to them and require this to be done before the mediation takes place. It does not always happen and some providers are happy for the mediation agreement to be signed on the day. This is what usually happens with self-administered mediations.

Some mediation agreements are self-contained documents. Others refer to terms and conditions or standard procedures and rules contained in other documents. Of course they have all to be read together.

Most mediation agreements cover the same key points but their provisions are not all the same. It is important to check what they say, for example, about how the mediation can be terminated, whether there is a presumption of confidentiality and in what circumstances a mediation can be extended.

It is important that the client has an opportunity to read the mediation agreement before the mediation day. It is surprising how often the advocate has not even sent the agreement to his client let alone taken him through it and asked whether or not he has any questions.

If the client has not seen the mediation agreement before the mediator comes into the room and asks everyone to sign it there can be a false start to the day. The client looks to his solicitor wondering what is going on. Usually the solicitor says: 'I have read it and it is standard form.' An experienced mediator will always ask the client whether they would like to read it before they sign. Nearly every client says that they would. Some read it very carefully, whilst others scan it.

The problem is that on the day of the mediation the client is already under pressure. He is feeling stressed because of the mediation itself. He is receiving a lot of new information. He may not be able to quickly take in the full meaning of the mediation agreement. If a client thinks that his solicitor has not kept him fully in the picture he might start to feel unhappy straightaway. This does not set the right tone for the mediation. If the client eventually settles and on reflection wishes that he had not he might start complaining to his solicitor that he had not realised what he was letting himself in for. If he has not been given a proper opportunity of considering the mediation agreement before signing it he may well have grounds for complaint.

There follows an analysis of a standard form mediation agreement clause by clause. The examples of wording have been taken from mediation agreements that are currently in use.

Clause: The parties

THE FOLLOWING PARTIES namely:

1. (represented by [   ])

2. (represented by [   ])

(collectively the 'Parties') hereby agree to appoint [ ] ('The Mediator'), to administer the mediation of the Dispute on the following terms and conditions:

Comment

13.02 It is essential to make sure that the parties are correctly described. This is particularly important when there are corporate entities or trading names. Exactly the same care has to be taken as when drafting commercial agreements. Sometimes, as part of a settlement, a parent company which is not actually a party to the dispute will join in, for example as a guarantor, or promise to procure that something happens, or other group members may agree, for example to waive any claims they may have. Quite often group companies will have given their authority to the company representative to bind them at the mediation. They may not actually be parties to the agreement to the mediation agreement. This can be important for the confidentiality provisions. It can therefore be sensible to widen the definition of party by including any related or subsidiary companies, etc.

Mediation rules

---

1. Mediation Procedures

1.1 The mediation shall be held and conducted according to this Agreement to Mediate ('Agreement').

1.2 The Mediator's standard Terms and Conditions as specified at http://sw com/terms-and-conditions are incorporated into this Agreement. Where there is any conflict between them and this Agreement, the terms of this Agreement shall prevail.

Comment

13.03 Administered mediations are conducted according to the rules of the service provider. Sometimes these are contained in a separate document or available on the website. They must be consulted.

One well-known mediation provider expressly provides that the legal representative confirms when he signs his name on the mediation agreement that:

'I have advised my client on the meaning and effect of this agreement, undertake to ensure that my client's fees are paid to [XXX] in accordance with the terms of this agreement, and acknowledge and agree that my firm is liable for the costs of the mediation in the same way as it is liable for disbursements incurred in the course of litigation and shall be a responsible to and shall indemnify [XXX] for payment of the fees set out herein in the event of my client's failure to pay pursuant to this agreement.'

Some of the rules contained in procedures can be quite prescriptive. For example, CEDR, in the 2014 edition of the Model Mediation Agreement, provides in clause 1:

'The parties agree to attempt in good faith to settle their dispute at the mediation and to conduct the mediation in accordance with this Agreement and consistent with the CEDR Model Mediation Procedure and the CEDR Code Of Conduct for Mediators current at the date of this Agreement.'

In the procedure, the parties agree that they will prepare and exchange a case summary for the mediation specifically and send the mediator one copy of the bundle of documents no less than one week before the date of the mediation. It expressly provides that the good faith of a party may be questioned if they do not submit documents on time.

In other words if you do not send in your documents on time your client is in breach of the agreement. Who said mediation was not like litigation?

Another well-known provider stipulates that 'each party will:

● Attempt to agree a bundle of relevant documents ('documents bundle') and supply the mediator with the documents bundle by the date set out in paragraph 3 of the Mediation Details.

● Exchange with each other and supply the mediator with a confidential mediation case summary ('case summary close') by the date set out in paragraph 3 of the mediation details.

The rules of some providers can also be prescriptive about who can attend the mediation. The JAMS rules provide: 'persons other than the parties and their representatives may attend only with the permission of the parties and with the consent of the mediator.'

Clerksroom provides: 'no other person shall attend mediation without the consent of the parties and the mediator'.

By contrast the ADR group says: 'every party should notify ADR Group and other parties involved in mediation of the names of those people intended to be present at the mediation session and indicate their capacity at the mediation is a principal, representative, adviser or otherwise.'

Clause: The Dispute

1.3 The Dispute shall mean [all matters in dispute between the Parties arising out of]

Comment

13.04   It is important to define the dispute. This serves several purposes:

- It focuses the parties' minds on what they are actually going to discuss and try and settle.

- It helps prevent disputes in the future if there is either no settlement at all, there is a partial settlement, or there is a settlement in this matter but further related matters give rise to litigation.

- In theory there should not be a problem because if there is a settlement the settlement agreement should adequately define what has been settled. In practice most parties want as wide a settlement in as final form as possible. Although in practice this does not always happen.

The reason why the definition of dispute is potentially important is because of the application of the confidentiality provisions (see below). It is not unknown for a party to allege after the mediation that some sort of an admission was made, which was not covered by the without prejudice or confidentiality provisions of the mediation agreement because what was being discussed is not what is now being litigated. It is also not unknown for parties to allege that whatever privilege or confidentiality attached to the mediation discussions was destroyed by some threat or unconscionable conduct by one of the other parties at the mediation. Some of these assertions may be genuine but more often they are tactical. They can still cause a lot of time, money and effort to be expended.

In practice there is rarely any dispute about the definition of dispute. If proceedings have been started there is usually a simple reference to 'all matters referred to or arising out of the pleadings in case number XX'. If there no proceedings then a little more care has to be taken. If there has been a pre-action protocol letter and response then that is often the document to which reference is made. It is analogous to a pleading.

In mediations where the issues have not been defined so formally either in pleadings or in pre-action protocol exchanges the dispute has sometimes been defined by reference to what has been set out in the position papers/mediation statements or in a list of issues or particularly detailed letter, as expanded by the position papers.

It is sensible when receiving the draft mediation agreement to suggest a definition of the dispute if one is not already included and to check the definition if one is included. Otherwise time can be can be wasted and anxiety generated at the start of the mediation.

Clause: Mediation

1.4 The mediation has been scheduled for an initial period of up to [4/8] hours ('Scheduled Period') starting at [   ] on [   ] at the offices of [   ]

Comment

13.05 It might be thought this would be otiose, but issues have arisen about when mediation starts and more particularly when it finishes. The significance of this point is not just confined to questions of costs and the mediator's fees. It is also important when considering the scope of confidentiality and formalities for concluding a settlement (see **paras 13.20** and **13.09** below).

All mediation agreements contain:

● details of when the mediation will begin at how long it will last; and

● provisions for termination of the mediation before the allotted time, either by the mediator or any of the parties.

There is usually a provision that the mediation continues if the parties want it to after the allotted time.

What is not expressly set out is in circumstances where there is no settlement, when does the mediation end? Some providers and some mediators produce a mediation record which they ask the parties to sign to confirm the start and finish time of the mediation and that it has not settled. Even in these circumstances there are questions:

● What happens if the parties agree to leave offers on the table, or to invite the mediator to telephone them the next day to explore settlement?

● Is the mediation still in session?

● Do the provisions of the mediation agreement about confidentiality and more particularly the formality of concluding a settlement still apply?

As explained in **Chapter 12** there has been litigation over these points. The experienced advocate will make sure that the position is clear and agreed by all parties and the mediator.

Some agreements expressly provide that, if the mediator is involved in any subsequent discussions or contact, the provisions of the mediation agreement still apply.

The question of when the mediation starts is usually less contentious. It only becomes an issue when one of the parties is late. Someone often asks when does the time start to run. Be prepared to learn that the time of the mediation started to run from the specified time in the mediation agreement (which at this time has often not yet been signed).

More importantly agreements often specify that its terms apply as soon as the mediator is appointed even if the mediation agreement is not signed. This imposes the obligations of confidentiality on all the parties from the start. Experienced advocates will make sure that any pre-mediation conversations that they have with the mediator are confidential.

Clause: Legally binding agreement

1.5 Any settlement reached in the Mediation will not be legally binding until it has been reduced to writing and signed by or on behalf of the Parties.

Comment

13.06   This provision is universal in civil and commercial mediations. It is designed to stop arguments about whether or not a binding settlement was reached at mediation. All that does is produce satellite litigation. This defeats the purpose of mediation, which is to bring an end to litigation.

In practice this issue frequently arises. The parties negotiate and make good progress but cannot come to a final detailed settlement. This is often because they run out of time and energy. Sometimes it is because they need further information or to involve someone who is not present at the mediation. Heads of agreement are proposed (this is discussed in more detail in **Chapter 14**).

Everybody needs to be clear and agreed about whether or not this provision continues to apply. The recent case of *AB v CD* provides a graphic illustration of what happens when it is not spelt out but the mediator stays involved in trying to help the parties conclude a settlement (see paras **12.04–06**).

---

2. Mediator

2.1 The Parties agree that [   ] will be the Mediator.'

Comment

13.07   There is no difficulty in identifying the mediator once appointed. The difficulty is agreeing who it should be in the first place. This is discussed in more detail in **Chapter 3**. The main point of this clause is to make clear the contracting parties are agreed.

Self-administered mediations are straightforward. The parties contract each other and the individual mediator. Usually the mediator will want to make clear that he is acting in an individual capacity and any liability that he may have towards the parties is his alone and not that of his firm or any organisation to which may be connected.

Administered mediations are sometimes more complicated. It depends on what the mediation provider is actually providing.

Clerksroom says:

> 'parties acknowledge that the mediator is independent and neutral, is not an agent or employee of Clerksroom and that the mediator does not give legal advice.'

This point really goes to the question of mediator liability, which is discussed in detail in **Chapter 12** and mentioned further below.

> 2.2. The Parties recognise that the Mediator is an independent contractor, there is no contract between the Parties and any firm to which the Mediator may be a consultant and no duty of care is owed by any such firm to the Parties.
>
> 2.3 The Parties confirm that they shall not bring any claim against the Mediator for breach of contract, breach of duty or negligence unless the Mediator has acted dishonestly towards them'

Comment

13.08   This topic is discussed in **Chapter 12**. For the moment it is sufficient to note that different mediators protect and limit their liability in different ways. Do not assume that all mediation agreements are the same. They are not. Clerksroom, for example, deals with the liability of the provider as follows:

> 'Save in the case of gross error or misconduct, the parties agree that they will respect the neutrality of the Mediator and any professional body to which the Mediator may belong, and not bring any claim, demands or proceedings against the Mediator.
>
> Further, the parties agree and acknowledge that Clerksroom shall not be liable for any alleged or actual loss or damage arising out of the appointment of the mediator or the conduct of mediation, whether in contract or tort, and agree they will not bring any claim, demands or proceedings against Clerksroom.'

CEDR provides that:

> 'the parties understand that the Mediator and CEDR do not give legal advice and agree that they will not make any claim against the Mediator or CEDR in connection with this mediation.'

ADR Group say that:

> 'nothing in these rules shall limit or exclude ADR Group's or the mediator's liability for any matter in respect of which it would be unlawful for ADR Group or the mediator to exclude or restrict liability. Subject to that proviso,

neither the mediator nor ADR Group shall be liable to the parties for any act or omission in connection with the services provided by them in, or in relation to, the mediation, unless the act or omission is fraudulent or involves wilful misconduct.'

The practical point is that the various mediation agreement, whether for administered or self-administered mediations,are all trying cover the same point ie exclude liability. They do it in different ways. The effective advocate has to be aware of what the scope of the purported exclusion is and how effective he thinks that it would be if tested.

---

3. Mediation Fees

3.1 The mediation has been scheduled for an initial period of up to [4/8] hours ('Scheduled Period') starting at [   ] on [   ] at the offices of [   ] at a cost of £[   ] per room. All sums referred to in this Agreement are exclusive of Value Added Tax.

3.2 The mediation fee ('Mediation Fee') shall consist of:

(i) the deposit payable for the Scheduled Period in the sum of [£   ] to include also all expected preparation time;

(ii) the additional sum of £xx.00 plus VAT for each hour (or part thereof) the Mediation exceeds the Scheduled Period up to 12 midnight and at £500 plus VAT for each hour (or part thereof) after then.'

Comment

13.09 All mediation agreements contain provisions for the charging of and payment of fees. They are not all the same. The advocate should check whether they include travel and preparation time. Increasingly travel time is included in the daily rate. It is not always and some mediators submit a supplemental invoice after the mediation.

The standard full-day mediation has been eight hours for many years. Some mediators now charge on the basis of a 10-hour day. This is possibly more realistic as most eight-hour mediations overrun by one or two hours as the parties hone the settlement agreement.

There is a tendency for parties to choose a shorter period. The usual half day is four hours but some parties choose three or five hours. They think that this will be cheaper. Sometimes it is if there is a settlement or the parties close the mediation at the allotted time.

In practice most half-day mediations overrun by an hour or so and sometimes more. This is usually because it takes longer to draft and agree the settlement agreement than people predict. As a rule of thumb it has been found that, as an example of optimism bias, people underestimate by 40 per cent the amount of time that it will take each to complete a task.

Parties rarely walk out at the exact time fixed for the end of the mediation. Discussions usually carry on. The advocate must be clear whether or not the mediator can charge extra if he has not been expressly requested to continue. Some mediation agreements provide that the mediation will continue beyond the finish time unless the parties say that they do not want to continue. Most mediators ask the parties to expressly confirm that they want to carry on.

> 3.3 This provision shall not disentitle any party to recover the costs of the Mediation in any subsequent assessment of costs whether or not there has been a concluded settlement of the dispute, which is the subject of the Mediation.

Comment

13.10 Nearly all mediation agreements provide that the parties shall split the mediation cost equally. As part of a settlement, the paying party may agree to reimburse the mediation cost to the receiving party. Sometimes one of the parties pays all the costs. This usually happens where the potential paying party is a company, for example an insurance company, and wants the matter to go to mediation or the other side says it does not have the money. A variation is where one party does not pay the whole of the cost but does pay a higher proportion than 50 per cent.

If a settlement is reached it usually deals with costs of the mediation by including an amount for them, either as part of a global sum or as a contribution towards costs. The alternative is for costs to be assessed if not agreed. Where proceedings have started this is a straightforward procedure. If the mediation is taking place before the issue proceedings this formula can still be used and an application can be made to the court for costs to be assessed.

If no settlement is reached this provision preserves the party's position on costs. In other words if cost orders are made in favour of one of the parties it can include the costs of the mediation in its claim for costs that it seeks to recover from the paying party.

Sometimes insurers in particular try and make the costs of the mediation irrecoverable if the case does not settle. In other words costs are not in the case.

> 3.4 If the Mediation exceeds the Scheduled Period, the parties acknowledge and agree that any additional time incurred is not included in the deposit amount and that such additional time will be charged for.

Comment

13.11 Usually the mediator in these circumstances asks the parties to sign a mediation report form recording the start and finish time of the mediation so that there is no argument about how much the additional time should be charged for.

> 3.5 The Parties are required to inform the Mediator, either before or during the course of the mediation session, if they do not wish to exceed the Scheduled Period.'

Comment

13.12   The sensible mediator will remind the parties that the scheduled time is about to expire and let them know that he will be charging additional time. Sensible advocates clarify whether or not the mediator is on the clock if he is not said anything, and the stipulated finishing time is about to or has in fact passed.

Clause: Legal Aid

3.6 Where a party is CLS Funded, the legal representative acknowledges that authority has been obtained from the Legal Services Commission in relation to the Mediation of this dispute, and that such authority will cover the full cost of the mediation.'

Comment

13.13   With the changes to the legal aid system this is less of a problem in practice than it used to be.

Clause: Expenses

3.7 Incidental expenses (Mediator's travel costs, refreshments etc) and disbursements will be charged at cost.'

Comment

13.14   Given the competitive nature of the mediation market it is usually possible to have these included in the day rate. Clients usually want to know how much they will have to pay for the mediation action and do not like little extras.

If the mediator is charging expenses, check whether or not he is going to drive and if so, what his mileage rate will be and whether or not he will be staying in a Five-Star hotel and travelling first class. These expenses can mount up and cause a disproportionate amount of angst.

3.8 The Parties shall pay all invoices within 7 (seven) days of receipt by cheque or by electronic transfer to the account shown on the invoice and in any case before the date of the Mediation.

Comment

13.15   Most mediation agreements make the legal representatives liable for the payment of fees and cost of the mediation as well as the clients. Most lawyers require their clients to put them in funds. It is not a good idea to argue with the mediator about payment of his bill before the mediation starts.

It is almost unheard of for mediators to agree that their costs can be paid after the mediation. Occasionally they may do this but it is not, as some solicitors argue, standard practice.

> 3.9 Interest at the prevailing judgment rate will be charged on overdue amounts.

Comment

13.16 Mediation providers and mediators reserve the right to do this but in practice rarely do so.

> ## 4 Consulting with legal advisers
>
> 4.1 A party does not require legal representatives to attend the Mediation, but is free to choose whatever representation it wishes.

Comment

13.17 The question of whether or not a party should have legal presentation at mediation is discussed in detail **in Chapter 6**. If proceedings have started and solicitors are on the record it is unusual for there to be no legal representation at all. Experienced users of legal services such as insurers may dispense with legal representation. Sometimes an in-house lawyer attends or the contract director.

It is increasingly common for there to be only either a solicitor or counsel present and not both. This is also discussed in more detail in **Chapter 6.** If counsel is going to be at the mediation alone, he needs to obtain authority from the solicitors to sign the mediation agreement as the legal representative of the party.

For smaller disputes and where proceedings have not been started it is common for parties to represent themselves. In family, workplace and community disputes it is the norm for parties to represent themselves and for no other no legal representatives to be present at all.

> ## Clause: Legal advice
>
> 4.2 Where a party is not legally represented, such party is advised to obtain independent legal advice before, during and after the Mediation and prior to finalising any agreement reached pursuant to the Mediation.
>
> 4.3 The Parties recognise that the Mediator does not offer legal advice or act as a legal adviser for any of the parties of the Mediation nor will he analyse or protect any party's position or rights.

Comment

13.18 This clause or something like it is standard. In practice it may not hold much weight at all. Evaluative mediators do give legal opinions when they give their view on the merits of the case. The European Code of Conduct expressly provides that mediators should address any questions of imbalance of power. Most mediators say that they do abide by the European Code of Conduct. A copy can be found at http://ec.europa.eu/civiljustice/adr/adr_ec_code_conduct_en.pdf.

In practice this clause is honoured more in the breach than in the observance.

---

5 Private sessions

5.1 The Mediator may hold private sessions with one party at a time. These private sessions are designed to improve the Mediator's understanding of the party's position and to facilitate the Mediator in expressing each party's viewpoint to the other side.

5.2 Information gained by the Mediator through such a session is confidential unless (a) it is in any event publicly available or (b) the Mediator is authorised by that party to disclose it.

Comment

13.19   Many but by no means all mediation agreements contain a provision that what parties say to a mediator in a private session or caucus will not be disclosed by the mediator to anyone else at the mediation without their consent. It is often assumed that this is the principle upon which the mediation is being conducted. Advocates must check specifically:

- what the mediation agreement says about this; and

- with the mediator during each private session, what he can tell the other side and what he cannot. Some mediators like to work on the principle everything is presumed to be disclosable unless they are told that it is not.

This clause also makes it clear that the mediator could call for a private session whenever he likes. So can a party. Most civil and commercial mediations are conducted on the caucus basis. In other words, most discussions take place in private sessions rather than in joint sessions. There are mediators who prefer to try and conduct as much of the mediation in joint session as possible. There is anecdotal evidence that this is a growing trend and certainly some commentators urge mediators to do this.

---

6 Confidentiality

6.1 The Parties recognise that the Mediation is for the purpose of attempting to achieve a negotiated settlement and as such all information provided during the Mediation is without prejudice and will be inadmissible in any litigation or arbitration of the dispute.

6.2 Evidence, which is otherwise admissible, shall not be rendered inadmissible as a result of its use in the Mediation.

6.3 The Parties will not issue a witness summons or otherwise require the Mediator or any other person attending the Mediation under the auspices of the Mediator to testify or produce records, notes or any other information or material whatsoever in any future or continuing proceedings.

6.4 All documents, statements, information and other material produced prior to or during the course of the Mediation, save to the extent that these documents have been disclosed already and are in the domain of the litigation, whether in writing or orally, shall be held in confidence by the parties and shall be used solely for the purposes of the Mediation.

Comment

13.20 Mediation is promoted as a confidential process. So is arbitration. The question of how confidential mediation really is in practice is not as straightforward as the wording of these provisions would suggest. This is discussed in more detail in **Chapter 12**.

The key points to note are:

- The mediator cannot be called as a witness.

- Documents produced for the purpose of the mediation not disclosable unless they would be disclosable in any event.

- Any document that would be disclosable under the normal rules is not protected from disclosure by the fact that it was referred to or used at the mediation.

The safe working assumption is that what occurs at mediation is covered by the ordinary rules about 'without prejudice' communications. There is no special privilege called mediation privilege as a matter of law but there might be an extra duty of confidentiality as a matter of the contract between the parties contained in the mediation agreement (see **Chapter 12**).

Clause: Pre-mediation confidentiality

6.5 Any communication by or through the Mediator before the commencement of the Mediation or after its termination shall, unless expressly agreed in writing by the Parties, shall be subject to the same confidentiality provisions as set out elsewhere in this Agreement.

Comment

13.21 This point has already been discussed in relation to confidentiality at **Chapter 12**.

---

7 Termination of the mediation

Either of the Parties or the Mediator shall be entitled, in their absolute discretion, to terminate the mediation at any time without giving a reason.

Comment

13.22 This provision is not as straightforward as it appears. This is because the courts have had regard to whether or not a party's conduct at the mediation was reasonable or not. This is discussed in more detail in **Chapter 8**. However, refusing to negotiate at all or walking out after a short time for no apparent reason may fall into the category of unreasonable conduct. It may also amount to a breach of warranty of good faith, which is contained in most mediation agreements.

Mediators who want to end the mediation before the allotted time must in practice have a good reason for doing it otherwise they may be in breach of contract.

Complaints have been made against mediators who have done this and fees have been reimbursed. Some clauses are rather fuller for example:

'Mediations shall terminate when:

- a written settlement agreement is executed by the parties, or

- a written notice of withdrawal is given by any party, or the time set the mediation has expired without agreement for continuation or resumption, or the mediator decides and notifies the parties that continuing with the mediation is unlikely to result in a settlement, or is undesirable or inappropriate for any other reason.'

(Independent Mediators)

In most mediations one of the parties, and sometimes both, tell the mediator at some point in the day that they might as well terminate the mediation and leave. This is almost always an expression of extreme frustration. Usually the mediator does not agree with them and asks them to stay. Usually they do and usually a settlement is reached. This is discussed at **Chapter 10.**

Walking out before the end of the allotted time may amount to breach the warranty of good faith.

---

8 Warranty

8.1 The legal representatives warrant that:

(a) they have carried out all necessary checks as recommended by the Law Society and/or the Bar Council to verify their clients' identity; and

(b) advised their clients of the obligations of disclosure on the part of legal advisers and/or mediators under the Proceeds of Crime Act 2002 (POCA).

Comment

13.23   This is a warranty given by the legal representatives. For their own protection, sensible advocates make sure but they are able to give them with a clear conscience. The rules about mediators making disclosure under POCA have been much relaxed. However, most commercial mediators will have encountered some complex arrangements, which were not easy to fathom. A private word with the lawyers usually ensues.

Clause: Authority

8.2 The parties warrant that they or their representatives have full authority to negotiate and enter into a legally binding settlement agreement disposing of the dispute at the Mediation.

Comment

13.24   The question of authority in mediations is in practice one that arises very frequently. The whole purpose of the mediation is to achieve finality by negotiating a legally binding settlement on the day. This means that there has to be someone present who can do this.

The warranty is in absolute terms. An experienced advocate will check with the client what limitations there are on authority and communicate these to the mediator at an early stage.

---

9 Signature of this agreement

9.1 This agreement is to be signed by the instructed legal representative of each party attending the Mediation (if represented) on behalf of that party.

9.2 The legal representative is liable for the fees of the Mediation in the same way as they are liable for disbursements incurred in the course of litigation.'

Comment

13.25 This makes the solicitor liable for the Mediator's fees. Always collect money on account.

Signed..   Signed ....

                                        Representative

Name ....   Name ....

Signed..   Signed ....

                                        Representative

Name ....   Name ....

Accepted to act as Mediator :-

Date...

Signed .... ('the Mediator')

Observer

Signed ....

Other Attendees

....   Who sign only for the purposes of confirming their agreement to be bound
....   by the provisions of Clause 6

Conclusion

13.26 To conclude:

● Read the mediation agreement.

● Do not assume that mediation agreements all say the same thing.

● Send the mediation agreement to the client beforehand and ask him to read it and raise any questions.

Chapter 14

Settlement Agreement

This chapter discusses:

- How to record the settlement
- Heads of terms
- Tomlin orders
- Settlement agreements

The danger zone

14.01 After a long day the parties have shaken hands. The deal is done. Except that it is not. Nearly every mediation agreement stipulates that the parties are not legally bound until they have signed a document recording settlement.

However, the clients think that the job is done. They are either:

- relaxing and congratulating themselves on getting a deal. The danger is that they now switch off and lose interest. They become impatient and want to go home and celebrate. They exert pressure on their representatives to draft the settlement agreement quickly; or

- they are carrying out a post-mortem on whether or not they should really have agreed and asking themselves whether the deal can be improved even now. They are not switched off. They are switching themselves back on to full negotiation mode. They will be putting pressure on their representatives to improve the deal during the drafting.

Mediators know that it always takes longer for the parties to draft the settlement document than they think. This is because:

- the well-established optimism bias leads people to habitually underestimate by about 40 per cent how long it will take them to complete any task;

- there is a tendency for drafting to just take longer as people concentrate on the detail;

- the tendency, even if there is no pressure from the client to do so, that lawyers have to try and improve the deal for the client in the drafting. All professionals want to try and do a good job for their clients but late-night perfectionism creeps in especially amongst Chancery barristers;

- people are tired.

The advocate has two tasks at this time:

- drafting the settlement agreement – this is much easier of course if barristers are present, as they usually take on the job; and

- keeping the client engaged and on-side. If the advocate is out of the room drafting the settlement agreement on his computer on the upper floors the client can feel alone and slightly abandoned. Experienced mediators are alert to this danger and go to chat to clients. Advocates can always ask the mediator to keep their clients entertained.

Who should do the drafting?

14.02   A number of points should be taken into consideration when considering who should draft the agreement:

- If barristers are present on either side they should do it. They are more experienced in drafting settlement agreements and consent orders and they like doing it.

- If only one barrister is present ask him to do it.

- If no barristers are present then the team with the largest legal representation should do it. If there are two representatives, the more senior can draft the agreement while the more junior keeps chatting to the clients to make sure they stay engaged and on side.

- If the mediation is being held in the offices of one side's solicitors or barristers, they usually undertake the drafting because they have access to the technology.

- If one side has brought a draft agreement that gives them a head start and they should finish off the first draft.

- If one party is represented and the other is unrepresented, the representative should do the drafting.

- Drafting by committee is never a good idea. This is true in any circumstances and is particularly true at mediation. It is much better if one person prepares a draft for consideration by everyone. Amendments can then be discussed and agreed.

The Practical Law Company Dispute Resolution section advises that: ' It may be helpful to convene a joint meeting, to allow the parties to sit at the table and finalise the agreement' In practice this is not a good idea, for the reasons given above. All that happens is that the negotiations reopen and continue. Once an agreement has been agreed in principle it is essential to have it recorded in writing as soon as possible. When the parties can see exactly what they are agreeing, amendments can be made and details clarified.

Usually mediators do not involve themselves in drafting until there is a disagreement over a particular provision or wording.

Draftsmen should remember at all times that their clients have come to a settlement. The clients want finality and they do not want to stay all night.

Heads of agreement: solution or problem?

14.03 The preference at nearly every mediation where there is a settlement is for the parties to sign a completed agreement. Clients want to walk away knowing that everything has been done and finality has been achieved. This is however, not always possible:

- **People run out of time**

  Decision-makers have to leave to catch trains. The case handler at the insurers needs to be telephoned for final consent and he has left for the day.

- **People run out of energy**

  This is far more common than running out of time. People just become too tired. This does not just happen to the clients. Tiredness can afflict barristers and solicitors who are being asked to produce and approve detailed documentation. It is especially significant if, as part of the settlement, parties agree to do something different, for example exchange shares in a company or transfer land. The legal documents required to give effect to these transactions are probably not available at the mediation.

- **The unexpected occurs**

  The litigators who are present may not feel sufficiently familiar with the newly relevant area of law to be able to advise. Of course well-prepared advocates will have foreseen this and every other possibility, but even the best prepared advocates can be caught out by the imaginative twists and turns that negotiations can take.

  In extreme cases the parties having been in a dispute with a broken relationship effect a reconciliation and decide to enter into a fresh licence agreement or new supply contract. In their newfound commercial enthusiasm they want the paperwork signed now before everybody changes their minds. The contracts lawyers have all gone home. What to do?

- **People run out authority**

  It is unrealistic to expect that the representatives of corporate bodies, insurers or funders to have been given unlimited authority to settle. Even if they had been given a limited authority it may still be subject to ratification by a higher level of seniority. In these circumstances the best that can be achieved is a contingent or conditional agreement.

Legally binding or not?

14.04 At this stage someone suggests that Heads of Agreement be signed. The essential question is whether they are intended to be legally binding or not. If they are intended to be legally binding:

- They must be clearer and fuller than if they are not.

- The advocates have to make sure that they are capable of having legal effect.

- All the usual formalities and ingredients for a legally binding contract have to be observed and included, ie offer, acceptance, consideration, certainty, and intention to be bound.

If they are not intended to be legally binding what is their purpose?

• They serve as a record of the stage that negotiations had reached.

• They are an indication of a degree of psychological commitment but there is no legal obligation to complete an agreement on these terms.

Non-binding heads of agreement give the parties the opportunity for second thoughts and renegotiation. Nobody can complain if this happens.

Temptation: Oscar Wilde misleads

14.05   Advocates may be emboldened and encouraged by Oscar Wilde's advice: 'There are terrible temptations which it requires strength, great strength and courage to yield to.' The temptation for both clients and lawyers to improve the deal during the drafting has already been identified and it may be terrible. When facing this temptation advocates and lawyers should remember:

• Most clients think that the deal is done and want to go home.

• Some clients will want their representative to effectively renegotiate parts of the deal during the drafting. They must be warned of the dangers of doing this. In the end, advocates must follow their clients instructions, but if this happens expect a long night.

• It is the clients who are paying for the representatives' time. They may end up paying for the mediator's time as well if the mediation exceeds the allotted duration.

• In most mediations the process of convergence that evolves during the negotiation towards settlement improves relations which were fractured at the start of the day. Generally people feel better about each other. Draftsmen must be alert to the danger of poisoning relations by prolonged disputes over drafting. The clients may want to do business again with each other in the future or at least be able to nod at each other in the street.

• As time passes people become tired. They go around and around in circles about the same issue. There is a danger that the draftsmen start a mini-war and demonise each other. There is a risk of contagion. They start to quarrel and have negative feelings towards each other. This is particularly true if the lawyers think that they have not had sufficient opportunity to display their lawyerly expertise during the commercially influenced day. Their clients may start to be infected. This is where the mediator should be called in.

Heads of terms: avoiding pitfalls

Include all relevant terms

14.06   Apart from the usual ones about parties, dates, consideration, etc, it is essential to include a provision making it expressly clear how any proceedings are going to be disposed of. This emerged from the case of *Brown v Rice* [2007] EWHC 625 (Ch). This was a case between a Trustee in Bankruptcy and the bankrupt's wife over a property. The case did not settle at mediation but both parties left offers open until the next day. There was a dispute about whether or not an offer had been accepted the next day in a telephone call and therefore a legally binding settlement concluded. The judge found that no legally binding offer could have been made because the terms of the offers left on the table did not specify how the action would be disposed of.

Everyone signs

Given the circumstances in which heads of agreement and offers are produced, ie late at night when everybody is exhausted, it is a good idea to make sure that all those involved in the decision making sign the document. This includes the clients and legal representatives, including counsel. This makes it harder for anybody to say afterwards that they did not understand what was being said. Sensible draftsmen also include an acknowledgement by the client that they have being advised on the terms and meaning of the agreement and by the advisers that they have in fact given this advice.

'Sleep easy' clause

It is a sensible precaution to include a clause that obliges everybody to act in good faith to amend any obvious mistake of omission or commission in the document. This is separate from the clause that imposes an obligation on the parties to perfect the document, for example by entering into a deed of security in a form to be agreed and in the absence of agreement settled by conveyancing counsel.

The wise advocate takes with him a selection of these boilerplate clauses so that they are available as and when needed. A selection of suggested clauses can be found under 'Settlement Agreements' in the precedents section on the Practical Company Law website.

Entire agreement clause

14.07 In the mediation agreement the parties agree to mediate in good faith. It can be dangerous to assume that everybody is doing that. As mentioned in **Chapter 6**, people do not always tell the truth. The way to deal with this is to provide that all material terms are contained in the agreement and no reliance has been placed on any representations or information not contained in the agreement – in other words include an entire agreement clause.

In practice this advice can be difficult to achieve at the end of a hard day's negotiation. The better approach is to identify the key information relied upon and for it to be warranted as correct.

Contingent agreements

Occasionally a final settlement agreement can be drawn up, whether as part of a consent order or as a standalone document, that is still dependent on another event, for example:

- further approval from the Board of Directors, which has to sign off; or
- a further step has to be taken, for example the surveyor may have to draw up a detailed plan before the contractor can replace the garden fence.

In these circumstances include a warranty by the party taking the further step that they will do it within a specified time and that, if it is a case of seeking approval, they will recommend that approval be given. Where a further step has to be taken jointly, for example instructing a surveyor, both parties should warrant that they will co-operate in good faith to do this by a fixed date. If one of the parties does not co-operate they are deemed to have consented to the choice or instruction of the other party.

Conditional agreements

These are distinguished from contingent agreements, although of course they are to an extent contingent because they are not final completed agreements. Here the provisions are triggered by something. As soon as it is triggered, everything else flows, for example, a pension provider agrees to start making payments as soon as the claimant's financial adviser tells them of the identity of the new provider.

The advocate must be as certain as he can that the condition is something that in the future can be met, but he must have a backup provision if the condition cannot be met. This usually happens because of an unexpected change in circumstances, for example a government change to the rules for pension transfers, which no one had foreseen.

Pre-action mediations

14.08 If proceedings have not been started, the settlement document will have to be a settlement agreement which will not be incorporated into a consent order of the court. This means that the default provisions will have to be drafted differently because the parties will not have the benefit of the enforcement methods under for example, a Tomlin Order.

Post-action mediations

14.09 The settlement is nearly always incorporated into a consent order. The usual form of consent order is a Tomlin Order. This has the advantage for the parties of not being a judgment. This can be particularly valuable to the paying party who does not want a judgment registered against him or have to disclose it to a potential lender if he is going to have to raise finance to fund the settlement.

For the receiving party, the two advantages of a Tomlin Order are conventionally:

- It is not necessary to commence a fresh action in order to enforce the settlement. The usual wording provides that: 'All proceedings be stayed except the purpose of carrying to give effect the terms of the schedule.'
- The terms can be confidential. In a Tomlin Order the order is on the face of the document and refers to the terms contained in a schedule. The schedule was

always attached to the order. Although it could be expressed to be confidential, it was kept on the court file. In fact because it was open to public inspection confidential schedules were often disclosed.

The solution to this problem was to refer in the schedule to a document signed and dated by the parties. That was not filed at court. This procedure has now been incorporated into the standard procedure for Tomlin Orders by some courts. The schedule is identified as the terms contained in a document dated and retained by a named firm of solicitors, usually the claimant's solicitors. There is no need to send the schedule to the court and in fact some courts will return the draft order if it is sent for sealing with a schedule attached.

The usual wording is:

● in the order:

> 'on the terms of settlement contained in a document signed by the parties and dated [DATE] retained by Messrs [NAME]'

● on the document:

> 'this is the document containing the terms of settlement referred to in a consent order signed on [DATE] '

> signed by [   ] and [   ] dated [   ].

Interest

The receiving party should be aware that interest does not automatically accrue on any late payments due under a Tomlin Order. This is because it is not a judgment. If there is default in paying and judgment is entered, interest will automatically accrue. It is therefore important to provide the interest will be payable on any late payments in any event.

Sealing the order

14.10   There is a fee to pay to court on the sealing of the order (as of October 2014 it is £50). There is no point in arguing about who is going to arrange for the order to be sealed. Usually the claimant is the receiving party and is anxious that the order be sealed as soon as possible. It is slightly demeaning to suggest that the other side can pay the fee.

Conclusion

14.11   To conclude:

● Make sure that someone with the necessary authority to sign is present.

● Make sure that you take the clients through the settlement agreement line-by-line and that they understand it. Try and do this in the presence of a third party such as counsel or an assistant.

- Mark the copy that you have been through with the client to the effect that you did this and note the date and time on it.

- If your client is ready, willing and able to sign, have them sign the document and give the signed copy to the mediator. If the other side are prevaricating they can see that you have signed and all that they have to do is sign and the deal is completed.

Checklist for Settlement Agreement

Who is to be a party to the agreement?

Who is the client settling with?

Are there other parties who you would like to bind into the settlement? For example, a defendant should endeavour to ensure all claimants and potential claimants are tied in.

As with defining the parties to the mediation agreement, particular care should be taken with identifying group companies.

Otherwise the benefits of reaching a settlement may be lost when a similar claim comes in from a related, but not explicitly identified party.

Third parties

What about any relevant third parties, for example, joint tortfeasors? Are they to be released from future claims or are rights to bring claims against others being preserved?

What about sideways litigation, where the parties to the settlement become involved in further litigation when one of them takes action against a third party, who joins in the other.

Consider including non-sue clauses, or at least an indemnity from the litigating party for all costs, expenses and damages etc.

What is the scope of claims being settled?

What claims does the settlement agreement cover? For example, how do you deal with existing but unknown claims and future claims?

Formalities

What formal requirements are necessary to ensure a binding settlement? For example, does the agreement need to be in writing or in a deed (for example, where no consideration is passing)?

Consider execution formalities and whether the execution clause will be effective to bind the parties.

Disposal of court proceedings

Deal with notification to the court and formalities required to dispose of any court proceedings. Is the action being stayed, dismissed, discontinued or discontinued on agreed terms (so that enforcement can take place within the existing court proceedings)?

Warranties

One or both of the parties may have relied upon information provided by the other or an assumed set of facts or circumstances when deciding whether or not to make this settlement agreement. If this was fundamental to their decision consider including a warranty that the information was accurate and complete.

A very common example is when the paying party pleads poverty. The receiving party relies on this information when assessing the recoverability risk. The paying party is often asked to warrant that its statement of assets and liabilities is true.

Is settlement conditional or unconditional?

Settlement may be, for example, conditional on payment so that the settlement agreement only becomes binding and effective on the payment of the settlement sum.

Default provisions

Will the innocent party be able to enter judgment for the full amount relief claimed in the proceedings if there is breach of the settlement terms?

Payment arrangements

What about the method and timing of payments? For example, it may take time for the paying party to raise the settlement funds and/or have the payment approved, but the timing of the payment may be highly significant to the client. How will payment by instalments be structured.

Interest on late payments

Are express provisions for interest on late payments needed?

Tax implications of the settlement

Check whether the settlement payment attracts VAT or has any further tax implications.

Legal costs

Make express provision for the parties' legal costs under the settlement, remembering to deal with any existing costs orders in the proceedings.

Confidentiality

Is an express confidentiality provision required in the settlement agreement? Should there be a carve out?

In some cases an agreed form of joint public statement, to be issued on conclusion of the settlement, can be beneficial.

Governing law and jurisdiction

As with any contract, issues of jurisdiction and governing law of the contract and the forum for any claims should be carefully considered.

Capacity and authority to settle

Ensure that the person(s) who will be signing the settlement agreement has/have authority to bind the company and to enter into the agreement, and include relevant provisions in the settlement agreement dealing with this.

Resolving disputes

The whole point about having written agreements is to remove the chances of further argument and dispute. Sometimes, even with the best drafted agreement, there can be genuine disagreement about what it means. Some mediators volunteer to adjudicate on any such disputes. If that is what the parties want then:

- it must be included in the settlement agreement to have binding effect; and
- the mediator's charges should be defined and the power if any he has to make a decision as to who should pay his charges.

Joint and several liability

If the parties have joint liability they are each liable for the full amount. If they have several liability they are only liable for their respective share.

Joint and several liability is a hybrid; the defendants are jointly liable to the claimant but as between themselves their liabilities are several, therefore if the claimant pursues only one defendant and recovers the whole amount that is due, that defendant can pursue the other defendants of their contribution.

Several defendants

The question of joint and several liability is more likely to be of interest to the defendants than the claimants in practice. Those advising defendants should bear in mind the Civil Liability (Contribution) Act 1978. Section 1 provides that a person who is liable for damages suffered by another may recover a contribution from any other person who is liable in respect of the same damage.

The term 'liable in respect of the same damage' is given its natural and ordinary meaning not the extended meaning previously given by the courts until the case *of Royal Brompton Hospital NHS Trust v Hammond (No 3)* [2002] UKHL 14.

Section 1(4) provides that a person who has made or agreed to make a payment in a bone fide settlement of any claim against them in respect of any damage is entitled to recover a contribution from a person who is liable for the same damage, provided that the former 'would have been liable assuming that the factual base of the claim against him could be established'.

It is essential to remember that this section only applies to a claim for damage and not one for debt. A joint or joint and several debtor who has settled the claim by paying the whole amount can recover a contribution from the other debtors by way of restitution.

Advisers must be careful when making settlement in a multi-party action, if the paying party intends to recover some or all the settlement from other parties, that a settlement may subsequently be held to have been unreasonable if the action for a contribution is defended. The case of *John F Hunt Demolition Ltd v ASME Engineering* [2007] EWHC 1501 (TCC) illustrates this.

Advisers also need to remember that if a party settles a claim it will not cap liability for a contribution to the damages under the 1978 Act. This is why care has been taken in connection to what has been described as sideways litigation. The case of *Carillion JM Ltd v Phi Group Ltd* [2011] EWHC 1379 (TCC) is an illustration of the problem

Claimants beware

Claimants advisers must be careful not to inadvertently lose or waive their right to a recovery from other potential defendants. Section 3 of the 1978 act provides that:

'Judgment recovered against any person liable in respect of any debt or damage shall not be applied to an action, alter the continuance of an action, against any other person who is (apart from any such bar) jointly liable with him in respect of the same debt or damage.'

It is thought that judgment includes a consent order.

Section 3 will not apply if a settlement is reached but there is no subsequent judgment. If this happens, release of one jointly liable tortfeasor or contractor will release all the others unless there is an express or possibly an implied reservation of the claimant's rights to pursue them.

Chapter 15

After the Mediation

This chapter discusses:

- What happens if the parties have not agreed
- Further discussions
- What happens if the parties have agreed
- Settlers' remorse

The parties have not settled: what next?

15.01 Mediations can end without a settlement in a variety of circumstances:

- **Almost there**

  The mediation had been productive. Good progress had been made towards settlement. For some reason the final gap could not be bridged. Generally the parties are enthusiastic about what is happening and optimistic about the future.

- **Nowhere near there**

  This is the opposite of the above scenario. No real progress has been made. Perhaps only one round of offers has been exchanged. There has been no development of thinking or approach. Neither side is showing much appetite for continued negotiation either on the day or later.

- **Meltdown**

  One of the parties walked out early. This is usually because:

  - they did not like the tactics of the other side;

  - they had received an unwelcome and potentially mind-changing surprise;

  - they decided that they had used up all the negotiation capital, both energy and goodwill, as well as reaching the limit of their financial ability to settle. It was the end of the road; or

  - one party has stated that they are making a final offer on a take it or leave it basis. If the other side do not take it they are leaving. They are not bluffing and they do.

- **Run out of road**

  The parties make good progress during the day but they have not actually settled. They reached the deadline and someone crucial had to leave for a train or another appointment. Or they were constructively negotiating but they became stuck and could not see the way ahead. They are positive about what is happening on the day and are disappointed.

Failing to settle is a not a failure – or is it?

15.02 Commentators say that not reaching a settlement on the day at mediation should not be regarded as a failure either by the mediator or the parties. They warn mediators about judging success solely by their settlement rate. Mediation can be regarded as success even if there has been no settlement. Communications have been reopened. Issues have been clarified and sometimes even narrowed. There may have been a partial settlement.

All this is true but in practice if the parties have attended mediation with the genuine intention of achieving certainty and finality they will be disappointed if they have not settled.

Of course not everybody who attended mediation is disappointed:

• The paying party may in fact be glad of a stay of execution. He does not have to pay today. He may be able to afford to pay in the future or in fact escape payment if he has a lucky day at court.

• Legal representatives who earn fees by litigating may be disappointed but that disappointment will be tempered by the prospect of further earnings. This will be true of most lawyers, even if they do not express themselves in quite the same way as the junior in a well-known set of chambers who was seen banging on her leader's door shouting with a song in her voice that the mediation had failed.

Don't let the mediation become an obstacle to settlement

15.03 The golden rule for both advocates and mediators is to try and avoid the fact that the mediation has not produced a settlement becoming an obstacle to settlement. No one wants the process of mediation to setback the process of settlement. Mediators therefore will often encourage the parties to:

• have another joint meeting before people leave for the day – the purpose of this is to review progress and identify the obstacles which prevented final settlement;

• think about taking negotiations further and even working out a provisional timetable;

• adjourn the mediation and have another go after a period of reflection or the gathering of fresh information;

• consider other methods of ADR such as ENE or MED/ARB; and

• leave offers on the table, book another day's mediation or speak on the telephone in 24 hours' time to review the position.

Leaving offers on the table

15.04 This is the most common way of leaving the negotiating door open. It has to be done with care. Most people agree to do it. After all if an offer to settle was good enough for the offeror at 8 pm on Monday, why will it not still be good enough at 8 pm on Tuesday? The offer should:

- be in writing and signed by the client as well as the representative;

- stipulate exactly what it is – there should be no uncertain or missing terms;

- stipulate the time for acceptance;

- stipulate the method of acceptance, which is usually by email to the offeror's solicitors; and

- stipulate how the proceedings are to be disposed of, in cases where proceedings have been started.

A prudent advocate will confirm in writing as soon as he can after the mediation what offer his clients left on the table.

The requirements for an offer left on the table and the difficulties that can arise, are described for example in the case of *Brown v Rice,* discussed at **para 12.14**.

Further discussions

15.05 The essential question is whether or not any further discussions are to be seen as a continuation of the mediation, or, if not an actual continuation, then carried out on the same terms as the mediation, ie the terms of the mediation agreement .The two most relevant provisions are those about:

- confidentiality; and

- the fact that no legally binding settlement is concluded until a document is signed by all parties.

It is good practice to mark the document containing the offer that has been left on the table with words to the effect that the terms of the mediation agreement still apply. If they do not apply, say so expressly. Otherwise the position is uncertain. This can give rise to litigation. As discussed in **paras 12.04–06**, the recent case of *AB v CD* [2013] EWHC 1376 (TCC) illustrates this very clearly**.** This was a case in which the parties to a mediation were disputing whether or not a binding settlement had been reached after the mediation day had concluded. There had been an exchange of emails and telephone calls both through and with the mediator and directly between the parties' solicitors.

The key question was whether or not the terms of the mediation agreement still applied. It contained the usual clause about the need for assessment to be recorded in writing. The clause provided that:

'If agreement is reached between the parties, the same shall not be legally enforceable unless incorporated into a written settlement agreement signed by them or their representatives who shall be deemed to have full authority to enter into such settlement agreement on their behalf.'

The mediation agreement did not contain a provision that the terms of the agreement should apply to any post-mediation contact through the mediator. As discussed in **Chapter 13** this is often included in mediation agreements.

The judge found that:

- The parties agreed to use the helpful services of the mediator on an ad hoc basis. There was no resumption or continuation of the mediation.

- The parties accepted that the mediation had failed.

- The ordinary rules of offer and acceptance applied to the making of the settlement agreement.

- The parties did conclude a binding agreement when the claimant's solicitor telephoned the mediator to communicate the claimant's acceptance of the offer of the defendant's figure for damages, together with the claimant's costs, to be assessed on the standard basis if not agreed, and the mediator then communicated that acceptance to the defendant's solicitors. It was by that second conversation that the agreement was concluded.

In practice if future contact is through the mediator, the terms of the mediation agreement will probably apply because most mediation agreements stipulate that any communication with the mediator prior to the mediation, during the mediation and after the mediation is covered by the terms of the mediation agreement. However, it is always better practice to stipulate if this is in fact the case.

If the terms of the mediation agreement do not apply, any subsequent settlement discussions will be covered by the ordinary rules of without prejudice communications. This means that a legally binding agreement can be made by e-mail or telephone conversations, as happened in the case of *AB v CD*. Unhappily for the parties and their solicitors there was confusion about whether or not a settlement had been made. It took satellite litigation to resolve the point. This rather defeats the whole purpose of mediation.

Do you involve the mediator not?

15.06   The main advantages of involving the mediator are:

- He is likely to make sure that the terms of the mediation agreement relating to the formalities of concluding a legally binding settlement and confidentiality apply. This does not automatically follow, as the case of *AB v CD* shows.

- He knows what was happening in both rooms. There may be confidential information he knows about each side's position, which he cannot disclose but that may be useful to him in trying to help the two sides bridge the gap.

- He remains a useful sounding board for the parties to test different offers against.

- He acts as a buffer between the two sides so that any feelings of annoyance or frustration felt by the advocates personally or their clients can be absorbed before being transmitted.

- He can encourage the parties and provide fresh momentum

The disadvantages are:

- It can cost money. Mediators usually but not always charge for their additional services.

- If a good working relationship has been established with the other side it can save time to speak direct.

- If the parties are keen to conclude a settlement they can do it over the telephone or by email under the normal without prejudice rules without worrying about the formality of both sides signing a document.

The parties have settled: what next?

Tell the court

15.07   If proceedings have been commenced, the parties must tell the court at once if the case is settled and there is no need for a hearing or trial. The Directions Questionnaire contains a reminder to do this.

Practice Direction 39A.4 stipulates that when a trial date has been fixed and the case settles the parties must notify the listing officer of the trial court. This can be done by letter. If a court order embodying the settlement is sealed, a copy of the sealed order should be sent to the listing officer.

In the middle of trial, even after all the arguments have been heard and judgment not yet given, the court must be informed of the settlement or even the possibility of a settlement.

(See *HFC Bank plc v HSBC Bank plc* (2000) *The Times* 26 April (CA) and *Gurney Consulting Engineers v Gleeds Health & Safety Ltd (No 2)* [2006] EWHC 536 (TCC).)

Post-settlement blues

After the tension of the litigation and then the mediation leading to settlement, the parties can feel deflated and rather at a loss. So can the lawyers. It soon passes. If the client was happy with the settlement, which they usually are after a good night's sleep, a congratulatory letter to the client is in order. If they were not so happy, even after a good night's sleep, then an understanding letter to the client is in order. In both cases the wise advocate summarises the reasons why the decision was taken to settle.

Three scenarios an advocate wants to avoid

Settler's remorse

15.08   This can apply to either the receiving or the paying party. It is a close relative of buyer's remorse, a syndrome, well known in auction rooms. People become caught up in the excitement of the moment, whether at auction or more rarely at mediation, and decide to go for it. They pay more money than they intended to. They experience the thrill of achieving what they wanted. The next day they wake up and reflect on the cost.

To try and avoid any such second thoughts escalating the advocate should:

- write to the client the next day summarising the decision taken and the reasons for it and the advice given;
- if counsel advised the client to settle, record this; and
- send a copy of the letter to counsel so that he knows that he is party to the decision.

Non-compliance

After they have made an agreement, one of the parties sometimes does not comply with it, either because they do not want to or cannot. They may be simply trying to renegotiate some extended terms of payment or they may have decided that they want to overturn the whole agreement. In both cases they are in breach of the agreement. The different methods of enforcement are discussed at **para 15.12.**

The basis for challenge

15.09   The usual grounds on which the parties have disputes after a settlement agreement has been reached, whether by where Tomlin order or not, are:

- there is no valid agreement. This is rare but it happens and is usually over whether there was offer and acceptance or sufficient certainty (see *AB v CD* and *Brown v Rice);*
- misrepresentation. This is not unknown, hence the practice of including warranties in settlement agreements;
- duress. This is also not unknown (see *Farm Assist*). The mediator is not there to make sure that the bargain is a fair one, unless there is a blatant imbalance of power;
- mistake is sometime alleged. This is the danger of mediations going for hours when everyone is tired;
- undue influence. This can be a problem when one of the parties is influenced by another, for example the wife of the bankrupt being pursued over a transaction is under the influence of her husband;
- unconscionable conduct. This does arise, usually in the context of discussions between the parties direct without lawyers present and in the worst cases without the mediator present either;
- uncertain terms. This is raised. It is often the result of hurried drafting by exhausted people;
- no offer and acceptance and lack of consideration. These two challenges can arise if the parties are unrepresented and the mediator is not legally trained or experienced in contract negotiations;
- incapacity. Doubts about whether a client is really understanding what is going on in a mediation do arise. This is usually with clients who are very old or who

have suffered behavioural problems for which they take medication. The two main worries are inability to concentrate and to remember what has previously been said . Mediators can usually be relied upon to raise any concerns they may have with the party's advisers;

- lack of writing where this is required as a formality. This can be a problem if ancillary documents are required to give effect to the agreement;

- lack of authority. This crops up more than it should. Advocates need to make sure that there are signed letters from companies confirming the authority of the directors;

- illegality. Thankfully this is rare;

- frustration and impossibility. These two do arise. Hence the need for a default provision as discussed in **Chapter 14**.

The only limit is the imagination of the defaulting party's legal advisers.

Warning to challengers

15.10 Anybody considering challenging a written settlement agreement should bear in mind that as a matter of public policy the courts have said that a 'clear compromise' agreement will be 'robustly upheld'. In the case of *Rothwell v Rothwell* (2008) EWCA Civ 1600 the Court of Appeal said:

'As a matter of public policy it is important that this Court should signify that if the parties arrive at a compromise, a clear compromise, within the mediation process, then that compromise will be robustly upheld by this court.'

Setting aside a settlement

If, despite these warnings, a party wishes to set aside a settlement, the following methods are available:

- If the settlement agreement is embodied in the court order a new action will have to be started seeking either:
  — an order to set aside the agreement; or
  — a declaration of invalidity.

  These sorts of actions can be just as expensive as the original ones an even more acrimonious because of feelings of betrayal. The original issues are not tried so to that extent the party is not achieving their day in court.

- If the settlement agreement is embodied in a final order or judgment but not yet perfected a party can apply for relief.

  If it is embodied in a final order or judgment which has been perfected it can be set aside:
  — by consent of all the parties; or
  — by new action alleging some grounds for an validating the agreement.

The court does have the discretion to set aside a consent order if it is satisfied that the consent lacked authority and the application is made in good time.

● If the settlement is contained in an interim order the court which made it can set it aside if it is proved that it was made under a mistake.

Enforcing settlement agreements

15.12   If there is a breach of the settlement agreement the following methods are available. Which ones are appropriate will depend upon the circumstances:

● If a settlement agreement was not embodied in a court order, the innocent party will have to start a fresh action for breach of contract.

● If the settlement agreement is ordered in a court order or judgment, the method of enforcement depends on whether there is:

— an order or judgment for the immediate payment of money. In this case the usual methods are charging orders, writs of possession or winding up orders;

— a Tomlin Order – without issuing fresh proceedings the innocent party can enter judgment or order; or

— an injunction by consent and undertakings to court. These can be enforced by an application to court.

● If one party tries to start fresh proceedings or tries to continue existing ones despite the settlement, the innocent party can claim as a defence that there is a settlement and apply for a stay of proceedings. This can be done by asking for the hearing of a preliminary issue that the proceedings have been compromised. There is no need to commence a fresh action.

● If one party disputes that there is a binding settlement at all the other can apply to the court to stay all further proceedings and apply for a declaration that a binding settlement has been made.

Suing a mediation advocate

15.13   Can a mediation advocate be sued? The answer to this is 'yes'. The ordinary rules of negligence and breach of contract apply. There is no representatives' or mediation advocates' immunity. The danger areas for mediation advocates are:

● Failing to explain precisely what the settlement agreement or, in order meant. Advisers are under a duty to do this as the case *of Frost v Wake Smith and Tofields Solicitors* [2013] EWCA Civ 772 makes clear.

● Failing to explain how the financial implications of the settlement affected the client. Often clients complain after the mediation that they did not realise how much would be deducted from the amount they receive and are disappointed at the net receipt they actually recover.

● Failing to explain throughout the course of the dispute and in particular the proceedings what the risks of going to trial were. This often results from a failure to review the case as it proceeds.

- Failing to make sure that, if counsel is instructed, he has been fully instructed. Too often this happens at the last moment. This can be because the client has not put his solicitors in funds to cover counsel's fees.

- Failing to make clear how the mediation has ended. This is particularly true where a final settlement agreement has not been signed. Heads of agreement may have been signed. A draft settlement agreement may have produced. All the issues are settled and a document signed but it is a contingent or conditional agreement. There is no obligation on a solicitor to make sure that a settlement is reached but there is an obligation to make sure the client understands whether one has been reached or not. See the case of *Frost*.

- Failing to advise the client whether or not to go to mediation at the appropriate time. This can happen if the representative takes an over-optimistic view of the client's chances of winning a trial and fails to take account of the views expressed by the court in recent cases that having a firm belief in the strength of one's case by itself does not mean that a refusal to go to mediation is reasonable.

- In particular, failing to advise the client of the potential cost consequences of refusing to go to mediation.

Remorseful clients may seek solace by bringing a claim against their advisers. If they cannot overturn the agreement and it is difficult to overturn a settlement agreement made after negotiation and with the benefit of legal advice they may decide that it was their adviser's fault.

15.14   Mediation is already producing a healthy annual crop of satellite litigation. This is not likely to dry up in the near future. Here is a non-exhaustive list of the types of complaints that have been made against advisers arising out of mediations:

- The clients were forced into a settlement either through pressure from the other side which their advocate did not protect them against or by their own advisers who for their own selfish reasons wanted a settlement.

- They did not really understand what was going on. They received too much information too quickly. It was not processed and explained to them by their advocates. The day went on too long and the clients were too tired, hungry or stressed. They should have been protected against themselves.

- The financial consequences of the settlement were not explained to them. In particular:

  — They did not understand what their net position would be after payment of all costs insurance premiums, success fees and the like.

  — They were not given a worked example.

  — There are expecting to receive more and no one told them but their expectations were misplaced.

- No one properly explained the impact of BTE or an ATE insurance or how third-party funders would recoup their investment.

- When the lump sum offer was made, the solicitors did not explain how that would be apportioned between costs and damages.

- When the offer was made to pay a reasonable contribution towards costs or the costs to be assessed if not agreed, it was not explained to them they would be liable for any costs not recovered from the other side.

- The advisers changed their mind without warning. Having told the clients that they were going to win at trial and had a very strong case, the solicitors seem to change their mind at mediation and press for settlement.

- The advocates did not seem properly prepared compared with the other sides' representatives and did not seem to be able to control the mediator or to stand up to him. They let him dictate what was happening on the day.

- They had not explained the implications of Part 36 offers.

- The solicitors failed to disclose to their own client what had happened so far in the litigation. In particular they did not tell them whether any Part 36 offers had been made or whether any interim costs orders have been made against the clients. It is astonishing how often clients learn for the first time at mediation what orders have been made against them (or sometimes in their favour) in the litigation to date.

- There is no doubt that mediation can be an anxious time for solicitors as they may have to disclose, through questioning from the other side, their own client or the mediator, matters that they ought to have told their clients about previously but failed to do.

Protective measures

15.15   Advocates can protect themselves by:

- carrying out a PMA with the client before the mediation and recording the conclusions in an attendance note which is sent to the client or in a letter recording the same things;

- making a written note during the mediation of advice given by the solicitors or counsel;

- making a written note of any comments about liability or the suitability of settlement proposals made by the mediator;

- making sure that the client writes out in his own hand any offers that he wishes to make at the mediation and keeping a copy of them;

- sending a summarising letter the day after the mediation; and

- making sure that he is familiar with the file, has the documents to hand, has spoken to or obtained advice from counsel (if counsel is instructed), participated in or absorbed the results of a PMA and has read and inwardly digested the contents of this book

Protection against lies

15.16   It is not unknown for parties at mediation, despite what they have agreed to in the mediation agreement about negotiating in good faith, to tell lies, whether by omission or commission. A common example is where they plead poverty in order to cast doubts in the other side's mind about the possibilities of recovery of any judgment that they might obtain at trial. They give recklessly or deliberately misleading information about their true assets and liabilities. Or, in a case where valuation of shares or property is important, they deliberately neglect to mention a material factor affecting the value. This could be either an understatement or overstatement of its value. In the heat of the mediation the other side does not have time to check so the deal is done on incomplete and inaccurate information.

Advocates can protect themselves and their clients against this happening by for example:

- always obtaining up-to-date valuations of any property in dispute or which might be available either as security or as part of the settlement or of the recovery if the matter went to trial;

- include warranties about the truthfulness of crucial information on which one side had relied when deciding to accept the offer advanced by the warrantor;

- obtain indemnities or guarantees from third parties. Templates should be brought along to the mediation so that they can be completed on the spot; and

- include a provision that in the event of default the innocent party can enter or obtain judgment for the full amount of the claim, with any counterclaim being dismissed. Care has to be taken not to be overzealous on the client's behalf and stray into the area of penalties. Take advice from counsel on the draft settlement agreement containing such provision in advance of the mediation.

Conclusion

15.17   If there is a settlement:

- record on the file and tell the client the reasons why a settlement was made;

- remind the client of the benefit of settlement – both financial and non-monetary – and the costs of litigation; and

- write to the mediator thanking him for his efforts.

If there is no settlement:

- record on the file and tell the client the reasons why a settlement was not made;

- urgently review with the client these reasons and explore whether the gap can be closed before the litigation timetable restarts and costs escalate;

- ask the mediator for his thoughts about closing the gap; and

- remind the client of the benefit of settlement – both financial and non-monetary – and the costs of litigation.

Part C
Mediation Advocacy Skills and Techniques

Chapter 16

Negotiation Fast Track Tactics

This chapter deals with:

- Background to the theory of negotiation
- Application of the theory to mediation
- What actually happens in negotiations at mediation

16.01 There are even more theories of negotiation than there are models of mediation and there is a growing and profitable worldwide industry of negotiation and people make a living selling their services as negotiators: hostage negotiators, diplomats, contract negotiators, troubleshooters – sometimes the list seems endless. There is an equally well-developed industry of analysing the activities of these practitioners and explaining what they do and how they can do it better.

Some of the negotiation theorists are also practitioners, but most practitioners are not negotiation theorists. They become good at negotiation by doing it, reflecting on it and doing it again.

There is a massive amount of information about negotiation. Much of it is contradictory, interesting, tedious, unintelligible, insightful, quantative, anecdotal, mind-numbing, eye opening, self-serving and potentially useful. It is easy to be overwhelmed.

This chapter tries be a fast-track through this information jungle to find out what can actually help advocates and their clients get more out of the mediation process through negotiation, remembering at all time that, while not every negotiation is a mediation, every mediation is a negotiation.

Advocates and their clients need to be aware of the theoretical influences that will be influencing the mediators that they appoint. If they know them they can recognise them and be prepared to accommodate them or otherwise deal with them.

We are all negotiators

16.02 Some commentators suggest that everything that we do in our daily lives is in fact a negotiation. This ranges from buying a cup of coffee on the way to work, to agreeing what time the children should go to bed, to arranging lunch with a colleague. Is such a wide definition really helpful? Is it so wide that it ceases to have any analytical value? Do people really behave in the same way when trying to agree what time to have lunch and where, as when they are trying to buy a company or more relevantly settle a court case? Leaving aside cultural differences are there any universal rules, norms or guidance that cover all these types of negotiation? Are the similarities between them greater than the differences?

The answer seems to be that there are some universal norms. This concept is discussed below. Professor Robert Cialdini has identified and popularised six key principles for persuading people. They are discussed below with a commentary on how they apply in civil and commercial mediations. Mediation advocates and their client should be aware of them so that they can use them when engaged in mediation and also be aware of them when they are being applied to them by others.

As previously described in **Chapter 4**, the dominant mediation philosophy is that based on principled negotiation, introduced by Fisher and Ury. That chapter also discussed in the commentary on how else it applies to civil and commercial mediations in practice.

A question

16.03 Advocates at mediation should ask themselves: Am I doing something different when I try and negotiate a settlement of a court case from when I am trying to negotiate the acquisition of a company or recruit a new member of staff?

This question is discussed at **para 16.16**.

How to influence people: the Big Six

Reciprocation

16.04 Sociologists claim that there is no human society that does not follow the rule of reciprocation and the sense of obligation that it engenders.

It is now well established that:

- if you do someone a favour they are more likely to do what you ask them to do when you ask them later. Charities have learned this lesson well. They include small gifts such as a pen or an enamel badge with their letters seeking donations; and

- when a person breaks the reciprocity rule he may incur the disapproval of other members of the group. This can cause someone who has received something to often give back more than they received. Why do they do this? The psychological impulse, ie the sense of unease and group disapproval, can outweigh the material or financial costs.

The principle of reciprocation or reciprocity has an evil twin: retaliation. An act of revenge incites a further act of revenge and so on. It all ends up in a spiral of feuding that can go on for generations.

In practice, at mediations:

- tit for tat behaviour is often displayed. This is corrosive of relationships and business opportunities. It makes litigation more difficult to conduct in a proportionate way as required by the Civil Procedure Rules. Costs escalate and become disproportionate. The disputants become more entrenched as they spend more time money and energy in retaliation. Advocates need to be able to dissuade their clients from instructing them to act in this way;

- reciprocity is one of the drivers of settlement negotiations. During mediation one of the parties often complains that it is making all the running. They complain that the other side have not moved as much as they have. It is all too one sided. Mediators constantly have to explain this perception to the parties. Advocates need to appreciate the power of reciprocity;

- the mutual exchange of information about the dispute and messages about settlement is a vital part of the mediation process. The effective management of mutual disclosure is the hallmark of a skilled mediator; and

- trading is, after all, the heart of any negotiation. The effective negotiator does not make concessions, he trades them.

Warning: beware of the fallacy 'if I am nice to them they will be nice to me.'

Commitment and consistency

16.05   Leonardo da Vinci said: 'It is easier to resist at the beginning than at the end.' In Western culture consistency is valued. Some psychologists regard the desire for consistency as a key motivator for our behaviour. It can even lead us to act against our own best interests. Consistency can offer a fast track through the complexities of life and enable us to make decisions more quickly. To help us decide, we can assume that what we want now is consistent with our earlier decisions. That makes it much easier to take a subsequent decision.

This has real implications for what happens at mediations:

- Once someone takes a stand their natural inclination is to act in a way that is consistent with that stand. This can make it far more difficult for them to review their position.

- They also look for means of reinforcing their stand. This brings confirmation bias into play (see **Chapter 18**).

- Mediators often ask the parties to write down their offer. They do this because it is well established that people who write something down feel more committed to it.

  This can be particularly true in workplace and community mediations where no legally binding agreement is drawn up, as usually happens in civil and commercial mediations. If the parties actually draw up their own agreement and write it themselves they are more likely to feel commitment to it. The human desire to be consistent is likely to lead to compliance with the written agreement they have produced.

There is a danger that the desire to be consistent can lead people to make decisions simply to be consistent rather than to reflect and even change their minds and adopt a better alternative. Clients therefore need to know when a consistency is foolish and likely to lead to them making a poor decision. Two signals have been identified:

- What your stomach tells you – in other words gut instinct.

- What your heart tells you – in other words what do your feelings tell you.

Many decision makers say, when trying to weigh alternatives and in particular an offer which is lower than the one they have previously said that they would accept: 'My head tells me to do this but my heart tells me to do something else.'

In other words rational and logical decision making is being replaced by instinct and feeling. The research into this phenomenon suggests that people experience feelings towards something in a nanosecond before they intellectualise them. By being aware of this and staying alert, people can use these signals as an early warning system before making a decision that they might regret later.

Social proof

16.06   This is also known as the herd instinct. In other words when trying to decide what to do people look to see what others have decided to do and do the same thing. This can have very negative consequences. There are many well-documented examples of a group of people watching somebody being attacked or collapsing in the street and not taking any steps. This is because people look around to see what they should do and nobody does anything. Individual responsibility is reduced taken over by the group.

This can be very significant at mediations:

- Most people in a dispute think that there are unique features about their dispute or case. There are, but the non-unique features usually outnumber them.

- At some stage in the mediation a client who is finding it difficult will say: 'This is going nowhere. They are not interested in settling. If that is their best offer I might as well take my chance in court.' It can be useful to point out that this is what happens in most cases in most mediations at this stage. Mediators often do this. The theorists call it normalising.

- At mediations, the parties and their advisers predict what will happen at court. This is, after all, part of working out their BATNA. It can be useful for the parties to be told that generally at court what influences the judge most is how the parties give evidence before him. Does he think that they are trying to tell him the truth or to deceive him?

- A mediator will often say in the Joint Opening Session that the statistics show worldwide that something like 70 per cent of mediations produce a settlement on the day. This manages the parties' expectations.

People respond to social proof in two ways:

- We seem to assume that if a lot of people are doing the same thing, they must know something that we do not. This is particularly true if we are uncertain. We are ready to place our trust in the collective knowledge of the crowd.

- The crowd can be mistaken because they are not acting on the basis of any better information but are themselves acting on the basis of social proof.

Social proof has an evil offspring: groupthink.

This is the negative side of team spirit. People like to be liked. They like to be part of a group. They like to co-operate. In the past if you were not part of the group you were more likely to be excluded and that could lead to you not surviving a at all. The urge to stay as part of a group is deep-seated.

This phenomenon is often seen at mediations. A team made up of clients, solicitor, barrister, witnesses, and expert has been working on a case together for some time. The may have had some triumphs or failures along the way. They have shared experiences and have to an extent bonded as a result. It becomes difficult:

- for the client who has invested his money and his confidence in his advisers to start questioning what they are telling him;

- for the expert to say that he's changed his mind. He does not want rest of the team to think that he is deserting them or letting them down; and

- for the lawyers to change their advice for the same reason.

Each of them may be starting to have doubts. This letter expressing they talk to each other about the best points in the case. They egg each other on and the group ends up with a more extreme view than the individuals hold individually.

However, it is the role of the advocate to, at all times, review the assumptions on which people have been acting and are acting. If the assumptions or information are changing then you should ask why people's minds on changing as well. Every group needs its Devil's Advocate.

Liking

16.07   People find it easier to say yes to people that they like.

Mediation advocates and their clients, therefore should ask themselves: 'If I want the other side to say yes why am I trying to annoy and antagonise them? '

This bias towards being liked can have negative effects. Researchers have shown the power of the halo effect. People automatically think that good-looking individuals are more talented, intelligent, kind and honest.

Various experiments have been carried out which show that good-looking people:

- are more likely to receive favourable treatment in the legal system;

- are twice as likely to avoid jail sentence as unattractive ones;

- who are victims, receive more compensation than unattractive victims;

- if in distress, receive more help than unattractive people even from their own gender; and

- even if children, are more likely to be perceived as more intelligent.

The possibly realistic but unwelcome conclusion is that mediation advocates should be tall and good looking. So should their clients.

This desire to be liked has four off -shoots: similarity, flattery, contact/co-operation and conditioning/association.

Similarity

16.08   Apart from physical attractiveness, people tend to like people like them. This can also be important at mediations:

- When establishing rapport, mediators spend time trying to find links such as knowing people in common, living in the same area, sharing the same educational background, supporting the same football team, having same number of children, etc. Advocates should encourage this and not try and interrupt it. Small talk is rarely only small.

- Skilled persuaders mirror and match the other person's behaviour, body language, tone of voice and vocabulary. Advocates will want to be aware of this in the Joint Opening Session.

Flattery

Most people like to be liked. We are all susceptible to flattery , compliments and praise. We also tend to like people who give us flattery compliments and praise.

Proverbially women are supposed to more susceptible to flattery than men .This is not true.

Example 16.1

In one experiment on men, they received comments from a person who wanted a favour from them. They received a range of comments. Some men received only positive comments, others negative and others a mixture. The conclusions from the research were:

- The person who gave only positive comments was liked best of all.

- This was true even when the recipients of the praise realised that he wanted a favour from them.

- Praise did not have to be true. Recipients liked flattery just as much even when the a compliment was untrue.

This insight could be of value to mediation advocates as most people at most mediations are men.

Contact and cooperation

16.09   We know what we like and we like what we know. Familiarity with something makes it more acceptable to us. Often this happens without people realising it.

In one well-known experiment the faces of different individuals were flashed onto a screen very quickly. The speed at which this was done was so quick that the observers could not remember seeing any particular face. But some faces were flashed up more than once. When the observers met the people later the ones they liked the most were ones that whose faces they had seen most often more.

Repeated experiments have shown that people get on better together when they have cooperated in a joint venture of some sort. Conversely the more people like each other the easier they find it to cooperate.

The significance of this for mediation is:

- Like it or not making peace is a cooperative effort.

- Negotiating a settlement of the dispute is not a tug-of-war. Everybody has to contribute towards the mutual goal of settling the dispute.

- A hostile adversarial approach is likely to engender a hostile adversarial atmosphere which will make co-operation more difficult and therefore settlement more difficult. Hired gun advocates need to bear this in mind.

Conditioning and association

Everybody at mediation is familiar with the plea: Don't shoot the messenger! This is why mediation trainers tell mediators never to take bad news to the parties, only to bring good news. Bad news tends to taint the bearer.

It is unrealistic for mediators only to bring good news. This is why they need to cultivate a good bedside manner when they have to bring bad news. Advocates need to do the same thing.

The opposite can also happen. It was established in the 1930s that people like each other more if they ate together and were more responsive and supported things that they experienced while they were eating. Hence, the importance of dinners and lunches in negotiation and diplomacy. This has not really caught on at mediations. Some mediators insist that:

- the parties start the day with breakfast of croissants and coffee together; and

- at lunch that they eat together.

In practice parties at mediation do not usually want to spend time together. Their advocates might be quite happy to do so but not the clients.

Warning: guard against being swayed by liking somebody too much, especially if the reason for liking them is unwarranted. It is much safer to separate the person (who you like) from the problem you are trying to deal with. This is not quite what Ury and Fisher meant but it has the same result.

Authority

16.10   Virgil said: 'follow an expert'. The ancients are often identified as sources of universal wisdom – in this case they were wrong. Following experts is likely to lead in most mediations to bad decisions.

Taking advice from experts and critically assessing it is another matter. Always ask, when someone is giving advice: why is this person giving me this advice? Many experts when giving advice can be influenced by the same cognitive biases that can influence their clients. As has been said many times, if one only has a hammer then every problem looks like a nail. Experts will see solutions through the prism of their own expertise. This is as true of legal experts as it is of technical ones. Mediators are often struck by the difference in approach from advocates with different legal specialisms.

As Winston Churchill said: 'Where you stand on something depends on where you sit.' This is why at mediations and even at trial there is often the clash of the experts. It is surprising how, apparently, people with similar levels of knowledge and experience looking at the same facts can have radically and indeed fundamentally opposed points of view. On examination this often turns out to be because they are making different assumptions. It is the origin of the assumptions that can often explain the apparent conflict. When experts are able to identify shared assumptions the scope of the differing conclusions is usually substantially reduced.

The susceptibility of human beings to authority has been well demonstrated. The shocking conclusions of the well-known Milgram experiment have been widely publicised. Although there has been recent criticism of the experiment and doubt cast upon the validity of some of the results it is still regarded as establishing that people will obey authority even when it offends their personal norms.

The Milgram experiment

In this experiment the students were divided into two groups – guards and prisoners:

- The guards were told that they were to administer electric shocks to the prisoners. The prisoners were in fact actors who simulated pain.

- The prisoners were asked mental arithmetic questions. If they gave the wrong answer they received an electric shock.

Except of course that there was no electric shock actually administered. The guards just had the dials with the levers so that they could administer a shock. The guards did not know that the dials and levers were not connected up. They thought that the shocks were really being administered.

The findings were that:

- two-thirds of the guards administered shocks to the full strength even when their dials showed that this was in the danger zone. They even did so when the prisoners were shouting that they had a bad heart and pleading to be let out;

- there were no difference between the genders;

- the guards found it difficult to resist the instructions of the white coated instructors in the labs who told them that they had to keep on administering the shocks; and

- all of the guards who were showing signs of reluctance to administer greater shocks refused to do so when encouraged by one of their own group, but most of them did so when instructed by one of the instructors.

> There have been many other examples of this tendency.
>
> The same phenomenon has been found in operating theatres, where junior medical staff have been reluctant to question the judgement of the senior surgeon even when it was obvious that he had made a mistake.

At mediations, treat all expert opinion whether from technical experts or senior lawyers, including recently retired judges who practice as mediators, with due respect and even more due scepticism.

Titles

16.11 These can influence people's perception. They can cause people to look up to someone, sometimes literally.

> In one experiment a visitor was introduced as someone from Cambridge University:
>
> • to one group of students he was introduced as a professor; and
>
> • to the other group of students he was introduced as a postgraduate researcher.
>
> The two groups of students were then asked to estimate the height of the visitor. The professor was estimated to be to thee and half inches taller than the postgraduate researcher.

This can have practical consequences at mediation:

• Is a party or his advisers being unduly influenced by the fact that the mediator is a QC or retired High Court judge?

• Does it matter that the representative on the other side is a professor and the leading authority in the field?

Clothes

Experiments show that a person wearing a uniform will be able to control more people than a person wearing ordinary clothes. A person wearing a security guard's uniform telling people to pick up litter will be paid much more attention than someone in ordinary clothes. It does not have to be such an obvious uniform. A suit and tie will do. Researchers found that more people will follow someone wearing a suit and tie in crossing traffic lights at red than follow someone wearing a casual shirt and jeans.

This effect is reinforced by other accessories, such as expensive watches, pens and cars. Many studies have shown that other motorists are more deferential to drivers of big expensive cars. Hence the proliferation of large Mont Blanc pens at commercial mediations.

How should you guard against this? Some authority figures have genuine authority, for example, senior judges or doctors. But even then their authority may not be relevant to the issues actually under consideration in the dispute. There are two key questions, which can be asked:

• How much of an expert is this authority?

• How truthful can I expect this expert to be here?

This is how Robert Cialdini formulates the question. A less provocative way of putting the question is to ask: why is this expert advising in this way on this occasion? However, what the question is addressing is how much has the expert been influenced by any of the biases that are identified in the next chapter.

Scarcity

16.12   The scarcity principle is seen in daily life all the time. People talking to someone face-to-face will interrupt the conversation to take a call from an unknown caller. Why? The availability of the person they are speaking to is guaranteed. The availability of the unknown caller is not.

The scarcity principle means that an opportunity seems more valuable when its availability is limited. The idea of potential loss is very influential in the way people make decisions. People are more motivated by the thought of losing something than by the thought of gaining something of equal value.

Why is it so powerful? There appear to be two reasons:

• Humans have a weakness for shortcuts. This can be beneficial. It helps us quickly judge the worth of something. Typically, things that are difficult to acquire are often of higher quality.

• As opportunities become less available, people see it as losing freedoms. People are very reluctant to lose freedoms that they already have.

Psychological theory calls this psychological reactance. When possession of something that we already have is threatened, we desire it more. Apparently it all goes back to the period of childhood known as the 'Terrible Twos'. This is the stage in infant development when children start to become aware of themselves as individuals.

Mediators often observe plenty of behaviour reminiscent of the Terrible Twos at mediation. Advocates must learn the skills of the wise parent.

In summary when the freedom to have something is limited, the item becomes less available, and people experience an increased desire for it.

Example 16.2

The classic example of this is the Worchel experiment. In this, identical biscuits were placed in two jars. Ten biscuits were put in one jar and two in the other and people were asked to say which tasted better. They rated the biscuits in the jar with only two in it as better, despite the fact that they were exactly the same as the biscuits in the other jar ,which contained ten.

This principle goes some way to explaining why at mediations:

- the paying party finds it more difficult to make concessions than the receiving party. A paying party already has the money. The receiving party wants to receive the money: all they have at the moment is a claim do to it.

- towards the end of the day the tempo increases. Time is running out. The opportunity to settle is becoming more limited. There is not exactly an outbreak of auction room fever but the parties start to sprint towards settlement after jogging along all day. Advocates need to be careful that the speeding parties do not trip themselves up.

16.13   Currently in the mediation world there are two main competing theories of negotiation: positional and principled.

The conventional wisdom is that positional negotiation is a bad habit, which is to be discouraged and if possible given up, but it is recognised that it is an ingrained habit, which many people like to indulge. It may be unavoidable.

By contrast, it is said that principled negotiation is much better. It may not come naturally to people but once it has been explained to them and they have been trained in it they will see its benefits, which are overwhelming.

The well-known thought experiment, known as the Prisoner's Dilemma, illustrates the difference between competitive and cooperative negotiation.

Example 16.3

There are two prisoners, held in separate rooms with no chance of communicating with each other. They are being questioned about a robbery. The questioner offers each of them the deal. He has enough evidence to obtain a conviction of breaking and entering but not of armed robbery which he suspects they did commit. Each prisoner is given the choice of confessing and not confessing to the armed robbery. The proposal is:

- if you confess but your partner does not you give evidence for the prosecution and go free. Your partner is sentenced to 20 years;

- if you both confess you each get 10 years;

- if neither of you confesses you are each sentenced to two years for breaking and entry.

What should the prisoners do? If one confesses and the other does not, he goes free and the other gets 20 years. Total prison time served 20 years. If both prisoners confess, thinking that is what the other will do in order to walk free they both get 10 years. Total prison time served 20 years. If both stay silent each receives two years. Total prison time served four years.

Competitive bargaining does not produce the optimal outcome for both prisoners. It has a one in three chance of producing an optimal outcome for one prisoner and the worst outcome for the other.

Cooperative behaviour, ie it is in the best interests of us both not to say anything, produces the optimal outcome, but the question for each side is: do I trust the other side enough to do the best thing for both of us?

Positional negotiation

16.14   This method is seen as the traditional way of negotiating. It entails parties taking a position and arguing about why they are right and the other party is wrong.

What happens is that a party takes a position and defends it. The other side does the same. They adopt the maxim that attack is the best form of defence and spend their time attacking each other's position. Each side becomes more entrenched and seeks to reinforce its position by repetition of its best points and repeated attacks on the other side's weakest points. They send out a small concession to test the other side's defences. Each concession seems to be accompanied by a fresh re-statement of their best points.

They are very keen to be reassured and confident that the other side fully understands the reality of the situation. By this they mean that the other side understands the weaknesses of its position, which they accommodatingly offer to explain at great length.

There is no judge to decide who is right and who is wrong and a battle of attrition ensues.

What is wrong with positional negotiation?

Critics of positional negotiation say:

- Positional negotiation is just argument. It is an inherently competitive process. It is not in essence different from presenting a case in court except there is no judge to decide who is right and who is wrong. There is no third party to declare who is the winner and allocate the spoils.

- Even if a settlement is reached it is usually after a bruising process.

- Relationships are damaged.

- People do not feel that they have had their day in court or been acknowledged.

- There is a high risk of settler's remorse the next day. The parties feel browbeaten. There may have been overbearing behaviour, to which one side now regrets having succumbed. The parties are not invested in the process or the outcome.

- Positional negotiators engage in aggressive tactics, indulging in lots of point scoring, attacking the other side's case or position concentrating on their weak points. Deadlines are set. Unreasonable demands and non-negotiable offers are made. A lot of bluffing and brinkmanship takes place.

- The parties seek to maximise their gain at the expense of the other side. They are looking for a victory, not a solution, and see negotiation as a zero-sum game, ie what I gain you lose. There has to be a winner and a loser.

- The critics say that it is nothing more than horse-trading or poker playing by another name. In essence it is a contest with a winner and a loser. Sometimes there are two losers. Rarely if ever are there two winners.

Why do people like it?

16.15 However, it has to be recognised that positional negotiation is often used and is liked by many negotiators, including lawyers and their clients. Why is this? There are several reasons:

- It is what most people know. It has certainly been practiced for centuries. It is used in markets and bazaars all over the world.

- It appeals to the competitive instinct, which many people have.

- Although it can be hard on the nerves and temper, it is easy on the brain. Not much creative thought or analysis is required to haggle.

- It can never be completely avoided, even in the most principled of principled negotiations. As its supporters say: you can expand the pie as much as you like but eventually you have to decide how big the piece is.

- You do not need a TPN or indeed an intermediary of any sort to horse trade or haggle.

- In the context of mediation many lawyers find it conducive to their adversarial cast of mind and training.

- In practice, parties and their representatives at mediation do talk about winning at mediation. This is not just the same as getting a good result. That can be measured by achieving a settlement above their expectations. They mean coming out on top or doing better than the other side.

Principled negotiation

16.16 This philosophy of negotiation was developed by the HNP in the 1980s by Roger Fisher and William Ury and others in the Harvard Business School. It has achieved worldwide influence and has become the mantra for many mediation trainers. The vast majority of mediators practising in the UK will have received training based on this philosophy. Some will have customised it in the light of their experience. Mediation advocates must be familiar with it and prepare themselves and their clients for what they can expect from the mediator.

The key text is *Getting to Yes* by Fisher and Ury, which was first published in 1981. It is a very readable and accessible explanation of the philosophy and worth reading by anyone wanting to be involved in mediation in the UK. Readers of *Getting to Yes* or the other HNP publications might be led into thinking that this approach is a panacea. Certainly it is credible and attractive and it does work. But how far does it work in practice in the UK in the 21st century?

Its intention is to introduce a process, which produces a wise agreement in an efficient manner, which should improve but at least not damage the relationship between the parties. Fisher and Ury define a wise agreement as:

'one that meets the legitimate interests of each side to the greatest possible extent possible, resolves conflicting interests fairly , is durable, and takes community interests into account.'

It achieves this by applying the four principles mentioned at **para 4.03.**

- separate the people from the problem;

- focus on interests not positions;

- invent options for mutual gain; and

- insist on using objective criteria.

It also introduces what is in reality a fifth principle, which is that of calculating the Best Alternative to a Negotiated Agreement (BATNA) and the Worst Alternative to a Negotiated Agreement (WATNA).

Separate the people from the problem

16.17   What this means in essence is:

- Do not see the other side as enemies. Regard the problem as the enemy not the other side.

- Do see the other side as human beings. They will share many characteristics with you such as the need to be acknowledged and respected. They will fall into the same cognitive traps (see **Chapter 18**) and they will get tired and frustrated as the mediation day goes on just like you.

- Do try and put yourself in their position. If you were them how would you see the situation?

- Do not let your opinion of them as individuals obscure the problem that you have to solve. It is easy to be distracted by your own feelings about how they have behaved or what values they represent (see the checklist of cognitive biases **in Chapter 18**).

- Be prepared to explain how and why you take the opinion that you do and also to listen to the other side when they explain their point of view. In other words be prepared to communicate. Often at mediations the parties are locked in a dispute because they have lost the ability or the willingness to communicate with each other.

This is sensible advice. In reality:

- Few aggrieved parties at mediation can resist trying to make the other side feel guilty.

- Few lawyers can resist trying to show that they are better lawyers than those on the other side.

- Sometimes the problem is the people.

- It is not easy to reconcile this precept with the exhortations that behind every dispute there is a broken relationship and the assertion that suppressed emotions sabotage settlements.

- There is increasing emphasis by some mediation commentators on the importance and benefit of the emotional (or irrational) part of our brains when compared with the rational part. The power of emotion in decision making has not only been acknowledged but encouraged and used. This places greater demands on the mediation advocate. He needs to be aware of the mind traps that he, his client, the other side, and indeed the mediator can fall into. These are discussed **in Chapter 18.**

Focus on interests not positions

16.18   This is another way of saying what Donald Trump said: 'When I have got what the other guy wants we have got a deal.'

The negotiator will:

- find out what the other party wants – what his interests are, and also be prepared to tell the other side what his are. In doing this both sides are beginning to discover the extent of the common ground;

- establish rapport. They engage in small talk with the parties asking them how they to the venue where they come from and so on;

- ask questions. This is a special skill in mediation and in negotiation generally and was discussed in **Chapter 6**; and

- listen carefully to what is being said. This is usually referred to as active listening. This was discussed in **Chapter 6**.

In mediation theory, a distinction is drawn between positions, interests and needs. There is a further distinction, which is goals:

- *Positions* are defined as public assertions of rights and arguments designed to achieve a particular outcome for a party.

- *Interests* are defined as what will actually benefit the party.

- *Needs* are defined as those things which a party must achieve. They may not be actually a matter of life and death. But they are a matter of commercial and psychological survival.

- *Goals* are what a party wants to achieve in order to meet his needs. It is an essential part of negotiation. Stuart Diamond, in *Getting More* (Penguin, 2011), argues that without setting a goal and sticking to it throughout negotiation there is little chance of there being a successful outcome. Setting goals improves performance and the likelihood of achieving the goal by 25 per cent. Specific goals are better than general goals, for example: 'We want 50 per cent of costs,' is better than 'We want a contribution towards our costs,' but 'We want £75,000 for out costs' is better still.

Mediators are trained to moves the parties from positions, to interests and eventually to needs. It is by satisfying parties' needs that settlements can be achieved.

16.19   The way to find out what the other side's interests are is by asking questions and listening. This sounds obvious and easy. But in practice people find it hard to do it. Why is this? The reasons were discussed in **Chapter 6**, but briefly are:

- People at mediation are much readier to talk than to listen. This can be because they are nervous and talking is for many people a way of relieving stress. They can be impatient. They will, as has been said before, want to be acknowledged and therefore to tell their side of the story.

- Listening is much harder than people think. It is not just a question of restraining your impatience and not saying anything. Listening means paying close attention to what is being said and what is not being said. Mediators are trained in 'active listening'. Lawyers who are intending to represent clients at mediation should also try it.

- Asking questions is harder than people think.

- In practice, parties see this sort of self-disclosure as a sign of weakness. They are afraid that by giving the other side information about themselves they are supplying ammunition to be used against them. This is particularly true at the start of the mediation.

- As trust develops with the help of the mediator during the day, this mutual self-disclosure becomes easier. Good mediators realise that developing trust is a fundamental part of their job and start the process of early on. Effective advocates also know this and try to help the mediator by showing trust and asking for guidance. They do not resist the mediator.

Warning: remember that the other side will also be asking questions and listening. So be prepared to answer them. Thinking in advance about what the other side or the mediator may ask will make this much easier on the day. It is all part of trying to see the situation from the other side's perspective.

Inventing options for mutual gain

16.20 Mediators often refer to this as growing the pie, or more formally as creating value. It is excellent advice. All mediators are trained to try and do this. They call it a win-win situation. That phrase is now rather hackneyed. Experienced mediators do not use it or, if they do, do so with invisible quotation marks around it.

In practice parties at mediations find this difficult. They may be very creative in their normal personal or business lives but when it comes to thinking about how to solve the dispute that they are in, imagination is replaced by judgmental indignation at the other side's conduct and intentions. In other words they demonise each other.

The fundamental question

This raises the question identified in **para 16.03**, ie whether negotiations to settle a commercial dispute are different in kind from negotiations to conclude a commercial deal. Is it a fundamentally different process when negotiating to buy a company than to settle a case of breach of warranty in the share sale agreement?

There is no difference

There are those that say that it is the same. What you are trying to do in both situations is get someone to do something that you want them to do and they do not want to do. As the potential purchaser, you want the vendor to sell at your price not his. It is the same with settling the warranty claim. The claimant wants the warrantor to pay on the basis of his calculation of loss not the warrantor's basis.

In both types of negotiation the same negotiation tools are used. A brief list of them comprises:

- prepare;
- keep the emotion out of it;
- identify and focus on your goals;
- find out who the other side are – establish rapport, acknowledge their position, strengths and weaknesses;
- identify and focus on the decision maker;
- identify norms or standards or objective values;
- ask open questions;
- keep an open mind; and
- keep your eyes and ears open – observe and listen actively.

In addition:

- Although positional bargaining is discouraged in mediation and commercial negotiation generally it is present in all negotiations. It is very present in commercial negotiations particularly when the negotiations are about price.
- Principled negotiation is also present in both dispute resolution and commercial negotiations. Mediators and parties engaged in principled negotiation look for creative solutions. This is the same sort of activity that takes place in commercial negotiation. The usual question is: how can we make this deal work for both of us? It applies in both dispute resolution and commercial negotiations.

There is a difference

16.21   The arguments against this view are:

- Legal disputes are essentially disputes are about people's rights. Commercial negotiations are not. They are about people's ambitions and interests. Rights as such do not come into play.
- Legal disputes take place within the law. Mediation is said to be conducted in the shadow of the law. If the parties cannot come to a settlement, a decision on what happens in the future is imposed by a third party, ie the judge or arbitrator. That is the default position. There is no equivalent default position in commercial negotiations. Either a deal happens or it does not. There is no third party who can intervene and impose an outcome on the parties.
- Parties in a dispute negotiation bring to the negotiation a lot of baggage. There is accumulated grievance, conflict and tension, and there may even be outright hostility. It is rare in commercial negotiations for there to be outright hostility. There may be some tension and grievance based on previous dealings but usually there is not a sense of grievance, score settling or the wish to extract revenge.

- The timescales are usually completely different. Most legal negotiations take place within deadlines imposed by the court. This is not the case in commercial negotiations. There may be deadlines, for example the end of the financial year, but usually they are susceptible to extension in the way the court deadlines are not. This gives a different atmosphere to the negotiations. They are in that sense more open-ended.

- Parties in dispute resolution negotiation do play the blame game. There is a tendency to find fault and attribute blame for what has happened in the past. This is much less, prevalent in commercial negotiations.

- In summary the commercial negotiations take place in a different environment with a different background to those negotiations designed to resolve a conflict, especially where legal proceedings have already started. These differences are so significant that they make the process fundamentally different.

Why is this question important?

16.22   It is relevant to the question of how an advocate and their clients should behave towards the other side at mediations. Do you are argue points or discuss proposals? How do you open negotiations in a mediation? This is dealt with in more detail in **Chapter 10**. The key question is: If you wanted to buy someone's company would you open negotiation by accusing them of being unreliable and dishonest? If the answer is no, then why do it in a mediation?

In principled mediations the mediators will try and encourage the parties:

- to break away from a mono-solution – there is always more than way of tackling a problem;

- not to be too quick to dismiss an idea; and

- to proactively think of ways in which both sides can gain value.

One favourite technique mediators use is brainstorming. This and other techniques was discussed in **Chapter 9**.

Another criticism of this approach is that it is not always possible to grow the power or to generate value. In many civil and commercial disputes the argument is about money and the solution will be found in money. It is all a question of who pays how much to whom and when.

This is not to deny that there is a role for creative thinking but it is confined to how to structure payment arrangements. It is not about creating options for mutual gain. Examples of these types of dispute are:

- A dental practice has not paid the maintenance fees to its IT contractor. Under the terms of their licensing and servicing agreement, the IT contractor is entitled to suspend service. It does. The dental practice cannot access its patient records or appointments. There is no dispute that the monies are due. The dental practice has not paid. To avoid court proceedings they attend mediation.

- An accountancy firm has not paid for its weekly supply of copier paper. They have done business with the supplier for many years. There is no dispute about the terms of business. They have missed four payments. The supplier does not receive the fifth payment and issues a statutory demand. He just wants his money.

- Many commercial mediations deal with parties who have been in business for some years and have conducted business with each other in the past. They both want to stay in business. Relations have deteriorated to such an extent that not only do they not want to do business with each other in the future, they do not even want to say good morning to each other at the mediation, let alone have a Joint Opening Session. There is a complete and absolute breakdown of trust.

  Mediators who make suggestions that they might want to do business together in the future may be on the receiving end of a variety of responses ranging from the obscene to the disbelieving. Some parties have been known to regard such enquiries as an insult their intelligence.

Insist on objective criteria

16.23   Although the HNP model of principled negotiation can sound idealistic, it does recognise that there is always going to be an element of conflict of interest at some stage in a negotiation. When this happens the danger is that the parties default to positional bargaining. The mediation becomes a battle of wills. To avoid this danger the fourth principle is recommended which is to agree how various proposals should be judged. This can be done by adopting by mutual consent, fair standards and a fair procedure. For example:

- Two neighbours in a dispute over boundaries and rights of way across each other's land may agree that the sensible solution is to exchange land. Rather than argue about the value of their respective plots of land they can agree to appoint three independent valuers and pick the average figure.

- In a building dispute over the quality of the work that has been done and what further works are needed to finish the job, the parties can appoint a third party independent surveyor who will inspect, draw up a specification and certify the work when completed.

- Reason can be applied. If one party proposes a figure of £500,000, ask how the figure is made up. Examine the rationale. This can be helpful in moving the debate away from the personal and subjective to the technical and objective. Of course the other party may ask the same question. Lawyers should therefore be ready to both use reason and to be open to reason.

Other objective standards include market value, precedent, professional standards, cost, or equal treatment. This approach takes the debate away from a personalised, competitive apportioning of blame for what has happened in the past to a co-operative search for an objective, technical answer for the future.

In practice parties often dispute the objective criteria. They are tempted to choose criteria that support their own position. These can more subjective than objective. This is where the skilled mediator can help and why the effective advocate builds a good working relationship with the mediator as early as possible in the process.

Know Your BATNA

16.24   This is not one of the four principles listed by Fisher and Ury of principled negotiation but is central to the philosophy. As they say in the book when describing a BATNA:

'*That* is the standard against which to any proposed agreement should be measured. That is the only standard that can protect you both accepting terms that are too unfavourable and project from rejecting terms it would be in your interest to accept.'

They advocated it as an alternative to a bottom line figure as indicating when you walk away from negotiations. Not having a developed BATNA means that there is a danger of accepting an unfavourable settlement. This happens because the party is fearful of accepting, because he has indeed not worked out what the alternative is.

Fisher and Ury argue that the BATNA is not just a defensive weapon. For them it is a weapon that brings additional strength in negotiation. They explain the process as:

- inventing a list of actions you might conceive taking if no agreement is reached;
- improving some of the more promising ideas and converting them into practical alternatives; and
- selecting, tentatively, the one alternative that seems best.

Below is a worked example of a BATNA in which values have been given to alternatives. It is based on a professional negligence claim where the claimant must prove breach, causation and loss.

	BATNA	PATNA	WATNA
Probability	70%		
	Claimant wins on breach, causation and loss	Claimant wins on breach and causation but only partial loss	Claimant loses on causation
	£	£	£
Damages	500k	300k	NIL
Costs spent	100k	100k	100k
Costs recovered from other side	75K	65K	75K (paid to other side)
Irrecoverable costs	25k	35k	100k
Total gain	475k	265k	−175k

So 'walk-away' figure is:	£475k x 0.7	£332.5k
	+	£53k
	£265k x 0.2	(£17.50k)
	+	
	(£175k) x 0.2	
		£368k

| NB if you put a value on other non-monetary factors such as opportunity cost this figure is reduced | (£50K) | (50K) | (£50K) |

It is then recommended that having worked out the BATNA for one side, the BATNA for the other side is calculated.

16.25 Some negotiation theorists advise calculating the reservation or walk away price. This is usually defined as the amount of money or list of non-monetary items or a combination to which the claimant would be indifferent between settlement at mediation and any of the alternatives.

The range between the two figures is the ZOPA or the Zone Of Possible Settlement.

There are four main criticisms of this concept:

- If the parties are in a legal dispute their BATNA is in fact the same as their WATNA, which is actually going to trial.

- The BATNA stands for the BEST alternative. In the real world, best and worst outcomes are not the ones that are usually achieved. Very rarely does anyone win hands down or lose completely. More helpful concepts are PATNA (Probable Best Alternative to a Negotiated Agreement) or RATNA (Realistic or Reasonable Alternative to a Negotiated Agreement)or even MLATA (Most Likely Alternative to a Negotiated Agreement).

- It focuses too much on walking away from negotiations. Fisher and Ury say expressly in the book:

  'the better your BATNA, the greater your ability to improve the terms of any negotiated agreement … it will it is easy to break off negotiations if you know where you're going. The greater your willingness to break off negotiations, more forcefully you can present your interests and the basis on which you believe that an agreement should be reached.'

  Apart from sounding suspiciously like a hardball tactic from positional negotiation it is defeatist. Settlements are not reached by walking away from negotiations. If the parties' goal it is to avoid going to court with the risks and costs that brings, walking away frustrates that goal. One of the most prized qualities in any negotiator is perseverance. Mediators are taught: 'Never give up'. Advocates should adopt the same mantra.

- Calculating BATNAs, etc in a single issue mediation can be straightforward. It is not in a multi-issue dispute, and most disputes have several issues, even if it is about how much the defendant pays the claimant an ascertained sum of money.

The whole idea of a BATNA, and indeed of principled negotiation, is predicated on the premise that parties will act rationally. There is very little room for irrational behaviour in this model. Unfortunately, as all mediators will say that, there is a great deal of irrational behaviour displayed in mediations. Sometimes it is by the parties, sometimes it is by their representatives. Mediators and representatives have to deal with the world as it is and people as they are, which is to say be tolerant and able to deal with a high-level of irrationality.

To be fair to Fisher and Ury they do recognise the need to cope with irrational behaviour by emphasising the requirement to focus on interests not positions and importing objective criteria.

The question then arises: how do you cope with the irrational? The answer lies in three different places:

- the type of negotiator you are (**Chapter 17**);
- the traps they fall into (**Chapter 18**); and
- the techniques they can use (**Chapter 9**).

Conclusion

16.26 To conclude:

- Learn and remember the Big Six: reciprocation, commitment and consistency, social proof, liking, authority and scarcity.
- Re-read and bear in mind at all times the eight core principles of negotiation in **Chapter 1**.
- Do not give up, and stay calm.
- Remember: settlements are not reached by walking away from them.
- It is the client's deal: let him do it if he wants to. He may have reasons that he has not disclosed to you.

Chapter 17

What Type of Mediator Are You?

This chapter discusses:

- Negotiating styles
- Negotiating tips and tricks

What type of negotiator am I?

17.01 Negotiation and mediation advocacy trainers emphasise the importance for advocates and negotiators of knowing what type of negotiator, style of negotiator or personality type they are. Some even say that advocates should also know the personality type or negotiation style of their own clients and the other side. In practice this is not possible.

Anyone who spends time negotiating or with his mediation advocate will, if they reflect on what they do, learn something about their own personality and style. They will already have some knowledge of this from their own personal and professional life. Some people find it useful to have a personality assessment.

There is nothing wrong with taking a test such as the Myers Briggs test or the Kilmann test. It would be a brave advocate who suggested to his clients that they might do the same. If the other side have also taken such tests they are not going to disclose results.

It also reveals a confusion about the role of personality in negotiation. To find out someone's personality is a serious matter. It requires at least nine different tests, which takes several hours and expert interpretation. What happens if the personality revealed by the tests is one that is regarded as inimical to negotiation? If it can be changed by appropriate training how influential and dominant is it as a driver in negotiation?

However, there is no doubt that the negotiation theorists' predilection for taxonomy is interesting and many practitioners like to read them and, at least on a superficial level, to know what category they are in. Two entertaining examples used by negotiation gurus are animals and colours.

Animals

Turtles	*withdraw* into their shell to avoid conflict. They are prone to giving up their own personal goals and relationships to achieve this.
Sharks	try to *force* the other party to accept their demands. They are not very concerned with relationships.
Foxes	*compromise* by giving up some of their own goals if the other party does the same. They value their own goals and recognise that the other party values theirs. They prefer to maintain relationships.
Teddy bears	*smooth* things over to avoid conflict and damage to relationships. They are more proactive than turtles.
Owls	want to *solve* problems. They understand the value of their own goals and relationships and that the other side value theirs. They look for solutions, which satisfy their own needs and the other side's.

Colours

Red	*aggressive* and seek to dominate and take what they want. They are not interested in relationships. Results are more important. Negotiations are one-off battles. They believe that life is a zero-sum game.
Blue	*submissive* and more prepared to give. They value business relationships more than results and the long-term more than the short-term. They believe that if they are nice to the other side, they will be nice to them in return.
Purple	a hybrid: they trade ie give (blue) in exchange for getting (red). They do not compromise by just giving up something but trade: if you can do this, I can do that. They are assertive but not aggressive (red) and reasonable but not timid (blue).

However, does it really help a mediation advocate to know that he is a red fox or a purple turtle?

In practice people cannot change their personalities. But they can change their experience, which has been defined as 'not what happens to you but what you do with what happens to you'. They can also learn new behaviour and unlearn old habits. This can be helped by some self-reflection.

There are two useful questions for advocates to ask themselves:

- What impresses me?
- What traps do I fall into?

Self-auditing is, therefore, a very useful habit for mediation advocates to acquire.

What impresses me?

17.02 Asking this question is something practitioners will have done during their professional careers as they have developed their skills and experience. They will have seen other practitioners and noted what they did well and what mistakes they made. It is the same with learning to be an effective mediation advocate.

For example, advocates should ask themselves how they and their clients react when another lawyer tells them that:

- your case is hopeless and based on a fundamental misunderstanding of the law;
- your client is dishonest or a liar;
- you and your client have no chance of winning;
- he is going to make only one offer and it will be non-negotiable; or
- his client has much more power and money than yours and can take this case all the way to the European Court.

These are all tactics designed to intimidate. How often are lawyers intimidated at mediation? What is the natural reaction – to capitulate? No, it is to fight back and meet fire with fire. Does this lead to settlement?

Observing and noting the mistakes of others can lead to reflecting on what did work. The chances are that if a particular approach or way of presenting information or proposals impressed them, it will impress the other side. In other words it is sensible for advocates to treat others in negotiation or mediation as they would want to be treated themselves. This is not rocket science but it is surprising how often it is forgotten.

Tips and tricks

17.03   The two essentials for a mediation advocate are

- be flexible; and
- be robust.

Be flexible

17.04   Flexible advocates do not change their mind every five minutes or have no plan or settled goals at all. They adapt to meet the conditions they are in on the day, just as top tennis players and golfers do. They play their game, their opponent and the conditions. Above all they are slow to rule anything out or in. They are quick to assess how far any suggestion, information or movement helps them achieve their goal.

Be robust

17.05   Robust advocates are not aggressive and obdurate. They are above all confident. That confidence comes from preparation. They know what their client's goals are, the costs and benefits of settlement and the costs and benefits of not settling. They are well prepared. They understand their clients and they enjoy their trust. They can withstand the inevitable attack from the other side and the reality testing from the mediator, and are self-confident enough to be able to acknowledge their weaker points without conceding their stronger ones. They do not become upset at the antics of the other side or the fumblings of the mediator and do not threaten to walk out or emote with frustration.

Flexible and robust advocates have learned the negotiator's adage: 'Broken noses alter faces, circumstances alter cases.' They adapt and carry on. In doing that they take note of the following points.

Never make a concession

- Always *trade* a concession. Remember that the most important word in the negotiator's vocabulary is: 'IF'.

- Always make *conditional* proposals. Unconditional proposals lead to unilateral concessions.

- Do not say: 'We will increase by £10,000'. Say instead: 'If you can come down £30,000 we can go up £10,000' or 'If you can give us more time to pay, such as an extra six months, we can afford another £20,000.'

Avoid threats and blackmail

- Threats and blackmail may sound tough and impressive, but they destroy the confidentiality of the mediation discussion. They rarely promote settlement. Instead they lead to a counter-threat and a threat spiral forms.

- If somebody is worried about the repercussions of not settling, they do not need to be reminded of it publicly. If it is thought that they might not be giving it sufficient weight in their risk/benefit analysis, a private word with the mediator will suffice. His discussion of the benefits of settlement with the other side will not be seen as a threat.

- Of course, some parties and their advocates regard every negative comment or criticism, however slight or justified, as a threat and any description of the adverse consequences of not settling, no matter how neutral or well-founded as blackmail.

- Do not be one of these. Naïve is the word that word that springs to the mediator's mind when he hears advocates complaining: 'That's blackmail'. Advocates and their clients need to be robust.

Example 17.1

In a recent mediation, which involved backdated documents, one side's solicitor suggested that the way to break the deadlock was to remind one of the solicitors on the other side that he faced the prospect of being struck off.

The mediator asked: 'How would you respond if you were told that?'

His colleague who was representing a co-defendant said 'I would just stand up and walk out.'

The threat was not made. The matter settled.

Be tough but not aggressive

- In the context of mediation being tough means being firm and consistent. Politely, calmly and unfailingly insist: 'Until you are going to give me something I am not going to give you anything.'

- Remember the fundamental importance of the principle of reciprocity (see **Chapter 16**).

Don't bluff

- Negotiators are told not to bluff. The reason is that, if the bluff is called, all credibility is lost, but other negotiation theorists such as Professor James J White say that misleading the other side is the very 'essence of negotiation'. What is the right approach?

- Lying is out. However, some bluffing goes on all the time in every mediation. Parties routinely overstate their confidence in their case, their determination and ability to take all the case all the way to trial.

- A degree of over-emphasis is pardonable. However, if one side regards the other as simply bluffing and blustering it impedes the generation of any settlement momentum, and if they regard them as lying it can be fatal to any chance of settlement.

- Remember the importance of trust in **Chapter 16**.

- Parties can end up painting themselves into a corner when they overstate their demands and the redness of their red lines.

- Do not be too emphatic. The skilful advocate always leaves a way out for himself and his client. The really skilful advocate leaves a way out for the other side as well.

- Wait until proposals have been presented and discussed before declaring anything off-the-table or non-negotiable. Remember all those demands that were set in stone that ended up as the sand of the beach of settlement lapped by the warm waters of collaboration.

Don't blame

- Playing the blame game wastes energy and time at mediations. However, most parties and their advocates do it even when they say that they are not going to. Why?

- It is easy. No fresh information or thinking is required.

- It is comforting.

- It is an expression of the natural inclination of everyone one in a dispute to demonise the other side.

- In litigation, attributing blame is mixed up with establishing liability. There are usually clear legal tests for establishing liability.

- The only interesting question is whether the parties think that they will be met. By the time that they come to mediation they know the strength of their own case, or they should do, and they have an appreciation of the strength of the other side's case. Neither side is going to radically change their mind at mediation. The trick is to find a settlement that takes into account both sides' appreciation of risk and benefit.

People do things for their reasons not yours

- Mediations are not mini-trials. Why do litigation lawyers both barristers and solicitors treat them as though they were?

- They have failed to grasp the essential truth of negotiation that you will never persuade the other side to do something for your reasons, you have to persuade them to do it for their reasons.

- First, you have to find out what they really are. Skilful questioning and listening of the sort described in **Chapter 6** both by the advocate directly and through the mediator will help establish this.

Self audit: the Rackham Carlisle test

17.06 Extensive research by Neil Rackham and John Carlisle into the characteristics of above average negotiators concluded that they:

- explore more options;

- spend more time considering areas of potential agreement (although both types of negotiators spend most of their time considering their differences);

- spent twice as much time considering long-term rather than short-term issues (although both spend over 90 per cent of that time on short-term issues);

- set objectives within a range rather than at a fixed point;

- do not mind in which order issues are considered;

- use far less irritators such as exaggerating their own proposals and denigrating the other side's, which do not persuade and are counter-productive;

- make far fewer instant counterproposals-they take their time;

- initiate far fewer defend/attack spirals;

- signal their own behaviour, eg 'Can I ask a question?'

- when they disagree, they give their reasons first and then state that they disagree;

- test their understanding more often;

- summarise more often;

- ask many more questions;

- give more information about personal feelings;

- do not dilute arguments with weaker statements; and

- review what has occurred during the negotiation.

Conclusion

17.07 To conclude:

- be flexible;
- be robust;
- always trade;
- remember the most important word in negotiation is 'IF'; and
- self -audit before and after each mediation: see **paras 6,24, 17.06** and **18.06**.

Chapter 18

Mind Traps Alert

This chapter discusses:

- How people make decisions especially in circumstances of uncertainty
- The influence of emotions on decision making
- Common mistakes that people make in assessing risk

A test

Here is a test. There are two boxes:

- In box A there are 100 coloured balls. 50 are white and 50 green.
- In box B there are another 100 coloured balls. You do not know how many are white and how many are green.

The challenge is if you put your hand into a box and, blindfolded, choose a white ball you win £100.

Which box would you choose your ball from?

Most people would choose box A.

Now choose a ball in the same way but this time you have to pick out a green ball and win £100. Which box would you choose?

Most people will again choose box A.

But this is illogical. In the first round you chose box A because you thought box B had fewer than 50 white balls and therefore more green balls. Therefore, logically, you should choose box B this time.

Risk and uncertainty

18.01 This is an illustration of a cognitive bias known as ambiguity aversion. Humans do not like uncertainty. Their distaste for it leads them to make hasty and wrong decisions. This tendency is aggravated by a confusion between risk and uncertainty which was mentioned in **para 7.01**.

With risk the probabilities are known, with uncertainty the probabilities are not known. When the probabilities are known a person can decide whether or not to take a gamble. When the probabilities are not known it is much harder to weigh up the competing choices and decide what to do. As was said previously, risk can be calculated – uncertainty cannot be calculated. Why do some people take more risk than others? In **para 7.08**, the importance of establishing a client's risk profile was discussed.

Why do some people take more risk than others?

18.02   Part of the answer is in the brain, The human brain has over a trillion brain cells. It consists of a mass of these neurons which form interconnected networks. These are formed into identifiable brain regions. In mammals the basic regions are:

● the cerebellum which looks like a cauliflower and is at the back of the brain;

● basal ganglia, an interconnected series of regions in the centre of the brain, and

● the cortex, which is the brain's outer layer and is the site of the higher mental functions.

There is also an almond-shaped region deep in the brain called the amygdala. The amygdala is vital. It processes memory and emotions. The configuration of a person's amygdala determines how easily they can tolerate ambiguity. The less uncertainty they can tolerate, the more conservative will be their voting or selection. In other words, what the test with the green and white balls proves is that people prefer known probabilities over unknown ones

Unfortunately advocates will not know the configuration of their clients' amygdalae, nor of their own, but what they can be aware of is how rational decision making using decision tree analysis will be influenced by other things. These are known as cognitive biases and heuristics. Reference to them is sometime made in books on mediation. The two biases that are usually featured are:

● optimism bias; and

● fundamental attribution error.

They are important in understanding how people behave at mediations, but there are many of them, over 150. A checklist of some of the most common is at **Appendix 1** to this chapter. There are some which any advocate should have a working knowledge of. These are on display every day in mediations and are listed with a commentary at **para 18.06.**

What are cognitive biases, heuristics and logical fallacies?

18.03

● Heuristics are mental shortcuts or rules of thumb that we all use to deal with everyday decisions and problems.

● A cognitive bias is a pattern of thought and behaviour that can be replicated and leads to the drawing of irrational conclusions.

● A logical fallacy is a missed or mistaken step in arriving at a conclusion.

They are not the same thing but they do have an impact on decision making and are often present at the same time. There is a tendency to criticise all of them as being negative and obstacles to accurate thinking and therefore to accurate decision making and action. This is not entirely accurate. Many of them have evolved over time to enable humans to cope with their environment and in particular with the threats that they faced. It has been said that the human brain is not designed to reason: it is designed to reproduce. Therefore it produces responses to dangers and opportunities that are intended to promote survival and reproduction.

We cannot completely control our emotions through thinking

18.04 As Dobelli says, thinking is a biological phenomenon. It has been shaped by evolution just as animals and flowers, etc have been shaped. However, things have changed. In particular, since industrialisation, and now perhaps digitisation, the brain that we evolved ie that of a hunter-gatherer, is of less use. Everyone faces a daily avalanche of information and sensation. How can we cope with it? Part of the answer is through the use of shortcuts and rules of thumb, ie heuristics. Advocates and their clients need to be aware of them because:

- they can be more confident that their decision making is as effective as it can be, ie it is directed towards achieving their goal whatever it might be and not being driven or influenced by something else; and

- they can understand and respond appropriately to what is said by the other side. Not everything is as it seems.

Research by psychologists and behavioural economists now provides a better understanding of what influences people when they make decisions. This is significant in understanding how people negotiate and interact with other parties in a negotiation – and every mediation is a negotiation.

Another test

> Here is another test, this time based on treating contaminated water.
>
> A river has two tributaries.
>
> If you use method A on tributary 1, the risk of dying from contaminated water falls from 5% to 2%.
>
> If you use method B on tributary 2, it reduces the risk reduces the risk from 1% to 0%.
>
> So which method should you choose A or B?
>
> Most people choose method B. This is a wrong decision. Under method A the reduction in the number of people who die is 3%. Under methods B the reduction in the number of people who die is 1%.
>
> This is an example of zero risk bias.

18.05   This illustrates that humans do not have an intuitive understanding of risk. They tend to concentrate on the magnitude of the impact of an event not the probability of it happening.

If, as Dobelli says, it is correct that our brains are designed to reproduce rather than search for the truth, then it is understandable why our thoughts are primarily used to persuade and convince. Those who succeed in persuading others gain access to power and resources, hence the power of the advocate.

But beware the traps. An essential part of mediation advocacy in preparing for and participating in mediation is knowing the client's case, the client's needs and also yourself.

Self audit

18.06   Here is list some of the most common biases and heuristics. This is not a complete list. Psychology is a young science, only about 150 years old. Behavioural economics is much younger. New cognitive biases are being discovered all the time. This checklist lists 30 common ones, for examples from Dobelli and Kahneman, which can be observed in every mediation.

Ad hominem fallacy

The belief that if you cannot trust someone, you cannot trust what that person says.

At mediations one side repeatedly makes remarks about the untrustworthy nature or conduct of the other and dismisses as unreliable whatever the mediator reports them as having told him.

Affect heuristic

An affect is an instantaneous judgment. You like something or you do not.

These reactions prevent people from considering risks and benefits to be independent variables. The affect heuristic leads people to treat them as emotionally the same. Therefore if you like some you underestimate the risks and overestimate the benefits. If you do not, you do the opposite.

At mediations mediators are anxious to know the outcomes of the risk/reward or cost/benefit analyses that the parties have carried out. As discussed in **Chapter 7** this sort of analysis has frequently not been completed. Time is spent at the mediation doing it. The results are often startling.

Anchoring

The tendency to rely to heavily or (anchor) on a past reference or piece of information when making decisions.

At mediations this is constantly observed with offers of settlement. Parties say that: 'We have moved from our figure of £500,000 by a long way, they have half as much from their starting figure.'

Authority bias

18.07   The tendency to allow the status and credentials of a person to influence the perception of information or advice he gives.

At mediations, advocates and experts display this: 'This is the strongest case I have ever seen in 25 years of practice'.

Choice supportive bias

The tendency to remember one's choices as better than they actually were.

At mediations people make statements such as: 'In the last case I was involved in we did not settle at mediation and took the matter to trial and they gave in at the door of the court.'

Closer examination of the net results for both sides often reveals that both sides were worse off.

Cognitive dissonance

This is where people reinterpret what has happened to justify the situation they are now in.

For example, people who apply for a job and do not get it rationalise this by saying they did not want it anyway and they did not like the company .

At mediations people, especially clients but also advocates, find it very difficult to acknowledge they may have been wrong.

Confirmation bias

The tendency to search for and interpret information in a way that confirms one's preconceptions.

At mediations parties constantly say things such as: 'What about the emails that show that John knew about Harry's plans?' They overlook the emails which show that they also knew of Harry's plans.

It is important to remember, as Aldous Huxley put it: 'Facts do not cease to exist because they are ignored.'

Curse of knowledge

18.08   The tendency to allow one's knowledge of the subject to reduce one's ability to think about the problem.

This happens all the time at mediations. The parties and their advocates get bogged down in the detail of the case, which they know intimately. They do not consider the underlying problem or the bigger picture.

Decision fatigue

Intensive decision-making can drain will power.

- In a well-known experiment, Roy Baumeister gave two groups of students tasks. The first group had to decide which out of a wide range of items they preferred. The second group simply had to write down what they thought about each item.

- The first group had to decide which item they would like to take away. The second group were told which item they could take away.

- He then asked them who could put their hand in a bucket of ice cold water and hold it there for as long as possible. This is a standard psychological test for measuring willpower and self-discipline.

- The deciders removed their hands first. They were simply too tired.

Studies have shown that when people's blood sugar falls they make different types of decision. For example, studies have shown that judges are more likely to grant applications for early release from prison in the morning or just after lunch than later in the afternoon. When their blood sugar fell, they did not have the same energy levels and were more inclined to make the conservative decision and not change the existing arrangements.

This is very important at mediations where blood sugar does go up and down during the day and tends to fall towards the end of the day, as the host venue's catering closes down. People usually hit the wall, at about 15.30 (see **Chapter 10**).

Default effect

18.09 People are drawn to make a choice based on what they already know and are comfortable with.

People tend to stick with the status quo because it is simply too much trouble to change. This inertia accounts for people sticking with low interest paying bank accounts and badly performing share portfolios.

At mediations this can inhibit creative structuring of settlements.

Empathy gap

The tendency to underestimate the influence or strength of feeling of either oneself or others.

At mediations, one party will often say that this is just business, but reveal that they are not taking decisions based on a business case: ' I know that it doesn't really make sense financially but it doesn't feel right'

Each side does not usually acknowledge this because they do not realise how cheated or let down the other side feel.

Endowment effect

The fact that people often demand much more to give up an object than they would be willing to pay to acquire it. In other words people value something more highly as soon as they possess it.

The client says: 'I cannot agree to transfer my shares for £2 million. They are worth much more than this. I know that the company has only been valued at £10 million, which makes my 10 per cent shareholding worth £1 million but they are worth more than that to me.

Or: 'I know that I have offered him £2 million for his 50 per cent shareholding but I will not sell my 50 per cent shareholding for £2million. It is not enough.'

False consensus effect

The tendency for people to over-estimate how much other people agree with them. People frequently believe that everyone else thinks and feels exactly like that.

We tend to regard people that are do not share our opinions as abnormal.

At mediations the parties routinely discount the possibility that the other side might have a point. They also assume that the judge will share their view of the merits of their case and the faults and moral turpitude of the other side.

Fear of regret

18.10   Here is another test.

> John owns £2,000 shares in company. During the year he thinks about selling them but does not. At the end of the year the shares are worth £500. Has lost £1,500 over the year.
>
> David own shares in another company. Earlier in the year he sold them and bought some shares in same company that John has shares in. If he had stayed with his original company he would be £1,500 better off.
>
> Who do you feel sorrier for?
>
> In a research project when people were asked this question 92 per cent chose David and 8 per cent chose John.
>
> They are both in the same position. They have both lost the same amount of money. The difference is that David took a conscious decision to buy the shares during the year but John decided to stay with what he knew.

If you do not follow the crowd you tend to feel more regret, hence last chances make people anxious and nervous and fear of regret makes them conform to the default position.

At mediations, parties find it difficult to think how their world might be different when asked to contemplate the consequences of not settling.

Framing effect

How a message is received depends on how it is communicated in the first place.

Kahneman conducted a survey in the 1980s. He presented two options for the epidemic-control plan. They told the participants that the lives of 600 people were at risk:

- Option A saves 200 lives.
- Option B offers a 33 per cent chance all 600 will survive and 66 per cent chance that no one will survive.

Although options A and B have similar outcomes with 200 survivors expected, most of the participants chose option A.

They re- framed the same options as:

- Option A kills 400 people.
- Option B offers a 33 per cent chance that no one will die and 66 per cent that all 600 will die.

This time nearly everybody chose option B

So depending on the framing of the option and the use of the word 'survive' or 'die', the decision of the participants who heard the options was changed.

At mediations everyone present does this all the time: asking questions in a way that will prompt the answer they want. Mediators spend quite a lot of time saying: 'Well, yes, but there is another way of putting it.'

Fundamental attribution error

18.11   The client says: 'They are only saying this because they are obstructive. They have always been awkward and acting in bad faith.'

This overlooks the fact that the reason people may be acting in a certain way is not because of their personality but because of the situation in which they find themselves.

At mediations parties habitually assume this. Mediators often have to ask: what would you do in their situation? When asked, most parties acknowledge that they might be doing the same thing.

Hyperbolic discounting

The closer a reward is to us the more we are prepared to pay for it. This is important in mediations when alternative settlements are proposed, some of which have longer instalment periods.

Here is a simple test.

Which of the following options would you choose?
• Option A: £1,000 in 12 months time
• Option B: £1,100 in 13 months time?

> Most people chose Option B.
>
> Which of these options would you choose?
>
> - Option A: £1,000 today in cash
> - Option B: £1,100 in a month's time.
>
> Most people choose option A.

It is inconsistent. The reasoning goes: 'I already waited 12 months so another month doesn't matter. This contrasts with: 'I can have the money now.' The power of now cannot be overestimated.

At mediations the timing of payments is often discussed and a lot of mind clearing has to take place for both sides to see the real value of money. The paying party frequently underestimates the drawing power of cash.

Impact bias

Tendency to overestimate the length or the intensity of the impact of future feelings.

At mediations people say: 'We could never agree to that. Members of our community know about this dispute. We have a good reputation, not like them.' In fact the community are already talking about something else.

Information bias

The tendency to seek information even when it cannot affect action.

At meditation there are always pleas for more information. Sometimes these requests are genuine and the missing information, when supplied, does remove an obstacle to settlement, but often it does not. The requests are more usually a pressure tactic or displacement activity.

Parties will often say earlier in the day: 'We cannot make a decision because we do not know …', but settlement is made later in the day even with the information still missing.

Introspection illusion

18.12   This is the belief that reflection leads to truth or accuracy.

People tend to be confident in their own beliefs. This leads them to have three reactions when someone does not share them:

- They are ignorant. They do not have the necessary information. If they had the same information they would have the same opinion.
- They are stupid. They have the necessary information but cannot draw the necessary conclusions.
- Bad faith: they have the necessary information but they are being deliberately obstructive and confrontational.

In fact, research shows that introspection is not reliable. People see what they want to see in themselves. Their belief in the accuracy of their own introspection causes them to feel superior.

At mediations this can cause parties to demonise each other. This can delay the generation of the modicum of trust, which is necessary to get any deal done.

Irrational escalation (also known as **sunk cost bias**)

The tendency to justify increased investments in a decision based on cumulative prior investment, despite new evidence suggesting that the decision was probably wrong.

At mediations, parties say: 'We have already spent £100,000 on costs, we might as well go to trial. I would rather spend the money on lawyers than pay it to them.'

Optimism bias

The tendency to be too confident in one's predictions, in particular the tendency to overestimate one's chances of success.

18.13 Two research studies illustrate this:

Study 1

The same factual information was given to two groups of Harvard students. One group was told that they were advising the claimant. The other was told they were advising the defendant. They were asked to predict the outcome of the trial in terms of liability and quantum. The claimant group consistently predicted higher chances of winning and higher amounts.

Study 2

The groups were given the facts of actual cases and asked to predict the outcome compared with what happened at trial. Both groups, whether acting for the claimant or the defendants, gave themselves a higher chance of winning than in fact turned out at trial.

At mediations advocates and their clients do this all the time. Sometimes they are bluffing. Often they are not. They are just being optimistically biased.

Paradox of choice

Choice is seen as a hallmark of freedom and progress. People like having a wide range of choice. But too much choice destroys the quality. The more choice people have, the more uncertain they are about the choices that they have made and the greater the anxiety and dissatisfaction

Pseudo-certainty effect

The client says: 'I know that you have told me that my chances are at best 50/50 but frankly I would rather take my chances in court.'

Clients who face the prospect of financial ruin if they go to court and lose often say this. As the example 'Illustrating the endowment effect' shows, people are more inclined to be risk averse in order to gain something and risk seeking to avoid giving up something that they already have.

Reactive devaluation

18.14   This is the tendency of one side to reject any suggestion from the other side simply because it came from the other side.

At mediations people do it all the time. The client says:'If we need a third-party surveyor to value the property we cannot use anybody that they choose or suggest,' or, 'we cannot agree that their suggestion of the grant of an option would be a good idea.'

In fact mediators spend a lot of time defusing this response when they take proposals on settlement to a party. Sometimes mediators go further and present a proposal or idea as their own rather than the other side's.

Selective perception

The tendency for expectations to affect perception

At mediations, the client says to the mediator in the first private session: 'I do not think that this mediation is going to work. The other side are not here in good faith. It is going to be a waste of time.' When a settlement has not been reached, the client says, 'I told you it was really a waste of time'

Expectations do affect performance.

Story bias

The tendency to see meaning in details, which can lead to false understanding and a predisposition to risk taking. The meaning is added afterwards. This is where another bias, **hindsight bias,** comes into play.

This bias underpins the narrative model of mediation and also much of the therapy-based philosophy. It also undermines their rationale.

Ultimatum game

The belief that you choose to accept or refuse an offer based on logic rather than on status.

An example of this has been given in **para 5.06**.

In mediations the importance of satisfying peoples' sense of fairness and of co-operating to achieve this is often overlooked until the day is well advanced

Zero-risk bias

This is the tendency to neglect probability and instead of concentrating on the likelihood of an event to concentrate on the magnitude of the impact of the event.

At mediations people will say: 'But if I win at trial they will be ruined. They have ruined me so I will ruin them.'

They say this even when they have been told that their chances of winning are 50/50 or 60/40 at best.

The biases in action

18.15 *This is the Opening Statement by the advocate for the claimant:*

> 'Thank you Mr Mediator I would like to say how grateful we are to you for acting as a mediator in this case. I only have a few words to say to my opponent.
>
> You must understand that while we are here with an open mind to listen to what you have to say about settlement we are supremely confident in our case. We do not just say that. We have thought long and hard about it and that is our conclusion. It is an objective assessment, which has been considered by our Legal Director and the Board of Directors. Our barrister, Mr Knowall, who as you know is the leading QC in this area of law, has advised us that we have an overwhelming chance of winning at court. It is one of the strongest cases that he has ever seen.'

Comment

This paragraph displays:

- optimism bias – we are supremely confident;
- blind spot bias – open mind, an objective assessment;
- authority bias – Mr Knowall a leading QC; and
- introspection illusion.

> 'You have also seen our expert's report which supports our case by Prof Smith who again is one of the leading experts in this area. We are sure that when he has the joint experts meeting with your man, I'm sorry I cannot remember his name, he will be able to explain to your man why his conclusions are in error. His suggestion that they should appoint a third expert to facilitate their discussion is frankly absurd'

Comment

18.16 This displays:

- authority bias – Professor Smith is the leading expert;
- confirmation bias – expert's report;
- optimism bias – why his conclusions are in error; and
- reactive devaluation: his suggestion.

'I'm not going to descend into arguments about facts and law. The position is clearly set out in the pleadings and the witness statements filed so far.

We do not understand how you can have persuaded your lawyers to act on a conditional fee agreement basis. Either they have not been fully instructed or they have not appreciated the legal difficulties that they face in this case.'

Comment

- False consensus effect – we cannot understand how you can have persuaded.

'We accept that there is a difference of evidence, which the judge will have to resolve in court but frankly we cannot see how your managing director can hope to persuade the court that he is anything other than a liar. We can tell you that Mr Noel is looking forward to cross-examining him in the witness box. We are sure that you have advised him about the risks of perjury. Indeed your companies have conducted themselves throughout in a dishonourable way which will open them up to criticism by the judge at trial.'

Comment

18.17   This displays:

- ad hominem fallacy – your MD is a liar;
- false consensus bias; and
- authority bias – Mr Knowell is looking forward to ….

'We do not need to remind you that our clients are a hugely successful multinational company. They can afford to take this matter all the way to trial without any difficulty whatsoever. We do have grave doubts about whether you can afford to do that. We do not mind admitting that recoverability of the costs order, which we will inevitably obtain, is something that has been factored into our costs and therefore when approaching this mediation. However, we have already spent in excess of £250,000 on this litigation so that we might as well go to trial.

As I said we are here to listen to you and see if you can persuade us but frankly unless you we so no reason to depart from our previous offer to which as you will know is solely calculated on a nuisance value. In fact we doubt very much whether there is anything that you can say that would persuade us.'

Comment

- Selective perception – we very much doubt …;
- optimisim bias – costs order which we will inevitably obtain; and
- irrational escalation – we have already spent £250,000.

'In fact if this case is not settled today my instructions are to withdraw the offer and to seek an order for security for costs against the claimants. This will cause you financial difficulty, but that is nothing compared with the financial crisis that you will suffer when you lose at trial.

I don't propose to say any more but would like cut to the chase and get with matters with the help of the mediator, who I'm sure has seen many cases like this before, because our CEO has a plane catch just after lunch.'

Comment

* impact bias– financial crisis;
* empathy gap; and
* false consensus.

Conclusion

18.18 To conclude:

* Self audit before during and after each mediation.
* You and your clients will be influenced by some or all of these biases. So will the other side and their advisers. So will be the mediator.
* Being aware makes you able to correct them and helps your client to come to the best-informed decision.

Checklist of biases and heuristics

Ad hominem fallacy: the belief that if you cannot trust someone, you cannot trust what that person says.

Affect heuristic: an affect is an instantaneous judgement. You like something or you do not. They prevent people from considering risks and benefits to be independent variables.

Alternative blindness: people tend not to compare an existing offer with the next best alternative.

Ambiguity effect: the tendency to avoid options for which missing information makes the probability seem unknown

Ambiguity aversion: humans do not like uncertainty. Their distaste for it leads them to make hasty and wrong decisions. This tendency is aggravated by a confusion between risk and uncertainty.

Anchoring: the tendency to rely to heavily or (anchor) on a past reference or piece of information when making decisions.

Association bias: (also known as 'shoot the messenger' syndrome.) Our brains like to make connections but sometimes the connections of false. For example Pavlov's dogs who learned to salivate at the sound of the bell while one at the site or smell or taste in food.

Authority bias: the tendency to allow the status and credentials of a person to influence the perception of information or advice he gives.

Blind spot bias: the tendency to see oneself as less biased than other people or to be able to identify more cognitive biases in others then in oneself

Choice supportive bias: the tendency to remember one's choices as better than they actually were.

Cognitive dissonance: this is where you reinterpret what has happened to justify the situation you are now in.

Confirmation bias: the tendency to search for and interpret information in a way that confirms one's preconceptions.

Curse of knowledge: the tendency to allow one's knowledge of the subject to reduce one's ability to think about the problem.

Decision fatigue: intensive decision-making can drain will power.

Default effect: people are drawn to it and should make a choice based on what they already know and are comfortable with.

Domain dependence: insights may not transfer as well from one field to another. Just because somebody does well at one thing or something works in one context does not mean it will work in another.

Empathy gap: the tendency to underestimate the influence or strength of feeling a of either oneself or others

Endowment effect: the fact that people often demand much more to give up an object than they would be willing to pay to acquire it. In other words people value something more highly as soon as they possess it.

Easy come, easy go: When people at mediation say it is just about money even when they are offered money or have to pay money that is not free of emotion and value judgements. Here is a test

---

After a hard years work you have a surplus £20,000 in your account. What you do with it?

- A leave it in the bank;
- B invest it;
- C make necessary improvements and repairs to your house; or
- D take a luxury holiday.

Most people choose a, B or C.

This time you win £20,000 on the lottery. Which choice you now make? Most people choose option D.

Envy: there's a difference between envy and jealousy. Envy is about a thing such as status, money or someone else. Jealousy is about the behaviour of someone else. Envy needs people. Jealousy needs thought.

False consensus effect: the tendency for people to over estimate how much other people agree with them. People frequently believe that everyone else thinks and feels exactly like that.

Fear of regret: If you do not follow the crowd you tend to feel more regret, hence last chances make people anxious and nervous and fear of regret makes us conform to the default position.

Feature-positive effect: what is present has more influence than what is absent. The information that is not there can be more important.

Also positive advice, eg 'Do this!' has more impact than negative advice 'Forget about that'!

Framing effect: Drawing different conclusions from the same information depending on how or by whom that information is presented.

Fundamental attributable error: believing that other people's behaviour is a reflection of their personality rather than as a result of their situation.

Hammer effect: this derives its name from what Mark Twain said: 'If your only tool is a hammer, all your problems will be nails.'

We tend to find solutions based on our own expertise.

Hyperbolic discounting: the closer a reward is to us the more we are willing to pay.

Impact bias: tendency to overestimate the length or the intensity of the impact of future feelings.

Information bias: the tendency to seek information even when it cannot affect action.

Introspection illusion: is the belief that reflection leads to truth or accuracy.

Inability to close doors: we find it difficult to our sacrifice an option. People prefer to have as many choices as possible. This makes it difficult to concentrate and dilutes the chances of success.

The sleeper effect: this is where we tend to forget the source of information or argument quicker than we forget information or argument.

Always ask who is giving this argument or information and why are they doing it? Why do they hold it?

Irrational escalation (also known as sunk **cost bias**): the tendency to justify increased investments in a decision based on cumulative prior investment, despite new evidence suggesting that the decision was probably wrong.

Omission bias: is being deliberately passive when there is a clear opportunity to be decisive and active.

Optimism bias: the tendency to be too confident in one's predictions, and in particular the tendency to overestimate one's chances of success.

Overthinking: what happens if people think too much is that they do not rely enough on their emotions and therefore cut themselves off from the wisdom of your emotions.

The Paradox of choice: The more choice you have the more uncertain you are about the choices that you made and the greater the anxiety and dissatisfaction.

Personification: people like to see other people are not figures. This is why charities have photographs of children not lists of percentages.

Planning fallacy: people systematically take on too much to do. People habitually take between 30 per cent and 50 per cent longer than they anticipate to complete a job.

Wishful thinking: people want to be successful and achieve everything that we would like to achieve and take on.

Primacy and recency effects: first and last impressions are very important. If you have to make a decision based on a series of impressions the primacy effect prevails. If however impressions were formed some time ago the recency effect prevails. If you saw a film or heard a speech a few weeks ago you remember the ending more than the beginning

Pseudo-certainty effect: the tendency to make risk-averse choices if the expected outcome is positive but risk-seeking choices to avoid negative outcomes.

Reactive devaluation: this is the tendency of one side to reject any suggestion from the other side simply because it came from the other side.

Selective perception: the tendency for expectations to affect perception.

Self-serving bias: this is where we attribute blame for failures to other factors and success to our own efforts and talents.

Simple logic: it has to be remembered that thinking is more tiring than sensing or feeling. Exercising rationality requires more self-discipline and will than simply relying on intuition.

Story bias: the tendency to see meaning in details, which can lead to false understanding and a predisposition to risk taking.

Sunk cost fallacy (see **irrational esclation fallacy**)

Twaddle tendency: filling the silence with meaningless words just for the sake of talking. Or, as Mark Twain said: 'If you have nothing to say, say nothing.'

Ultimatum game: the belief that you choose to accept or refuse an offer based on logic rather than on status.

Zero-risk bias: this is the tendency to neglect probability and instead of concentrating on the likelihood of an event to concentrate on the magnitude of the impact of the event.

Part D
Self-Advocacy: Representing Yourself

Chapter 19

Self-Advocacy

> This chapter discusses:
>
> - The differences when advocating for yourself
> - Common mistakes made by self-advocates
> - Checklist of points and tips for self-advocates

19.01 This chapter is intended for those who decide to represent themselves at mediation. They will have no legal training or prior experience of representing themselves at mediations; they are first-time advocates and they are acting for themselves.

Some of the matters discussed in this chapter have already been discussed in this book and are cross-referenced. There is some duplication. Please re-read the cross referenced sections.

The chapter deals with the work that the applicant has to do:

- pre-mediation;
- in the Joint Session; and
- in the private sessions

Why is self-advocacy different?

19.02 It is much harder to advocate for yourself rather than on behalf of somebody else for a number of reasons:

- As an advocate you want to be persuasive. As a self-advocate you are more invested in the case. You believe in it. The danger is that you think the sincerity of your own belief is sufficient to convince the other side that you are right. It is not.

- In order to persuade someone, you have to address points and issues that are influential on them. You have to look at the case from their point of view and see what they see. This is difficult when you are heavily committed to a particular view of the case. It always requires effort to look at a case through somebody else's eyes. Even third-party advocates find this difficult.

- The curse of knowledge can apply. To be an effective advocate you have to concentrate on the main points. You identify the key issues and marshal the supporting evidence. A process of selection has to be applied. When you know everything about the case and you live it day in day out it, is incredibly difficult to select in this way. You think that the other party needs to know everything that you know. If you try and tell them everything you will lose their attention. If they are not paying attention you cannot persuade them of anything.

- Inexperience shows. Most people attending a mediation have never been to one before. Many of them have never had to present a case on their own behalf before. Even if they have, they have not usually had to do so to a hostile audience, ie the other side and their advisers. It can be off-putting.

- If you believe in something is it is difficult to not feel emotionally engaged. This is particularly true if the other side aggressively challenges your belief. You feel personally under attack in a way which the third-party advocate does not. His client might feel under attack but the client is not doing the advocacy. They can concentrate on controlling their emotions. This is much more difficult to do if you are controlling your emotions and advocating at the same time.

Common mistakes of self-advocates

Talking for too long

19.03   People talk for too long for various reasons:

- They are feeling under stress. Talking can relieve stress. There is a whole industry of psychotherapy based on the idea that you should talk about your problems to make yourself feel better.

- At mediation, many mediators believe that the party should be encouraged to vent. They may invite clients to speak out.

- People feel nervous if there is silence. They feel that they have to fill it.

- People feel everybody is looking at them and they have to do something. That something is to talk. In fact the silence can be no more than people being polite and not interrupting.

- Of course, experienced lawyers on the other side know that many people, if given the chance to talk, carry on talking and end up talking themselves into problems. Many negotiation trainers emphasise the use of deliberate silence and pauses to let the speaker keep on talking and revealing more.

- Many people believe that you can talk yourself out of a problem, but in reality they often talk themselves into a problem.

Talking too quickly

Most people talk too quickly when they are nervous. You will be nervous. If you are not nervous at all you will not do a good job. The trick is not to be over-nervous. There is no need to have stage fright.

Lack of preparation

As George Bernard Shaw said: 'I have written a long book because I did not have time to write a short book.'

It takes time and hard work to prepare for any sort of speech. You have to give yourself enough time to do it. Most people cannot leave it until the last moment – experienced advocates may be able to, but not most people. Remember most people underestimate by 40 per cent how long it will take them to complete a task.

Stage struck

19.04   Self-advocates may be overwhelmed by the moment. They have a dispute, which they think they are right about, and they want to be heard. They may even think that they want to have their day in court. This is their chance. They have become so nervous that they freeze or babble away in a disjointed way.

Information management

An important part of the mediation process is the managed disclosure of information. The parties manage it themselves. They decide what they are going to tell the mediator or the other side and when. The mediator also does it. He is receiving information from the parties and with their consent deciding when it can be disclosed to the other side. He is also identifying information gaps, which need to be filled and telling each side what they may have to disclose to the other.

Giving too much information

19.05   Experienced mediation advocates and lawyers know about information management. Clients often do not.

Self-advocates assume that the more information that they give to the other side and to the mediator the better. The more that the other side know, the more that they will understand and the more that they will agree with you. This is a mistake. The listener is overloaded with information. Your weak points dilute your strong points. More can end up being less.

In a caucus, self-advocates talk at length to the mediator. They are so involved in the case that they feel the need to convince the mediator that they are absolutely right and to be reassured that he believes them.

Most mediators will allow this to happen in the early private sessions. They want the parties to feel that they have had a chance to vent. As the issues become clearer mediators become more directive about what they want to hear. Parties do not always respond to the clues and cues that the mediator is giving them. Mutual frustration can build up, with the parties thinking that the mediator is not listening to them and the mediator thinking that the parties are being evasive.

Self-advocates may be very ready to volunteer information to the mediator without being clear in their own mind what it is that they want the mediator to do with it. You have to ask yourself: why am I telling the mediator this?

- If the mediator has asked a question, the answer is obvious – you are trying to give the mediator what he wants. Even then you should clarify why the mediator thinks that what he has asked is important.

- Is he just asking for his own benefit? In other words, is he asking to clarify his own understanding or is he asking for information that he may wish to pass onto the other side at some stage?

- Is he, in a question, actually telling you something?

Even as a self-advocate, listen more than you speak.

Over-selling

Parties are often bursting with information in the early part of the mediation day. They have been waiting for this opportunity for a long time. They give fluent descriptions of their case and explanations of why they are confident that they will win at trial. They assure the mediator that they have the evidence to back up what they say. As the day progresses it often becomes clear that the information and evidence is not actually to hand.

The information may not be presented in the way that it is being asked. For example, they may not have the latest sale figures. They may only have available the last quarter's figures. Or they have left the information at home. Many mediators have been told by a party that there are pages and pages of emails which proved the point that the client is emphasising. When the mediator explains that this is useful in trying to show to the other side why they might want to reconsider their position and asks for permission to take the pages into the other room he is told that they have only brought six with them. This has two negative results:

- your point cannot be fully substantiated and therefore loses its impact; and

- your credibility is diminished.

Pre-mediation

19.06   Preparation is everything. It:
- increases self-confidence;
- clarifies the mind;
- ensures that you have the points and documentation read; and
- stops you worrying.

Contact the mediator

Email the mediator, introducing yourself and asking when it would be convenient to call him. Then speak to mediator on the telephone. Before the telephone call make a list of the questions that you want to ask him. Re-read **Chapter 3.** Ask the mediator what he requires from you and when he wants. That helps you work out a timetable the preparatory before the mediation day.

Steps up to mediation day

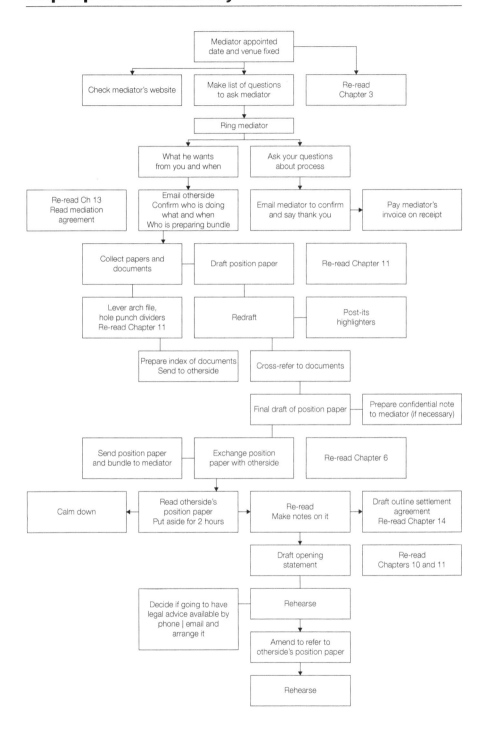

If the mediation agreement has already been received, make sure you have read it before speaking to the mediator so that you can any questions about it. If it has not been received, ask when it will be available.

Contact the other side

Email the other side to confirm who is preparing the documents bundle and any index, and when you are going to send them to the mediator and exchange position papers. There is no need to copy this to the mediator

Email the mediator

Email the mediator to confirm what he has said and to thank him for his time and advice. There is no need to copy this to the other side. Pay the mediator's invoice on receipt as this always creates a good impression.

Documents

19.07   You should prepare the documents as follows:

- Collect all your documents together. Put them in date order with the earliest at the front.

- If court proceedings have started, collect the various court papers including statements of claim, defence etc pleadings) and any court orders. Put them in a ring or lever arch binder. Lawyers call this a bundle in England and Wales. You can call it a mediation file.

- Once you have decided what documents to include number them in the bottom right hand corner.

- If you have time to do so,prepare an index and insert dividers. Do not index every letter. Do not put dividers in between every piece of correspondence.

- At the end of the chapter there is a template example of an index for a medium-sized bundle. This is for your use. It means that you will have everything to hand and be able to find it on the day. If you are preparing the bundle you can of course use it for that as well.

Re-read **Chapter 11**.

What to include

Think what you would like the mediator to read. Tell the other side and invite them to agree. Do not waste time arguing about this. Do not worry about trying to agree the contents of the bundle or the index with the other side. Send it to them for their information. Ask them if there is anything they want you to include,and, if so, include it.

If the other side is represented by lawyers, ask them to prepare and send the bundle. If they refuse to do this just send one yourself with an index and explain to the mediator what you are doing.

Tell them if there are any documents that you want to be included. If they object, just send them to the mediator anyway and explain why you are doing this.

Go back to your draft statement and mark any documents that are referred to with the number of the page in the bundle. Once again this is for your use.

If you decide to send a mediation statement to the mediator, delete any references which are helpful to you but not necessarily helpful for him. Mediators like short rather than long mediation statements and thin rather than fat files of documents

Mediation statement/position paper

19.08   A template for a mediation statement/position paper is at the end of this chapter.

Prepare a mediation statement (aka position paper)

You may decide not to exchange mediation statements, or you may decide not to use one at all. Preparing it will have these benefits:

- It will provide you with a draft script to use in the Joint Opening Session.

- If you decide not to have a joint session, it will provide you with a script to use in your first private meeting (caucus) with the mediator.

- It will make you think how you are going to present your side of the story. Doing this will force you to identify clearly what the key points are that you want the other side to understand (and eventually, if not publicly, accept).

- It will make you focus on precisely what you want by way of settlement and how that settlement can be structured.

Headings

Do not worry about headings. If there are pleadings they will have the headings used in the court file. It is conventional to put those headings on the top of the position paper and the index. There is no requirement to do it.

If there are no court proceedings, use headings like those shown in the template. You can refer to the two sides as claimant and defendant or by their actual names. Sometimes it is easier to use the words claimant and defendant even if there are no court proceedings. The mediator reading through the mediation statement will know who is making the claim and who is defending it without having to check back to see which party is which.

Re-read **Chapter 11.**

Prepare a draft Settlement Agreement

19.09   Re-read **Chapter 14** and see the template at the end of this chapter. Doing this now helps you focus on:

- what you actually want from a settlement;

- how it would in practice be implemented;

- things that you might have to double check; and

- preparing alternative versions stimulates creative thinking about potential solutions.

Give yourself the best chance of making a good impression, first by preparing the bundle of documents and the mediation statements as described above, and secondly by the way that you present yourself in the Joint Opening Session.

At the mediation

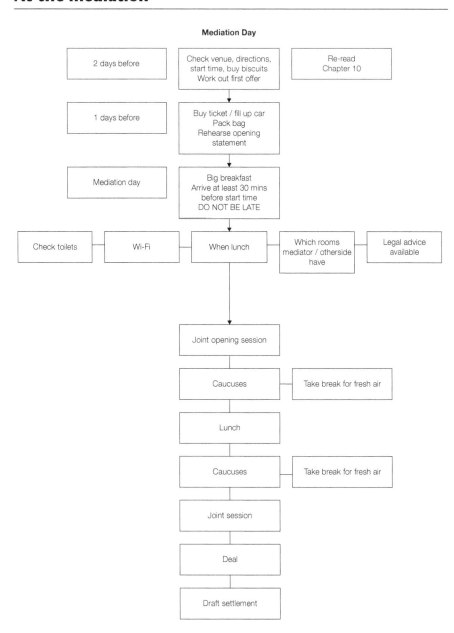

The Joint Opening Session

19.10 Many people worry about this and become anxious. It is important. It is a performance. The other side might appear negative and hostile but the mediator will not be.

The purpose of the Joint Opening Session and what happens has been described in **Chapter 10**. Re-read it.

Each party at the mediation is given the opportunity to make an opening statement if they want to. You do not have to make an opening statement if you do not want. Although it is conventional to do so and it is unusual not to say anything at all there is no requirement or obligation.

Sometimes a party, even if a barrister or solicitor is representing them, confine themselves to saying that they do not want to add anything to what is already in the paperwork or included in the position paper (or mediation statement). They just want to say that they are here to try and settle this matter with the help of the mediator.

Any issues that need to be expanded or explored can be done in private session with the mediator. If the mediator considers that it would be useful for there to be a joint session later in the day, he can suggest one.

Advantages of Joint Opening Session

The advantages of the Joint Opening Session for an unrepresented party are:

- You get to see the other side will. You may never have seen the decision maker on the other side before. You can assess them.

- You can make a human contact.

- They can of course do the same to you. Be aware that they will be weighing you up to see how good a witness you will make at trial. Are you credible? Do you get rattled? Can you withstand pressure?

Not being a lawyer helps

19.11 You are not a lawyer. Do not see this as a disadvantage. It is not. Instead make a virtue of not being a lawyer. You tell them that:

- you are not going to get drawn into legal arguments:

- you have been told that mediations are not mini-trials so you are not going to have one;

- the important factors at mediation are not legal ones but commercial and personal ones – that is what you will deal with; and

- if they have legal points they can make them to the judge.

By taking this line you are seizing the initiative and taking control of the agenda. You are also bringing the clients on the other side into prominence and demoting the lawyers to the sidelines. You will not encounter any resistance from the mediator. Many will thank you (inwardly if not expressly) for doing it.

You must be clear what you are going to say, having cut through the legal undergrowth to identify the path to settlement. Are you intending to persuade, argue or assess?

Mutual assessment

Ideally you should be assessing the situation from both sides. See their reality and yours. Remember Core Principle 4 (see **para 1.02**). Do not just look at the issues from your side. Showing them that you are able to see their point of view will win you respect from both them and the mediator and also free up your mind to be flexible, when thinking about settlement.

Poise under fire

In practice most parties at mediations cannot resist the temptation to tell the other side that they are wrong. They have to correct, clarify or just deny. Sometimes, although the mediator has asked everyone not to interrupt they cannot help themselves. Stay calm and silent

Do not:

• get drawn into any arguments. It is much more impressive to hear them out. Then calmly go through the points on which you disagree, explaining as you go why you think that the judge will agree with you;

• get drawn into extended argument. There will be more of them than you. You can end up facing attacks from different directions; and

• make life more difficult for yourself.

Say that you will deal with these points through the mediator.

• Remember that if you have chosen the mediator wisely (see **Chapter 3**), he will be bound by the European Code of Conduct. That requires him to address imbalances of power. He will not represent you but he will stop you being bullied.

Arrange yourself

19.12

• Make sure that you have your papers in front of you on the table. Have a note pad to hand to note any point you think is important from what either the mediator says or the other side.

• While they are talking: watch, listen, learn.

• Do not try and take a verbatim note. Jot down a few key words to jog your memory later. Be careful what you note and when you make a note. They will be looking at you for clues as what makes an impression on you. If you scribble intensely, they may think that you must be worried.

- Make sure that you have a glass of water to hand. You are nervous. Your mouth will be dry. Talking and tension makes it drier. Take a sip in mid-speech if you need to. Just say, 'Excuse me' and have a drink. This also gives you a moment to think. If there is no water in sight ask for some.

Visual aids

There are mediators and trainers who swear by visual aids. Power points, slides, recordings and flip charts: they love them. Beware: they are treacherous.

As a self-advocate do not use them. Their capacity for going wrong is too great. It will throw you off course. If you have any, tell the mediator and the other side. Say that you will play them at the appropriate time. If you do play them later you will have been able to set them up and run through them. At this time you will be concentrating on one thing: setting up the visual aid or recording. You will not be trying to make your Opening Statement at the same time.

Photographs and plans

The only exceptions are photographs and plans, but even those can be referred to and left with the other side to look at or supplied later through the mediator. It is usually better to supply them through the mediator. You can explain the meaning and relevance of them to him. If the mediator agrees that they are useful, he can take them to the other side and pass on your explanations.

If you are using plans, make sure that you show the scale and you have plenty of copies for people to mark up.

If you are using photographs, make sure that you have the time, date and location to hand. For really key photographs make multiple prints. They still have more impact than images on an iPad.

How many points to make?

19.13 Pick your best three points and concentrate on them. Three points in five minutes is a lot more effective than 15 in 25 minutes. Many advocates think that they have to include every possible point. They are scared of missing something out. This is particularly annoying to judges in court and there is no point in doing it at mediation. The big danger is that the other side loses their concentration and the quantity of so many points dilutes the impact of the strong ones.

Resist the urge to give expression to your secret desire to be a lawyer. You have seen them on the screen and you have a good idea of what works. In practice it is all very different, especially at mediation.

Be careful of 'Googlelaw'. There is a lot of useful information and advice to be found on the internet, but it has to be assessed and interpreted. Do not start quoting from cases or law books in the Joint Opening Session. If you want to refer to this material, run through it with the mediator in private first. He will give you guidance on whether it will be helpful to the settlement process. Do not think that you will be able to persuade the other side on the law or the facts. Even if they think that you may have some good points, they are not going to publicly admit it. You do not need to prove them wrong. You just need them to pay you money.

Three tips for all advocates

19.14 The three tips traditionally given to all advocates are:

- stand up
- speak up
- shut up

At mediation you do not stand up. You *sit up* instead. But you do *speak up* and you do *shut up*. In other words: be confident. Even be assertive, but do not be aggressive and certainly do not be offensive. There are some cultures where if you are not screaming and shouting you are being a wimp and not really trying. Not at mediations in the UK,however. Histrionics do not impress.

Prepare and then prepare again and then again. Rehearsal is essential for a confident opening statement.

Sports psychologists who train competitors get them to visualise how they will perform. Do the same for the mediation. It works and it helps. Practice what you are going to say. Do it in front of a mirror so that you can see your body language, particularly your hands and eyes. Time yourself and mark the time splits on your notes.

Suggested openings and closings

Openings for the claimant speaking first

19.15 'GOOD MORNING. I am glad we got this chance to sort this matter out. I am only sorry that it has got this far. I do hope that with the help of the mediator we can see a way through to a settlement.

I am not a lawyer. I'm not going to deal with legal arguments and evidence. I have been advised that I have a strong case. I'm going to leave it there.

I realise that you think that you have a strong case. If you want to make legal points against my case and in favour of yours, I suggest that you do that before the judge.

Today is not the day for that. I fully take on board the purpose of today, which is to try to make a settlement and we are here to make peace not war.

The mediation process has been explained to me. It is my understanding that mediations are not are not mini-trials.

Settlement at mediation is not driven by legal factors but by commercial and personal ones. Those are the ones I'm going to deal with.

It seems to me with the help of the mediator that we have to tackle the following [3–5] issues.'

[List them and briefly comment on them.]

Openings for the defendant going second (where the claimant has been moderate and conciliatory)

'GOOD MORNING. I'm glad that we have got this opportunity tried to sort this matter out.

I listened carefully to what you said. I'm not going to go through all your points one by one and comment on them. I am not a lawyer. I am not going to deal with legal points. We can do that at trial if we have to.

If the mediator thinks that there is a particular issue that he would like to explore in the interests of achieving settlement then I will be happy to co-operate.

I understand that mediation is a process designed to try and bring about a settlement.

Settlements of mediation are not driven by legal factors but by commercial and personal ones. Those are the ones I will deal with now.

From my point of view I think that with the help of the mediator these are the following issues, which we will have to address today in order to achieve a settlement.

These are in addition to the points you have raised. [or] They include some/all of the points that you have raised.'

[List your points.]

'As I understand from what you have said both in your opening statement and in your mediation statement you also think that we have to address: [List their points]'

Openings for the defendant (where the claimant has been aggressive and adversarial)

19.16 'GOOD MORNING. I'm glad that we have a chance today the help of the mediator to sort this matter out and to try and achieve a settlement.

I have been told that the purpose of mediation is to make peace not war. I am not going to respond in kind to what you said in your opening statement. I will leave the mediator to deal with that.

I'm not a lawyer. I have been advised that I have a strong case of this matter goes to trial. I realise that you also believe that you have a strong case. The only person to decide which of our lawyers is right is the judge.

I have also been told that mediation is not a mini-trial. I am not going to deal with legal arguments.

I understand that factors that drive mediation settlements are not legal ones but commercial and personal ones and I will concentrate on those.

The benefits to both sides of settling this case seem to me to be:

- saving legal costs. By my calculations the total legal fees spent to date is [£XX] and by the end of trial will be [£XX];

- saving time. No matter who wins, we do not get compensated for the lost time and effort. I would rather be spending this on my business/life. Litigation may be stimulating profit for lawyers but it is downtime for their clients; and

- opportunity cost: frankly there are other things that I would rather be spending time and effort on. I'm sure that this is the same for you.

I think that with the help of the mediator we need to address the following issues: [List them]'

Closings for claimants going first

19.17 'Finally, as I have said, I understand that the purpose of mediation is to make a settlement. I understand what is involved in negotiating settlements. I understand that there are costs and risks of litigation on both sides. If at all possible I would like to avoid further costs and risk. It takes two to tango – I am here to try if you are. Thank you for listening.'

Closings for defendants going second (where the claimant has been moderate and conciliatory)

'I am pleased to hear that you're also in settlement mode. As I said at the beginning I'm sorry that we got to this stage but I hope that with the help of the mediator that we can settle things today.

I realise that it takes effort from both sides. I'm here in good faith to participate in the settlement process and hope that we can put this dispute behind us and move forward.

Thank you for listening.'

Closings for defendants going second (where the claimant has been aggressive and adversarial)

'As I have said, I could see the mutual benefits of settlement outweighing the mutual costs of fighting on. I hope that with the help of the mediator we can find at to settlement. I'm here in good faith to participate in that process.

I hope that despite what you said in your opening statement that you are as well. But if you're not then so be it and we can have an early lunch and get back to work.

I'm told that worldwide between 70 per cent and 80 per cent of mediations produce a settlement on the day. So why should we be in the minority?

Thank you for your attention.'

A template for a simple mediation statement/position paper is at the end of this chapter.

Conclusion

19.18   To conclude:

● Absorb the hints in this chapter.

● Give yourself plenty of time to prepare. Use the Flowchart at **para 19.09** as framework.

● Rehearse again and again.

● Take notes. Do not trust to memory, Even the most experienced advocate can easily forget something in the heat of the moment

● Do not worry that you are not a lawyer. Treat it as a strength, not a weakness.

● However, if you feel out of your legal depth, ask for time to take legal advice.

Appendix 1

Template for Index of Documents File/Bundle

Heading as in court papers

or

RED DOG

v

BLUE COW

INDEX FOR MEDIATION BUNDLE (THE CLAIMANTS/DEFENDANTS – if there is not a single bundle being used.)

Item	Description	Page
TAB 1	Pleadings	
1	Particulars of Claim	1–5
2	Defence	6–10
3	Reply to Defence	11–16
TAB 2	Contractual Documents	17–30
TAB 3	Correspondence with the Police	31–42
TAB 4	Experts Reports	
4	Report of Mr Brown	43–60
5	Report of Mr White	60–75
7	Joint Report	76–86
TAB 5	Correspondence about Settlement	86–95
TAB 6	Correspondence between the solicitors	95–101

Appendix 2

Template for Mediation Statement/Position Paper

RED DOG	**Claimant**
v	
BLUE COW	**Defendant**

MEDIATION STATEMENT OF THE CLAIMANT FOR USE AT THE MEDIATION ON
4 NOVEMBER 2014

WITHOUT PREJUDICE AND FOR THE PURPOSE OF THE MEDIATION ONLY

1   THE PARTIES

The claimant is Red Dog who is represented by Farmer Giles of SUE THEM SOLICITORS.

The defendant is Blue Cow who is represented by Mother Hubbard of Cupboard and Co Solicitors.

2   NATURE OF THE DISPUTE

Red Dog is suing Blue Cow for damages for breach of contract or the sale of some farm equipment. Some equipment did not work,. Other pieces of equipment did not belong to Red Dog. The value of the claim is £250,000.

3   CURRENT STAGE OF THE PROCEEDINGS

Proceedings were issued on 18 September 2013. A copy of them is at tab 1, pages 1–32. Formal disclosure has taken place. Copies of relevant documents are in the mediation file at pages 33–52. A case manager conference has been arranged for 10 November 2014.

4   THE ISSUES BETWEEN THE PARTIES

Red Dog (claimant) says that:

Blue Cow (defendant) says that :

Up-to-date valuations of the items of equipment at been prepared by Humpty Dumpty.

5   ATTEMPTS TO SETTLE

There was a without prejudice meeting to discuss settlement. The claimant walked out and threatened the defendant with bankruptcy. At that meeting the claimant offered to settle for £200,000 plus VAT plus costs, which at that time were estimated to be £25,000 plus VAT. The defendant demanded his costs of £75,000 plus VAT should be paid by the claimant.

Subsequent to that meeting, a Part 36 Offer was made by the defendant of £25,000 including interest and costs.

Last week there were telephone calls between solicitors of both sides. The defendant solicitor indicated that he might be able to persuade client to offer £35,000 plus costs. The claimant solicitor said that his client would not accept anything less than £200,000 plus VAT.

6   COSTS

Cost schedules have been exchanged and filed at court. Copies are at tab D pages 62–70.

The claimants have served notice of funding and indicated that they have an after the event insurance policy in place.

The defendant knows that the claimant recently had possession proceedings served on him by his bank. He has doubts about the claimant's ability to fund this matter to trial and to pay any costs order made against him to.

7   ATTENDING AT THE MEDIATION

Mr XX, the managing director of the claimant, will attend together with Mrs YY, the finance director, and Mr ZZ, the company accountant. Mr WW, who is the contracts manager and negotiated this purchase, will also be present.

8   CONCLUSION

The defendant acknowledges that both sides think they have a strong case. He has been advised that to go to trial he is likely to win but that there are always litigation risks as well as commercial benefits to settling rather than litigating to trial. He approaches this mediation in that spirit, and he hopes the claimant does the same.

Part E
Conclusion

Chapter 20

Conclusion

20.01   In a nutshell, the essential concepts for a mediation advocate are:

(1)   Mediation is about making peace not war.

(2)   Preparing for peace talks is not like preparing for litigation in court.

(3)   You make peace by negotiating.

(4)   The keys to settlements are found in people's minds not in their documents.

(5)   The barriers to settlement are also found in people's minds.

(6)   Therefore, make sure that you know:

- what is in the other side's head;

- what is your client's head; and

- what is in your own head.

(7)   How?

- ask questions and listen, really listen, to the answers; and

- self-audit.

(8)   The advocate's main job: minimise your client's stress.

The biggest single barrier to settlement at mediations is stress. Stressed people are not thinking about the future. They are thinking about the present and the past. Their creative problem-solving faculties are not engaged. They are defensive and critical, not open and creative.

(9)   How do you do it?

- Remember the three lessons of **para 1.15**:

(10) **Rebalance** preparation:

- walk the clients through the process;

- take the client through the mediation agreement;

- find out what the client wants and work out possible settlement proposals that could achieve the client's goals;

- complete a PMA;

- make sure that the clients are fully up-to-date on the financial implications on settling and not settling;

- have all the information to hand and know the file;

- work out before the mediation the opening and the closing offers; and

- stay energetic, good humoured, optimistic and in control. Do not wilt.

(11) **Re-orientate** away from forensic advocacy towards mediation advocacy, which is:

- different from court or tribunal advocacy;

- a set of techniques and attitudes to be learned, which will help you and your clients get the best out the mediation process;

- here to stay and will be a skill for which there is an increasing demand; and

- is not about the forensic demolition of the other side's case but about explaining perspectives and exploring proposals

(12) **Recognise** that:

- mediation is hard work. It is not a soft option compared with litigation in court. Advocates have to juggle the commercial and personal demands of clients under stress, the attacks from the other side and the questions from the mediator;

- it is much easier to criticise something than to create something; and

- mediation, like it or not, is a team effort. Advocates must be able to collaborate with the mediator and the other side to find settlements.

The bottom line

20.02 The opportunities for mediation advocates are expanding all the time. In an increasingly competitive market give yourself an edge by really knowing how to do it.

Index

Litigation – *contd*
  grounds for refusing mediation –
    contd
    Halsey factors, 8.12–8.14
    Halsey letters, 8.23
    overview, 8.11
    prospects of success, 8.21–8.22
    strike outs and summary
        judgments, 8.15–8.16
    use of alternative settlement
        methods, 8.17–8.18
  risk assessment, 7.04
  satellite litigation, 15.14
  Tomlin orders
    post-action settlements, 14.08
    sealing, 14.09
Logical fallacies, 18.03

Med/Arb, 2.21
Mediation
  agreements *see* **Agreements**
  arbitration distinguished, 2.35
  Civil Procedure Rules *see*
      Constraints on mediation
  contractual constraints *see*
      Constraints on mediation
  core concepts
    actual stages of mediation, 1.14
    classic stages, 1.13
    overview, 1.03
    what lawyers do, 1.12
  core principles
    discussion not argument, 1.08
    make peace not war, 1.04
    mutual recognition of reality,
        1.07
    negotiation and mediation
        distinguished, 1.06
    negotiation leading to action, 1.10
    overview, 1.02
    peace through negotiation, 1.05
    preparation for peace talks, 1.09
    reasons for settlement decisions,
        1.11
  defined, 1.02, 2.02, 2.27
  distinctive features
    confidentiality, 2.30
    party autonomy, 2.34
    presence of third party, 2.33
    scope of dispute covered, 2.29
    voluntary approach, 2.28
  eight dualisms currently observed,
      1.17

Mediation – *contd*
  grounds for refusing *see*
      Constraints on mediation
  need to know technique, 20.02
  percentage choice for best outcome,
      2.36–2.37
  procedure *see* **Procedure**
  related processes
    Arb/Med, 2.07
    judicial mediation, 2.18
    Med/Arb, 2.21
    mediation after last offer
        arbitration (MEDALOA), 2.22
    time limited mediations, 2.25
  styles *see* **Styles of mediation**
  venue *see* **Venue**
**Mediation after last offer
    arbitration (MEDALOA)**, 2.22
Mediation agreements
  appointment of mediator, 13.07
  authority to act, 13.24
  choice of representation, 13.17
  civil and commercial mediation,
      10.05–10.06
    importance of prior notice, 10.06
    signing, 10.05
  conclusions, 13.25
  confidentiality, 13.20–13.21
  defining the dispute, 13.04–13.05
  enforceability, 13.06
  entitlement to terminate, 13.22
  fees, 13.09–13.11
  general principles, 13.01–13.02
  incidental expenses, 13.14
  interest on unpaid fees, 13.16
  legal advice, 13.18
  liability for fees and costs, 13.15
  mediator liability, 12.17–12.19,
      13.08
  private sessions, 13.19
  procedural rules, 13.03
  signatures, 13.25
  time extensions, 13.12–13.13
  warranties, 13.23
Mediation bundles *see* **Documents**
**Mediation information and
    assessment meetings
    (MIAMs)**, 10.30–10.31
**Mediation Settlement
    Enforcement Orders (MSEOs)**,
    8.10
Mediation statements *see* **Position
    papers**